MW01155749

The Fifty Greatest Conspiracies of All Time

The Fifty Greatest Conspiracies of All Time

History's Biggest Mysteries, Coverups, and Cabals

Jonathan Vankin
and
John Whalen

A CITADEL PRESS BOOK
Published by Carol Publishing Group

A Citadel Press Book
Published by Carol Publishing Group
Citadel Press is a registered trademark of Carol Communications, Inc.
Editorial Offices: 600 Madison Avenue, New York, N.Y. 10022
Sales and Distribution Offices: 120 Enterprise Avenue, Secaucus, N.J. 07094
In Canada: Canadian Manda Group, P.O. Box 920, Station U, Toronto,
   Ontario M8Z 5P9
Queries regarding rights permissions should be addressed to Carol Publishing Group,
600 Madison Avenue, New York, N.Y. 10022

Carol Publishing Group books are available at special discounts for bulk purchases, sales promotion, fund-raising, or educational purposes. Special editions can be created to specifications. For details, contact: Special Sales Department, Carol Publishing Group, 120 Enterprise Avenue, Secaucus, N.J. 07094

Manufactured in the United States of America
10 9 8 7 6 5 4 3 2 1

Library of Congress Cataloging-in-Publication Data

Vankin, Jonathan
  Fifty greatest conspiracies of all time: history's biggest
mysteries, coverups, and cabals / by Jonathan Vankin and
John Whalen.
      p.   cm.
  "A Citadel Press Book."
  ISBN 0-8065-1576-7
  1. History—Miscellanea. 2. Conspiracies. I. Whalen, John.
II. Title: Fifty greatest conspiracies of all time.
D24.V36   1994
909.82—dc20   94-20251
                                                 CIP

To our parents

In America the majority raises formidable barriers around the liberty of opinion; within those barriers an author may write what he pleases, but woe to him if he goes beyond them.

—Alexis de Tocqueville

History is always written wrong and so always needs to be rewritten.

—George Santayana

Contents

Part III: They Died Alone

Part IV: Mondo Politics

Part V: Blood 'n' Guts

Part VI: Unified Field Theories

Part VII: Conspiracy, Inc.

Conspiracy, N'est-ce pas?

Tere really are, as one of our favorite writers, Jim Hougan says, two kinds of history, the safe, sanitized "'Disney version,' so widely available as to be unavoidable...and a second one that remains secret, buried, and unnamed."

This book is not a Disney production.

But we differ with Hougan, (investigative author of *Spooks* and *Secret Agenda,* two classic exposés of clandestine politics), on one minor point. The "second" version of history does have a name: "conspiracy theory."

The label itself is a reason why the secret history remains buried—if it is mere "theory" then it can't really be "history," correct?

Not in our view. In even the driest recounting of historical "fact" there is much theory—and in conspiracy theory there is much fact. This is not to say that we should all throw up our hands and admit that everything's subjective and that no one can ever figure out what's true or false. Quite the opposite. We hope that this book will help broaden the definition of what *could* be true because that definition is so narrow right now.

On the other hand, in our personal experience we have

naturally discussed our subject matter with a great many people
and have often been heartened by their openness to so-called
conspiracy theories. The problem is, they don't know the
details of very many. Even in the post-JFK era, when the stigma
on this subject has been at least partially lifted, there are still
relatively few avenues for exploring the secret history.

The "Disney" version of history could just as easily be called
the *"New York Times* version" or the "TV news version" or the
"college textbook version." The main resistance to conspiracy
theories comes not from people on the street, but from the
media, academia, and government—people who manage the
national and global economy of information.

There is certainly a lot of resistance there and the reasons
why are multifarious, complex, and probably deserve a book of
their own. A few of the main ones (vastly oversimplified) are:

- *Vested interests.* Conspiracy theories, by their nature, attack established authority. People in positions of authority
  fight back, as you'd expect they would.
- *Laziness.* A good conspiracy is tough to crack. It's easier to
  rewrite a press release and then act 100 percent certain that
  you know what you're talking about when someone calls
  you on it later.
- *Armchair psychoanalysis.* Pundits and pontificators tend to
  deal with conspiracy theories not on their merits, but as
  symptoms of the mental problems afflicting those who
  advocate them. Unfortunately, many of the most vocal
  conspiracy theorists do little to dispel this stereotype.
  However, the armchair Freudians rarely admit that their
  own views also have deep-seated psychological motivations.
  It is unsettling to face the possibility that, to quote the
  Firesign Theater, "everything you know is wrong."
- *Peer pressure.* Because most reporters, political scientists,
  and politicians shy away from conspiracy theories, few are
  willing to stick their necks out and risk being laughed at by
  their buddies.
- *Bad associations.* For years "conspiracy theory" was almost

synonymous with "Jewish conspiracy." Sadly, the anti-Semitic "theory" (if it can be called that) has been around for thousands of years and won't go away, lately finding unfortunate expression in the rantings of various Eastern European politicians and certain African-American orators. In somewhat disguised form, it even sneaks into the mainstream every now and then in the scribblings of select, well-known conservative columnists—even baseball players. In early 1994 there came a cry to ban recent inductee Steve "Lefty" Carlton from baseball's Hall of Fame for his statement in *Philadelphia* magazine that "twelve Jewish bankers meeting in Switzerland" rule the world.

A tragic canard, the Jewish conspiracy merits no further comment. Its existence, however, tends to unfairly discredit other conspiratorial interpretations of events that have nothing to do with making scapegoats of any ethnic or religious group.

- *Faith in democracy.* We'd like to believe our system of government protects us from the sorts of things that go on in more "backward" countries.
- *Denial.* Many conspiracy theories deal with the darker side of human nature and the capacity of "respectable" people to do some very nasty things. It feels better to pretend that if I'm OK, you're OK.
- *Conspiracy!* Let's face it, these things happen. And when they do, the conspirators are not likely to fess up at the first hint that they've been smoked out.

None of those reasons says anything about whether any particular conspiracy theory is true or false, worth considering or dismissing.

So what makes the following the *Fifty Greatest Conspiracies of All Time*? We confess, our criteria were rather flexible. Many were included for a combination of their importance and the availability of checkable facts to back them up. We chose others, frankly, for their entertainment value. If there's one problem we've found with conspiracy theories that bugs us more than any other, it's the determination of conspiracy theorists to take their subject matter *so* seriously that Gerald "Case Closed" Posner looks like David Letterman by comparison.

What we're mainly exploring here is a different way of seeing the world. Just as Henry Kissinger cracks us up every time he intones his shoot-from-the-hip opinions as if he's reading from a stone tablet, we also see a good deal of unintentional humor in the dissenting conspiratorial worldview.

One thing we do not want to do here is talk down to you or insult your intelligence. We'll let the George Wills and Ted Koppels of the world instruct you in what you're *supposed* to believe. All we ask from the reader is an open mind and a little intellectual courage. Even Walt Disney gave us nightmares sometimes.

Acknowledgments

This is a book that almost didn't happen. But it did, thanks to two people. First, our agent and friend, Ken Swezey, who stuck with the project for fifteen months before a contract was finally signed. And equally important is our editor, Kevin McDonough, who believed in the project and saw its potential. Our lasting thanks to them both.

This topic is deceptively difficult to write about. We're deeply indebted for research assistance to Ron Bonds of IllumiNet Press, one of the most daring small publishers in the country; to Kenn Thomas, editor of *Steamshovel Press*, one of the best in a strangely growing field of conspiracy-oriented publications; and to Jim Martin, editor of *Flatland*, part book catalog, part magazine, all quite fascinating (and a great place to start your conspiracy/alternative-politics-and-literature library). For readers who want to pursue this topic further, we recommend contacting IllumiNet at Box 2808, Lilburn, GA 30226; *Steamshovel* at Box 23715, St. Louis, MO 63121; and *Flatland* at Box 2420, Fort Bragg, CA 95437.

We also acknowledge the support of our former employer, Metro Newspapers, and particularly, Bob Hansen, Sharan Street, David Cohen, and Dan Pulcrano.

JONATHAN VANKIN'S PERSONAL ACKNOWLEDGMENTS:
The circumstances under which I wrote my portion of this

book were far from ideal, making the moral, emotional, and practical support of a great many people more valuable than ever. Three people deserve spots at the top of that list. First, my parents, Jean and Larry Vankin, who in addition to providing all the essentials of parenthood (love, inspiration, money, etc.), served as my personal research assistants—a task far exceeding the call of parental duty. My love and thanks always.

My most special thanks to Debbie Picker. She did so much for me that a mere thank-you for her love, understanding, and patience seems far from adequate. She was my partner through this rather memorable experience, and will be through many more, I hope.

Heartfelt gratitude—for a wide variety of personal reasons—goes to: my sister, Laura Vankin; Dan Reichert and Andrea Marcovicci (double to Dan, my closest friend over many years and miles); the Shimogaito family, Teruko, Yoshiko, and Takehiro; Al Edmonds; Hal March (still the world's coolest...); Gary Sherman; Louis Theroux; Eric London; Holli Richards; Brent Filson (still my mentor); Trevor Loring; Judge Sande Mazer Moss and Bill Deane; three generations of Pickers, Si and Lorraine, Ben and David; Coleen Curran (for everything); Lisa Stone-Norman; Ichiro Taniguchi; Ryuji Nakazono; Ann Walker; Matt Maranz; Jamesfinkle@twics.com; Jay Whearley; and I'm sure a large number of people I'll think of once the book has gone to press and kick myself.

Equally important, my thanks to the many people who have given me their time, inspired me, or in some other tangible way helped me along with what has now become a two-book project.

Clark Coolidge merits a special mention for, perhaps unwittingly, getting me started on this particular track. Mark Stewart should be mentioned in the same light. And thanks to: Evelyn Fazio; Kurt Andersen; Congressman Don Edwards (retired); Robert Anton Wilson; E.J. McCarthy; John Strausbaugh; Emily Reichert; Tom Snyder; Kerry Thornley; G. Gordon Liddy; Adam Parfrey; Paul Theroux; Jim Martin; Anthony Summers; Jason Neely; Jim Keith; Mickey Z.; R. U. Sirius and Queen Mu;

Suzanne Guyette; Mike Litchfield; Dave Emory; Greg Krupey; K-Talk radio, Salt Lake City; John Judge; Trowbridge Ford; William Bramley; Don Kennison; Al Kunzer; Jim and Ken Collier; Laura Lindgren; Don Oldenburg; Loompanics; Stuart Swezey and Brian King; Jo Glorie; Nancy Sayles; Dennis Hayes; Sally Robinson; and anybody else I've inadvertently, and with sincere apologies, omitted.

Finally, but perhaps most important for this book, my deepest gratitude to John Whalen, my collaborator (no "co-conspirator" jokes, please).

JOHN WHALEN'S PERSONAL ACKNOWLEDGMENTS:
It seems that everybody has a favorite conspiracy. My thanks to the many folks who shared their pet cabals, news clippings, suppressed files, hunches, ah-ha's, and other smoking guns.

Of course, a special thanks goes to my parents, Patricia and Frank Whalen, who took me to see *All the President's Men* at an impressionable age.

Ann Walker also deserves top billing. Her generosity, encouragement, and patience know no bounds, at least none that I've been able to test, and that's saying a lot.

Others who helped guide me through the dizzying labyrinths of conspiracy research deserve a nod of appreciation (although some of them may take umbrage at the loaded term, *conspiracy*). They include, in no particular order, Jim Hougan; Robert Gettlin; John Stockwell; Stephen Pizzo; Norman Solomon; Henry Lincoln; Peter Dale Scott; Joel Bleifuss; Robert Parry; Ben Bagdikian; Ed Connolly; Dave Emory; Pete Brewton; Al Kunzer; Ralph McGehee (for his indispensable computer database, CIABASE, order it ASAP: Box 5022, Herndon, VA 22070); Marc Cooper; and Ellen Ray.

And, of course, a special thank-you goes to Jonathan Vankin, an excellent writing partner without whom this book would have been half as long.

San Jose, California
February 1994

I

Your Tax Dollars at Work

1

CIAcid Trip

LSD was invented in Switzerland by Albert Hofmann, a researcher for Sandoz pharmaceuticals. It did not spontaneously appear among the youth of the Western World as a gift from the God of Gettin' High. The CIA was on to acid long before the flower children.

So, for that matter, were upstanding citizens like Time-Life magnate Henry Luce and his wife, Claire Booth Luce, who openly sang the praises of their magical mystery tours during the early sixties. Henry, a staunch conservative with close connections to the CIA, once dropped acid on the golf course and then claimed he had enjoyed a little chat with God.

While the cognoscenti had the benefit of tuned-in physicians, other psychedelic pioneers took their first trips as part of CIA-controlled research studies.

At least one person committed suicide after becoming an unwitting subject of a CIA LSD test, crashing through a high-story plate-glass window in a New York hotel as his Agency guardian watched. (Or perhaps the guardian did more than watch. In June 1994 the victim's family had his thirty-year-old

3

corpse exhumed to check for signs that he may have been thrown out that window.) Numerous others lost their grip on reality.

MK-ULTRA was the code name the CIA used for its program directed at gaining control over human behavior through "covert use of chemical and biological materials," as proposed by Richard Helms. The name itself was a variation on ULTRA, the U.S. intelligence program behind Nazi lines in World War II, of which the CIA's veteran spies were justly proud.

Helms later became CIA director and gained a measure of notoriety for his Watergate "lying to Congress" conviction and a touch of immortality in Thomas Powers's aptly named biography, *The Man Who Kept the Secrets.* Helms founded the MK-ULTRA program and justified its notably unethical aspects with the rationale, "We are not Boy Scouts."

At the time, the spook scientists suspected that LSD had the potential to reprogram the human personality. In retrospect, they were probably right—Timothy Leary spoke in similar terms, though he saw unlimited potential for self-improvement in this "reprogramming." The CIA and the military simply couldn't figure out how to harness the drug's power. Thank goodness. Their idea was not to open "the doors of perception" but to convert otherwise free human beings into automatons.

"We must remember to thank the CIA and the army for LSD," spoke no less an authority figure on matters psychedelic than John Lennon. "They invented LSD to control people and what it did was give us freedom."

Or did it? The acid-tripping intersection between the CIA and the counterculture is one of the areas where the on-the-record facts about MK-ULTRA meld into the foggy region of conspiracy theory. It has been suggested, even by prominent participants in the counterculture, that with LSD the CIA found the ultimate weapon against the youth movement.

Officially, the MK-ULTRA program ran from 1953 to 1964, at which time it was renamed MK-SEARCH and continued until 1973. However, U.S. intelligence and military operations with the same purpose had been ongoing at least since World War II and likely chugged ahead for many years after MK-ULTRA's publicly stated conclusion. MK-ULTRA encompassed an undetermined number of bizarre and often grotesque experiments. In one, psychiatrist Ewen Cameron received CIA funding to test a procedure he called "depatterning." This technique, Cameron explained when he applied for his CIA grant (through a front group called the Society for the Investigation of Human Ecology), involved the "breaking down of ongoing patterns of the patient's behavior by means of particularly intensive electroshocks," in addition to LSD. Some of his subjects suffered brain damage and other debilitations. One sued the government and won an out-of-court settlement in 1988.

Then there was operation "Midnight Climax," in which prostitutes lured unsuspecting johns to a CIA bordello in San Francisco. There they slipped their clients an LSD mickey while Agency researchers savored the "scientific" action from behind a two-way mirror, a pitcher of martinis at the ready.

Author John Marks, whose *The Search for the Manchurian Candidate* is one of the most thoroughgoing volumes yet assembled on U.S. government mind-control research, readily admits that all of his source material comprised but ten boxes of documents—but those took him a year to comprehend despite the aid of a research staff.

Marks writes that he sought access to records of a branch of the CIA's Directorate of Science and Technology, the Office of Research and Development (ORD), which took over behavioral (i.e., mind control) research after MK-ULTRA's staff dispersed.

Marks was told that ORD's files contained 130 boxes of documents relating to behavioral research. Even if they were all released, their sheer bulk is sufficient to fend off even the most dedicated—or obsessed—investigator. To generate such an intimidating volume of paper must have taken considerable time and effort. Yet curiously, the CIA has always claimed that its attempts to create real-life incarnations of Richard Condon's unfortunate protagonist Raymond Shaw—the hypnotically programmed assassin of *The Manchurian Candidate*—were a complete bust.

If their demurrals are to be trusted, then this particular program constitutes one of the least cost-effective deployments of taxpayer dollars in the history of the U.S. government, which is rife with non-cost-effective dollar deployments.

The CIA's most effective line of defense against exposure of their mind-control operations (or any of their operations, for that matter) has always been self-effacement. The agency portrays its agents as incompetent stooges, encouraging the public to laugh at their wacky attempts to formulate cancer potions and knock off foreign leaders.

Under this cover story, MK-ULTRA's research team was nothing but a bunch of ineffectual eccentrics. "We are sufficiently ineffective so our findings can be published," quipped one MK-ULTRA consultant.

Despite the findings of a Senate committee headed by Ted Kennedy that U.S. mind-control research was a big silly failure, and even though Marks—whose approach is fairly conservative—acknowledges that he found no record to prove it, the project may have indeed succeeded.

"I cannot be positive that they never found a technique to control people," Marks writes, "despite my definite bias in favor of the idea that the human spirit defeated the manipulators."

A sunny view of human nature, that. And indeed a consoling one. But the human spirit, history sadly proves, is far from indomitable. The clandestine researchers explored every possible means of manipulating the human mind. The CIA's experiments with LSD are the most famous MK-ULTRA undertakings, but acid was not even the most potent drug investigated by intelligence and military agencies. Nor did they limit their inquiries to drugs. Hypnosis, electronic brain implants, microwave transmissions, and parapsychology also received intense scrutiny. Marks, Kennedy, and many others apparently believe that the U.S. government failed where all-too-many far less sophisticated operations—from the Moonies to Scientology to EST—have scored resounding triumphs. Brainwashing is commonplace among "cults," but not with the multimillion-dollar resources of the United States government's military and intelligence operations?

For that matter, the (supposed) impetus for the program was the reported success of communist countries in "brainwashing." The word itself originally applied to several soldiers who'd fought in the Korean War who exhibited strange behavior and had large blank spots in their memories—particularly when it came to their travels through regions of Manchuria. Those incidents were the inspiration for Condon's novel, in which a group of American soldiers are hypnotically brainwashed by the Korean and Chinese communists and one is programmed to kill a presidential candidate.

Interestingly, the belief that one's psyche is being invaded by radio transmissions or electrical implants is considered a symptom of paranoid schizophrenia. But there is no doubt that the CIA contemplated using those methods and carried out such experiments on animals, and the way these things go it would require the willful naïveté of, say, a Senate subcommittee to maintain that they stopped there. Even Marks, who exercises the journalistic wisdom to stick only to what he can back up with hard documentation, readily acknowledges that the clandestine researchers "probably" planted electrodes in the brains of men. Marks points out that the electrode experiments "went far beyond giving monkeys orgasms," one of the researchers' early achievements.

The ultimate goal of mind control would have been to produce a Manchurian Candidate assassin, an agent who didn't know he (or she) was an agent—brainwashed and programmed to carry out that most sensitive of missions. Whether the program's accomplishments reached that peak will probably never be public knowledge. So we are left to guess whether certain humans have been "programmed to kill." In 1967, Luis

Castillo, a Puerto Rican arrested in the Philippines for planning to bump off Ferdinand Marcos, claimed (while in a hypnotic trance) that he had been implanted with a posthypnotic suggestion to carry out the assassination. Sirhan Sirhan, convicted as the assassin of Robert F. Kennedy, showed unmistakable symptoms of hypnosis. A psychiatrist testifying in Sirhan's defense said that the accused assassin was in a trance when he shot Kennedy, albeit a self-induced one. Author Robert Kaiser echoed that doctor's conclusions in his book *RFK Must Die!* Others, of course, have offered darker conjectures regarding the origins of Sirhan's symptoms.

James Earl Ray, the convicted assassin of Martin Luther King, also had a known fascination with hypnosis, and, more recently, British lawyer Fenton Bressler has assembled circumstantial evidence to support a theory that Mark David Chapman, slayer of John Lennon, was subject to CIA mind control. Way back in 1967, a book titled *Were We Controlled?*, whose unknown author used the pseudonym Lincoln Lawrence, stated that both Lee Harvey Oswald and Jack Ruby were under mind control of some kind. The book may have had at least a trace of validity: Something in the book convinced Oswald's mother that the author was personally acquainted with her son.

Did MK-ULTRA spin off a wave of history-altering assassinations—did it whelp a brood of hypnoprogrammed killers? The definitive answer to that question will certainly never reach the public. We are left, with John Marks, to hope on faith alone that it did not, but always with the uneasy knowledge that it could have.

Perhaps not through assassinations, and perhaps not even intentionally, MK-ULTRA definitely altered a generation. John Lennon was far from the only sixties acid-hero to make the connection between the mood of the streets and the secret CIA labs. "A surprising number of counterculture veterans endorsed the notion that the CIA disseminated street acid en masse to deflate the political potency of the youth rebellion," write Martin Lee and Bruce Shlain in *Acid Dreams*, their chronicle of both the clandestine and countercultural sides of the LSD revolution.

"By magnifying the impulse toward revolutionism out of context, acid sped up the process by which the Movement became unglued," the authors continue. "The use of LSD among young people in the U.S. reached a peak in the late 1960s, shortly after the CIA initiated a series of covert operations designed to disrupt, discredit, and neutralize the New Left. Was this merely a historical coincidence, or did the Agency actually take steps to promote the illicit acid trade?"

The tale of Ronald Stark, told by Lee and Shlain, may provide the connection between the CIA and the Left. Stark was a leading distributor of LSD in the late 1960s—the same time acid use was at its heaviest—and apparently a CIA operative. The Agency has never admitted this, but an Italian judge deciding in 1979 whether to try Stark for "armed banditry" in relation to Stark's many contacts with terrorists (among other things, Stark accurately predicted the assassination of Aldo Moro) released the drug dealer after finding "an impressive series of scrupulously enumerated proofs" that Stark had worked for the CIA "from 1960 onward."

"It could have been," mused Tim Scully, the chief of Stark's major LSD-brewing outfit (a group of idealistic radicals called the Brotherhood who grew to feel exploited by Stark), "that he was employed by an American intelligence agency that wanted to see more psychedelic drugs on the street." But Lee and Shlain leave open the possibility that Stark may have been simply one of the world's most ingenious con artists—a possibility acknowledged by most everyone to come in contact with Stark.

The CIA's original "acid dream" was that LSD would open the mind to suggestion, but they found the drug too potent to manage. Sometime around 1973, right before MK-ULTRA founder and, by then, CIA director Richard Helms hung up his trenchcoat and stepped down from the CIA's top post, he ordered the majority of secret MK-ULTRA documents destroyed due to "a burgeoning paper problem." Among the eradicated material, Lee and Shlain report, were "all existing copies of a classified CIA manual titled *LSD: Some Un-Psychedelic Implications.*

There exists today no on-paper evidence (that anyone has yet uncovered) that MK-ULTRA was the progenitor of either a conspiracy to unleash remote-controlled lethal human robots or to emasculate an entire generation by oversaturating it with a mind-frying drug. But MK-ULTRA was very real and the danger of a secret government program to control the thoughts of its citizens, even just a few of them at a time, needs no elaboration.

MAJOR SOURCES

Budiansky, Stephen, Erica E. Goode, and Ted Gest. "The Cold War Experiments." *U.S. News & World Report.* 24 January 1994.
Lee, Martin, and Bruce Shlain. *Acid Dreams.* New York: Grove Press, 1985.
Marks, John. *The Search for the Manchurian Candidate.* New York: Dell, 1979.

2

Get Castro!

If the Cold War incubated a kind of national hysteria, nowhere was the delirium more frenzied than in Florida of the early 1960s. Clandestine plots to topple Fidel Castro bred like mosquitoes in the Everglades. The U.S.-backed Bay of Pigs invasion, which ended in disaster, only compounded the tropical madness. As Cold War fever rose, the CIA launched one of its most scandalous episodes, a series of surreal attempts to assassinate Castro employing Florida's Cuban exiles and the nation's top Mafiosi.

As President Johnson later put it, "We were running a damn Murder, Incorporated in the Caribbean." Although three presidents had at least some knowledge of the CIA plots, in several cases the Agency appears to have operated autonomously—and against presidential authority.

In 1975, Senate hearings held in the wake of Watergate's revelations exposed the CIA's so-called "executive action" programs. The Senate Select Intelligence Committee, chaired by Frank Church, uncovered eight failed attempts to ice Castro and a handful of murder plots aimed at other heads of state.

11

Quite conservatively, the committee decided to dub its findings "alleged assassination plots." Moreover, according to the testimony of CIA Brahmins, all of the murder plots misfired. Notwithstanding these claims, there is reason to believe the hearings rooted up only a sampling of the Agency's political hits.

As good a place as any to begin the tale is with that elemental spook E. Howard Hunt, the CIA propagandist whose name became synonymous with Watergate, Bay of Pigs, and a scorecard of subterfuge that defined a quarter century. Returning from Cuba, the CIA officer drew up a list of strategic recommendations. At the top of the list: Whack Castro. The agency apparently took Hunt's advice, for in 1960 the CIA brain trust began plotting the Cuban leader's permanent "elimination."

To get the ball rolling, in August of that year the CIA's Office of Medical Services sprinkled a box of Castro's favorite Cuban cigars with a virulent toxin. The resulting stogie was so lethal that merely sucking on it would "terminate" the hardiest dictator within moments. Castro was to visit the United Nations in New York, and it is possible that the tainted cigars were to be proffered there. What happened next isn't clear. According to one report, the New York Police Department was informed by CIA officers of aborted plans to kill Castro with a box of *exploding* cigars, Three Stooges-style.

Other unrealized plans—including several intended to assassinate the man's character, if not the man himself—managed to be even less practical than the gag stogies.

- One early brainstorm involved spraying Castro's broadcasting studio in Havana with "super acid," a concentrated form of LSD, which, it was hoped, would cause Fidel to tune in, turn on, and go nuts during a public speech. A variation on that theme would have had the CIA's Technical Services Division lacing those all-purpose cigars with LSD,

thereby dispatching the unflappable Marxist on a proverbial bad trip.

- Another scheme proposed sprinkling Castro's shoes with
thallium salts, a potent depilatory that would cause his
beard, eyebrows, and pubic hair to fall out. His cherished
Latin machismo called into question, Castro would theoretically whither in stature and self-respect, like a fol-
lically deprived Samson.

- As for the more lethal plots, one idea called for Castro, an
avid scuba diver, to be presented with a wet suit by an
American lawyer then negotiating for the release of Bay of
Pigs prisoners. The Technical Services Division went so far
as to purchase a scuba suit and contaminate the respirator
with tuberculosis bacilli. Nothing if not scrupulous, they
also treated the suit itself with fungus spores that would
cause the rare skin disease, madura foot. Alas, the shuttle
diplomat took the initiative and gave Castro an uncontami-
nated suit, thereby defusing a plan that, if successful, would
hardly have fallen under the category of "covert operation."

- Another Ian Fleming-esque scheme called for an exploding
conch shell to be placed on the sea floor in an area where
Castro often went diving. Ultimately, this plan was
scrapped as impractical.

- In his autobiography, CIA operative Felix Rodriguez—a
close confidant of George Bush—says he tried three times
to enter Cuba on kill-Castro missions. The missions were
his idea and at the time he didn't know that the CIA was his
silent patron. In 1987, asked by the Iran-Contra committee
whether he took part in the CIA's attempt to poison
Castro's favorite smokes, Rodriguez replied indignantly,
"No sir, I did not. But I did volunteer to kill that son of a
bitch in 1961 with a telescopic rifle."

- Perhaps the most visionary proposal came from the fertile
mind of General Edward Lansdale, who supervised the
Kennedy administration's covert war on Castro. The gen-

eral hoped to spark a counterrevolution by spreading the word to devout Cuban Catholics that the Second Coming was imminent and that Castro was none other than the anti-Christ. At the appointed hour, Christ, Himself, would surface off the shores of Cuba aboard an American submarine as star shell flares illuminated the heavens. In a pique of Cold War rapture, it was hoped, the Cubans would rise up and spontaneously overthrow their satanic leader.

In light of these fantasies, it might be tempting to conclude that the CIA couldn't hit the broad side of a barn with a deluxe sniper scope. As in many an airing of the CIA's dirty linen, low comedy tended to soften public outrage, a circumstance in which Agency crypt keepers may have taken comfort.

However, the Agency's assassination program was anything but frivolously pursued. Concurrent with the earliest Castro plots of 1960, the CIA's deputy director, Richard Bissell, asked his science advisor, Sidney Gottlieb, to research assassination techniques. The fruit of Gottlieb's labor was a portable murder kit, complete with a lethal biological agent, hypodermic needles, and rubber gloves.

Gottlieb hand-delivered the kit to Africa, where the CIA station chief had been ordered to assassinate Congolese dictator Patrice Lumumba. Apparently, attempts to poison Lumumba failed. In 1975, the Senate Intelligence Committee found that the CIA had sponsored a separate hit on Lumumba using European mercenary assassins. That plan fell apart when the hit man turned out to be as out of control as "an unguided missile," in the words of the Agency's Congo station chief. According to the official story, Lumumba's own countrymen saved the CIA from having to do the dirty work, taking the initiative and murdering their leader in January 1961.

But doubts linger about the CIA's supposed hands-off role. In his book, *In Search of Enemies*, Agency veteran John Stockwell writes that one CIA officer boasted to him about driving around with Lumumba's body in the trunk of his car.

A few months after Lumumba's timely demise, Dominican Republic autocrat Rafael Trujillo was assassinated. Although the CIA had generously donated guns to dissidents who made it clear they intended to off Trujillo, it was, the CIA swore, local boys who lethally perforated their leader. Of course, it is quite possible they did it with the CIA-provided arms.

Author Dick Russell relates another possibility in his book about the JFK assassination, *The Man Who Knew Too Much*. Russell tracked down and interviewed a retired army colonel named Bill Bishop after hearing him described as "some kind of contract killer for the CIA." When Russell met him, Bishop blithely announced, "I made the hit on Trujillo....That's one mission I'm kinda proud of, because a lot of my associates said it couldn't be done."

If fortuitously timed assassinations bore few CIA fingerprints, plots in which the Agency took the initiative always seemed to go unconsummated, if we're to believe CIA luminaries like former director Richard Helms. For instance, in February 1960 Helms endorsed a plan to see that Iraqi junta chief Abdul Karim Kassem be "incapacitated" with a poisoned handkerchief. Although the whiz kids in the Technical Services Division whipped up a toxic hankie and forwarded it to Kassem, the general evidently never got a runny nose.

Considering the capriciousness of murder by sniffles, perhaps it's understandable that the CIA turned to the Mafia, old pros in the liquidation racket. In the case of Castro, it was a match made in, well, heaven; for the Mafia also had its heart set on killing the Cuban. Mob boss Meyer Lansky had already put a million-dollar bounty on Castro's head. Castro's rise to power in Cuba following the 1959 revolution didn't sit well with the mob, to put it mildly. The Cuban leader had confiscated the Mafia's lucrative casino operations in Havana, which were even more profitable than the syndicate's holdings in Las Vegas.

Of course, recruiting the mob was nothing new: during World War II, the Office of Naval Intelligence had used Mafiosi to guard the New York waterfronts against saboteurs and to

assist in the Allied invasion of Sicily. (For his trouble, mob boss
Lucky Luciano won an early prison release, and the American
and Sicilian Mafias got a new lease on life.) But to sic the
goodfellas on Castro must have seemed like the ultimate neat
idea. And as far as Cosa Nostra bosses were concerned, putting
a powerful government agency in the Mafia's debt had obvious
appeal.

So with the imprimatur of Agency director Allen Dulles, and
using "dirty tricks" freelancer Robert Maheu as a go-between,
the CIA made the mob an offer it couldn't refuse: a $150,000
reward for anyone "tough enough" to bump off Castro—but,
more importantly, government sanction to do the job. On loan
from Howard Hughes, Maheu had handled a number of
"sensitive" projects for the CIA. These included a bogus porno
film production starring a doppelgänger of Indonesian President Sukarno and a Richard Nixon—spearheaded propaganda
war on Greek shipping magnate Aristotle Onassis. (According
to Maheu, a hard-boiled Nixon, swept away by the intrigue,
barked: "If it turns out we have to kill the bastard, just don't do
it on American soil.")

In the autumn of 1960, two months before John F. Kennedy's
narrow electoral victory, Maheu introduced his pal, Vegas don
John Roselli, to the CIA's Jim O'Connell. In Miami, Roselli
introduced the two spooks to Chicago Godfather Sam
"Momo" Giancana and Florida's powerful mob boss Santos
Trafficante. Both Giancana and Trafficante had seen their
interests in Cuba fizzle when Castro shuttered the drug and
gambling rackets. Trafficante was especially peeved; he had
controlled Cuba's rackets before Castro locked him up in the
aftermath of the 1959 revolution. So as not to blow their cover,
the mobsters adopted suitably innocuous code names: Roselli
was "John Rawlston" and Giancana was introduced as "Sam
Gold." The redoubtable Trafficante retained a measure of his
ethnicity, becoming "Joe Pecora."

The industrious Technical Services Division set about producing a batch of botulinum toxin pills that would dissolve in

soup, coffee, or cocktails. After a few refinements and success-ful tests on monkeys, the CIA passed the pills on to Roselli in February 1961. The plan was to have one of Trafficante's well-placed Cuban contacts slip Castro the lethal Mickey. The first attempt went awry when the designated poisoner, a member of Castro's inner circle, lost his job. A second attempt in April failed as well, reportedly because Castro suddenly stopped frequenting his favorite restaurant.

After the Bay of Pigs rout in April 1961, the mob plot went dormant for nearly a year. When it was reactivated, Maheu and Momo were judged to be security risks and were left out. (Momo's boasting about knocking off Castro had reached J. Edgar Hoover's twitching ears, jeopardizing the CIA's de-niability.) Helms assigned a new Agency coordinator to the project, the hard-drinking, tough-talking William Harvey. Harvey formalized the Agency's "assassination bureau" under the code name ZR/RIFLE and on the Cuban front he now headed Task Force W, the CIA's anti-Castro mission. Phase two featured more poison pills, rifles, and explosives over the course of eleven more months—but all these plots failed as well. Castro kept on breathing. In February 1963, Harvey released Agent Roselli from his tour of duty. Neither Harvey nor Helms had informed CIA director McCone of Mafia phase two.

So what did the Kennedy brothers know and when did they know it? That became a subtle but emphatic theme in the testimony of Agency regulars before the Senate's Church com-mittee. Though CIA honchos tried to show that they were just following Kennedy directives, the committee never reached a definitive conclusion. In his biography of Richard Helms, *The Man Who Kept the Secrets*, Thomas Powers called these murky waters "the deepest secret of all—who gave the orders?"

We know that the mob plots began before the JFK's election, under the Eisenhower administration. More than a year after the first CIA-Mafia collaboration, Attorney General Robert Kennedy was briefed on the operation. Lawrence Houston, the CIA's house lawyer of the time, testified that the younger

Kennedy was "mad as hell" because his prosecutions of Giancana and other mobsters had been jeopardized. Houston testified that RFK declared, "I trust that if you ever try to do business with organized crime again—with gangsters—you will let the attorney general know." At that very moment, however, Harvey, Helms, and Roselli were thick as thieves.

But there's also reason to believe that early in his administration Jack Kennedy knew about the Mafia operation. According to JFK's sometime mistress, Judith Campbell Exner, who was also Giancana's moll, the president conferred with Giancana early on. Those contacts, Campbell said, "had to do with the elimination of Castro."

But there is evidence that the Kennedy brothers, though supportive of early assassination plotting, later took a dim view of the killing spree. Robert Kennedy reportedly told two aides that upon learning of the first Mafia plot, he "turned it off." He was mistaken. In late 1961, the president was clearly pondering the policy of murder when he asked journalist Tad Szulc, "What would you think if I ordered Castro to be assassinated?" When Szulc expressed his dismay, Kennedy agreed and said his advisors had been pressuring him to have Castro killed. According to Senator George Smathers, himself a fierce Castro opponent, JFK was "horrified" at the prospect of a Castro assassination and "complained that the CIA was almost autonomous."

Apparently the Kennedy brothers weren't informed of yet *another* series of CIA attempts to plug Castro beginning in the autumn of 1963. Harvey's replacement, Desmond FitzGerald (the idea man behind the poison wet suit and explosive conch shell), began cultivating an agent ideally placed to knock off the Cuban leader.

Rolando Cubela, a major in the Cuban army, was not only an intimate of Castro's, but a disgruntled one, unhappy with the growing Soviet influence in Cuba. In a deception remarkable for its audacity, FitzGerald (with Helms's approval) met with

Cubela in Paris, posing as Robert Kennedy's personal representative, without RFK's knowledge. (Cubela later told journalist
Anthony Summers that FitzGerald also claimed to be a U.S.
senator.) FitzGerald, without any authority to do so, promised
Cubela that the U.S. government would fully back a coup
against Castro. FitzGerald subsequently arranged for Cubela to
receive a "pen" that could inject a poison (Blackleaf 40) into a
certain blustering autocrat.

But while the CIA was talking termination with Cubela,
Kennedy had already softened his formerly hawkish Cuban
policy. To be sure, Robert Kennedy was still approving
"pinprick" assaults on Cuba, but the administration seems to
have changed its tack. In early 1963, with the U.S.-Soviet
nuclear test ban treaty under negotiation, the Kennedy administration began cracking down on "unauthorized" raids against
Cuba (and on Soviet ships anchored there) by the revanchist
exiles. CIA contact agents were among the anti-Castro Cubans
detained and prosecuted.

And, as Anthony Summers reported in his JFK assassination
study, *Conspiracy*, during the final months of his life, Kennedy
sent diplomatic feelers out to Castro. Through an American
advisor to the United Nations, Kennedy had begun to make
secret overtures to Castro—at precisely the same moment
FitzGerald was assuring Cubela that the Kennedys would back
an anti-Castro coup. Although stealth diplomacy didn't get very
far (Kennedy was assassinated two months later), the president's
former special advisor, historian Arthur Schlesinger, found the
CIA's timing peculiar.

As he told Summers: "The whole Cubela thing raises even
deeper questions. The CIA was reviving the assassination plots
at the very time President Kennedy was considering the possibility of normalization of relations with Cuba—an extraordinary action. If it was not incompetence—which in the case of
the CIA cannot be excluded—it was a studied attempt to
subvert national policy."

MAJOR SOURCES

Hinckle, Warren, and William Turner. *Deadly Secrets.* New York: Thunder's Mouth Press, 1992.

Hougan, Jim. *Spooks: The Haunting of America—The Private Use of Secret Agents.* New York: William Morrow and Company, 1978.

Powers, Thomas. *The Man Who Kept the Secrets: Richard Helms and the CIA.* New York: Pocket Books, 1979.

Rodriguez, Felix I., and John Weisman. *Shadow Warrior.* New York: Simon & Schuster, 1989.

Russell, Dick. *The Man Who Knew Too Much.* New York: Carroll and Graf, 1992.

Senate Select Committee on Government Operations with Respect to Intelligence Activities. *Alleged Assassination Plots Involving Foreign Leaders.* Washington: U.S. Government Printing Office, 1975.

3

Breeding Better People

The following two statements were authored in the same year, 1925, by two public figures generally supposed to have not much in common:

"Those who are physically and mentally unhealthy and unfit must not perpetuate their sufferings in the bodies of their children. Through educational means the state must teach individuals that illness is not a disgrace but a misfortune for which people are to be pitied, yet at the same time it is a crime and a disgrace to make this affliction the worse by passing it on to innocent creatures out of a merely egotistic yearning."

"It is better for all the world, if instead of waiting to execute degenerate offspring for crime or to let them starve for their imbecility, society can prevent those who are manifestly unfit from continuing their kind."

The latter opinion comes from Justice Oliver Wendell Holmes of the U.S. Supreme Court, writing for the majority in the case of *Buck v. Bell*. The former statement appeared in *Mein Kampf* by Adolf Hitler. Eugenics wasn't just for Nazis.

The "racial hygiene" programs of Nazi Germany were by far

21

the most catastrophic application of eugenic "theory," but they were neither the first nor last. In the early twentieth century, fourteen countries, including the United States, approved some type of eugenic legislation. In the first thirty years of this century, thirty of these United States passed sterilization laws. By one estimate, as many as sixty thousand people were "legally" sterilized. The true number can never be known because many operations in penal and mental institutions went unreported.

The United States of America, in fact, was the first industrialized nation to enact racial purification laws. In the late nineteenth century the states of Michigan and Massachusetts castrated numerous mental patients and young boys exhibiting such genetic imperfections as "persistent epilepsy," "imbecility," and "masturbation with weakness of mind."

Castration evidently hit a little too close to home for the average member of the public to stomach, so vasectomy became the preferred method for sterilizing males, and its equivalent, salpingectomy, became the preferred sterilization method for women.

Justice Holmes to the contrary, courts were not generally favorable toward sterilization laws. As early as 1912, the New Jersey Supreme Court struck down a law allowing for the sterilization of "feeble minded" people, including, according to the law's wording, "idiots, imbeciles, and morons."

"Imbeciles" and "idiots" were a virtual obsession for eugenics-happy legislators. Indiana's law was designed to "prevent procreation of confirmed criminals, idiots, imbeciles, and rapists." California's statute (California sterilized far more people than any other state) allowed, with a note from a doctor, the "asexualization" of "any idiot" as well as any prison inmate who had shown evidence that he was "a moral or sexual degenerate." An Iowa law targeted people "who would produce children with tendency to disease, deformity, crime, insanity, feeble-mindedness, idiocy, imbecility, epilepsy, or alcoholism."

Though courts often ruled against the eugenics laws, sterilization programs continued unabated, and most of the state laws stayed on the books well into the 1970s and 1980s, though they haven't been applied since the early part of the century when California, for example, sterilized 6,200 "feeble minded" people.

The status of "feeble mindedness" was determined largely by the then recent invention of the IQ test, as well as by scientists' rather arbitrary judgments of what counted as appropriate behavior.

By these standards not only "idiots, imbeciles, and morons" but entire ethnic groups were deemed "inferior." Interestingly, there is no available record of a scientist judging his or her own group "inferior."

Zany racial theorizing with a "scientific" foundation has gone on at least since the industrial revolution. With industrialization, the world's prosperity ballooned and it looked like there would at last be more than enough wealth to go around. At the same time, it created the need for a permanent class of unfortunates to operate the heavy equipment.

Consequently, the owners had to come up with some halfway respectable explanation of why they deserved Newport mansions and everyone else merited nineteen-hour days in the mill struggling to keep their digits out of the the widget-making machines. The answer was Social Darwinism, the pseudo-biological notion that certain types of people are born to breathe asbestos dust for six bucks an hour while others have "cellular phones and Malibu beach houses" somehow inscribed in their genetic code.

From the start, the most enthusiastic eugenics advocates emerged from society's upper strata. David Starr Jordan, president of Stanford University, also headed Cold Spring Harbor, the nation's first biolab devoted to building a better human. Mrs. E. H. Harriman endowed the Eugenics Records Office (ERO)—the eugenicists' think tank—with a $15,000 grant and reached into her own pocketbook to cover staff salaries.

John D. Rockefeller, whose progeny personified the American ruling class, was the ERO's number-two cash cow. The first "Race Betterment Conference" took place in Battle Creek, Michigan, at the initiative of Dr. John Harvey Kellogg, whose family business still leads the Western world in Froot Loops production (a contribution to the betterment of the species if ever there was one).

The plutocrats were in league with scientists, many with formidable reputations. These scientists expended immeasurable energy trying to "prove" that blacks were stupid, Jews were greedy, Mexicans were lazy, women were nutty and so on—as well as the corollary; rich, white people with good table manners and glowing report cards were genetically superior. This massive waste of time began when Victorian Englishman Sir Francis Galton published his observations that the most "eminent" members of British society, by and large, had very eminent parents. That might not seem like much of a revelation today, but apparently it was so mindblowing to Galton that he could think of no other causal factor than pure heredity. Charles Darwin himself paid homage to Galton's "admirable labors" in establishing that "genius...tends to be inherited."

Galton came up with the term *eugenics* to advocate breeding better humans. Like so many theoreticians of his day, he asserted, among other things, that blacks lagged behind whites on the evolutionary scale. This ugly bit of quackery, like a wart, won't seem to go away.

As recently as the 1960s, Columbia University psychologist Henry Garrett maintained that people of African lineage are in fact 200,000 years behind those of fairer complexion. In the midst of the civil rights movement he condemned desegregation, with its presumably inevitable sexual mingling of blacks and whites, as "breeding down."

The attempt to codify existing class structure in some kind of biological schemata drags on. And it is worth noting that the endeavor is *not* limited to Klansmen or fringey crypto-fascists (as is, for example, the bogus-scholarly project to establish that the Holocaust never happened). The elite media's warm reaction to such questionable outpourings as Harvard ant expert Edward O. Wilson's 1975 manifesto, *Sociobiology: The New Synthesis* and its 1978 follow-up *On Human Nature*—e.g., a fawning *Time* magazine cover story, and a Pulitzer Prize for Wilson—reveals an unsettling eagerness on the part of powers-that-be to embrace the idea that some people are inherently better than others.

The issue is hardly passé. The Pioneer Fund, established in 1937 to finance "study into the problems of human race betterment," according to its charter (and that's a *revised* charter), was still handing out grants in 1989. University of Delaware researcher Linda Gottfredson got $174,000 to study the supposed relation between race and job performance.

The Pioneer Fund is not racist, said its president, New York lawyer Harry Weyher. It is merely concerned about "problems of heredity in the human race."

From the conviction that some members of the human race have hereditary "problems" it is but a short leap to advocacy of eugenic action. William Shockley, the Nobel Prize–winning electronics pioneer, advanced a proposal in total seriousness to pay persons—black persons—with low IQ scores a cash incentive of $1,000 per point below 100 to have themselves sterilized.

But nowhere is the urge of the "establishment" to justify its existence in scientific terms embodied better than in the person of Konrad Lorenz. A trailblazer in the field of ethology, the study of how behavior patterns are supposedly fixed by genetics, and a source for some of Wilson's key points, the Austrian-born Lorenz was accepted as a member of Germany's Nazi Party on June 28, 1938. In 1942, Lorenz wrote a paper employing principles of ethology and calling for a "self-conscious, scientifically based race policy" administered by "our best individuals" with the aim of inducing "a more severe elimination of morally inferior human beings."

Sadly enough, exactly that program was already well under way at the time, under the guidance of the same "best individuals" who accepted Lorenz into their political party.

Lorenz's bestseller *On Aggression* contained most of the same ideas, albeit stated in more politically palatable language. *On Aggression*, Lorenz's popularized explication of his life's work in ethology, was described by one journalist as appearing "to confirm the prejudices of an authoritarian Right."

In 1973, amid protests from scholars worldwide who knew of his past affiliations and understood his enduring ideological affinity for those prejudices, Konrad Lorenz traveled to Stockholm, Sweden, to accept his Nobel Prize.

MAJOR SOURCES

Chorover, Stephan L. *From Genesis to Genocide: The Meaning of Human Nature and the Power of Behavior Control.* Cambridge, Mass.: MIT Press, 1983.

Parfrey, Adam. "Eugenics: The Orphaned Science" In *Apocalypse Culture*, edited by Adam Parfrey. Los Angeles: Feral House, 1990.

Reilly, Philip R. *The Surgical Solution: A History of Involuntary Sterilization in the United States.* Baltimore: Johns Hopkins University Press, 1991.

Much of this chapter was based on research compiled by G. Lawrence Vankin.

4

The Disaster Agency

The plague of hurricanes, earthquakes, and other natural disasters that beset America during the late 1980s seemed to mystify the Federal Emergency Management Agency (FEMA). While victims pleaded for attention, the bureaucracy charged with handling disaster relief fumbled and stalled. Alas, if only catastrophe had taken a more familiar form—say, nuclear war, border-storming "aliens," or rampaging radicals— FEMA would have known *precisely* what to do: Slam subversives into national detention centers, declare martial law, suspend the U.S. Constitution, and govern from underground bunkers until the apocalypse is contained and mopped up.

Most Americans had never even heard of this obscure government agency before syndicated columnist Jack Anderson reported in October 1984 that FEMA had prepared bizarre "standby legislation" that would, in the event of a national crisis, "suspend the Constitution and the Bill of Rights, effectively eliminate private property, abolish free enterprise, and generally clamp Americans in a totalitarian vise." In any self-respecting banana republic, such a document might be called a

27

blueprint for a coup d'état. FEMA called it "national security" planning.

Cold War delirium only partly explains FEMA's preoccupation with junta-minded plotting during the Reagan era. To understand how a disaster relief agency came to think of itself as a "junior CIA or FBI," as one critic put it, it's helpful to consider the mind-set that launched the Reagan Revolution. In 1981, Ronald Reagan and his arch-conservative troops marched into Washington determined to extinguish a conflagration that had, in fact, long since burned itself out. In the eyes of the president's aging posse, however, the flaming hippies, militant minorities, and draft-dodging radicals of the sixties and early seventies continued to pose a clear and present danger.

Thus was born FEMA. Or, more accurately, thus was it born again. Jimmy Carter had established the agency as a catchall for natural-disaster relief and civil defense planning. But under Reagan, FEMA immediately went off the deep end, eyeing peaceful demonstrators as potential bomb-throwing terrorists.

To head the agency, Reagan and presidential counsel Edwin Meese III (later U.S. attorney general) tapped their old friend "General" Louis O. Giuffrida, a stealth-obsessed ex-California National Guard officer who preferred to be addressed according to his former rank in that organization. Giuffrida was eminently qualified for what Reagan and Meese had in mind. Prepared for all contingencies, he had himself deputized so he could pack a sidearm at the office.

During the late sixties and early seventies, Giuffrida had served as Governor Reagan's terrorism advisor and at Reagan's request founded the California Specialized Training Institute (CSTI), a school for police and military commandos. To quote an early CSTI instruction manual: "Legitimate violence is integral to our form of government, for it is from this source that we can continue to purge our weaknesses."

Giuffrida and Meese (then Governor Reagan's chief assistant) helped develop a plan to purge California of its militant *and* peaceful protesters. Operation Cable Splicer, a variation of the army Garden Plot, a "domestic counterinsurgency" scheme, spied on suspected radicals and marshaled maximum force to squash riots and legitimate demonstrations alike.

But if the early seventies were heady days for military and civil defense planners, the budding 1980s turned out to be a veritable renaissance for cold warriors. As Reagan warned complacent Americans about the Evil Empire and the communist horde (which was bivouacked just south of Texas, the Gipper claimed), the Pentagon prepared plans for World War IV—mere World War III preparations being hazardously short-sighted. Giuffrida, meanwhile, battened the hatches at FEMA. Signs were posted warning employees that SECURITY IS EVERY-BODY'S BUSINESS. A new phone system was installed to record each number dialed, and memos were circulated reminding staffers that personal phone calls were *verboten*: "Calling to say you will be home late could result in a fine or separation from the job," advised one memorandum.

FEMA-sponsored conferences obsessed over the possibility of "radical environmentalists" teaming up with terrorists and doing unkind things to nuclear power plants. In fact, FEMA's R & D work made the CIA's LSD dabbling look like a 4H project. According to Donald Goldberg, who helped research Jack Anderson's column, government scientists advised FEMA on mob control techniques such as "injecting terrorists with stimulants and tranquilizers to manipulate their actions in times of crisis, or zapping them with microwaves to alter their perceptions."

Given the dense trench-coat atmospherics, it was probably inevitable that one Lieutenant Colonel Oliver North would find a home away from home in Giuffrida's FEMA. As White House National Security Council liaison to FEMA, the Iran-Contra point man reportedly collaborated with Giuffrida in drawing up secret wartime contingency plans, possibly including the scheme to commandeer the Bill of Rights. Although North denied helping draft such a plan, Congressional Iran-Contra investigators never adequately grilled him on the matter. When

Texas representative Jack Brooks asked North about his work for FEMA, Senate panel chairman Daniel Inouye gavelled Brooks to silence, insisting that the question dealt with classified matters. Such was the persuasiveness of FEMA's national security stamp.

FEMA's wartime crisis strategy was tested in a series of simulated war games conducted in conjunction with Pentagon maneuvers. In early 1984, FEMA, military, and other government officials met in portentous secrecy to plan a "readiness exercise" code-named Rex-84.

FEMA coordinated Rex-84 with the military's Night Train 84 operations, which deployed thousands of troops in Honduras near Contra supply bases in April 1984. The FEMA portion of the simulation involved an international crisis, presumably a U.S. invasion of Nicaragua, which supposedly would set off "uncontrolled population movements" (as one declassified FEMA memo described it), with hordes of "refugees" swarming over the Mexican border into the United States.

According to an August 1985 article in *Penthouse* magazine co-authored by Goldberg, during the exercise FEMA would round up some 400,000 fictional "aliens" in a six-hour period and detain them (or, rather, *simulate* rounding up and detaining them) in military camps throughout the United States. FEMA apparently justified the concentration camps by presuming that terrorist moles would be peppered among the refugees.

But as Goldberg noted, the Mexican border's daunting terrain made an influx of gate crashers on the order of hundreds of thousands highly unlikely. In fact, more than one critic has suggested that Rex-84 was really a drill to practice rounding up crowds of *American* citizens. It would have been a game plan not unlike Cable Splicer or Garden Plot, designed to quash public protests in the event of a controversial government deed—an invasion of Central America, for example.

Indeed, Giuffrida had once considered tossing Americans into concentration camps. In a 1970 paper written as an army student, Giuffrida devised a hypothetical plan for incarcerating black radicals, describing how to build and run detention camps.

That Rex-84 dealt with more than merely apprehending illegal immigrants is certain. A heavily censored FEMA memo obtained by the *Miami Herald* described the Alpha Two phase of the exercise, as a test of "emergency legislation, assumption of emergency powers...etc." In other words: martial law.

The joint FEMA-military martial law plan was more than a simulation. Shortly before the Rex-84 drill, the Pentagon Joint Chiefs of Staff had prepared an internal document itemizing the military's purported authority to proclaim martial law in times of crisis, take over local policing, and even run the courts. It was a dubious claim at best. The Posse Comitatus Act forbids the military from operating in the United States, a prohibition backed by Supreme Court precedent.

But Giuffrida was already on record as a martial law booster. In a 1972 CSTI course manual on civil disorder, Giuffrida described martial law as "the legal means available to control people during a civil disorder," including "the replacement of all civil government by the military."

The "standby" emergency legislation that columnist Anderson exposed prescribed nothing less than an American police state. Called the Defense Resources Act, the draft plan would presumably gather dust on the shelf until a time of crisis, when it would be presented to a preoccupied Congress for speedy approval. In fact, the benevolently titled legislation granted the president near-dictatorial powers, including the authority to censor communications, ban antigovernment strikes, nationalize industry, seize private property for "the national defense," and authorize loyalty oaths to the state.

To augment the Defense Resources Act, FEMA prepared a draft presidential executive order to be invoked by the commander in chief during an "emergency." The order would put FEMA in charge of all government agencies. According to the *Miami Herald*, the executive order activated the aforementioned legislation, thereby removing Congress and constitutional democracy from the equation entirely.

Alas, FEMA's ambitious plans were truncated shortly after the Rex-84 games, when Attorney General William French Smith complained about the agency's attempted power grab. In a letter addressed to North's boss (and fellow Iran-Contra player), Robert McFarlane, Smith warned that FEMA was trying to anoint itself "emergency czar." And, as Smith demurred, FEMA's generous definition of crisis encompassed "'routine' domestic law emergencies." Smith's objections apparently killed the draft executive order.

Though the full scope of the Rex-84 games remains obscure, the Ollie North connection is particularly interesting, given that North was simultaneously working with the Pentagon and the CIA on plans for combat forces in Central America. Was FEMA plugged into the Iran-Contra scandal coordinated by North? Because Congress chose not to pursue that avenue of Contragate, we don't know for certain. However, allegations have been made. Daniel Sheehan, crusading (perhaps recklessly so) attorney with the Christic Institute law firm, suspected that Rex-84 served as cover for illegal arms shipments to the Nicaraguan Contras. Citing unnamed sources (including one described as a member of FEMA's legal division), Sheehan claimed that FEMA distributed "hundreds of tons of small arms and ammunition" to civilian militiamen in "state defense forces" in the United States.

From the early days of the Reagan administration, FEMA had prodded state legislatures to form state defense forces, which would act as paramilitary police in the event of a national crisis. Militia in several states were recruited by placing ads in *Soldier of Fortune*-style magazines. In several instances state defense forces subsequently had to be purged of neo-Nazis, white supremacists, and other unsavory characters.

According to Sheehan, FEMA's plan was to distribute the guns and ammo to state defense forces as part of the Rex-84 war games. The militiamen would return only half of the artillery and would smuggle the remainder to the Contras, thereby circumventing the congressional ban on lethal aid to the Nicaraguan guerrillas.

Though the scheme certainly sounds like a "neat idea" worthy of the North brain trust, it's hard to imagine how even FEMA could justify parceling out guns and ammo for the sake of a war *simulation.* Because Sheehan never got a chance to argue his case in court (a judge threw out the Christics' sweeping lawsuit, calling it "frivolous"), his theory has to be filed under the category of "interesting speculation."

Other speculation about FEMA having its fingers in the Iran-Contra cookie jar revolves around a tip to Senate investigators in 1983 that C-130 and C-141 cargo planes were bound for Texas. Because the planes were rigged with troop seats, Senate staffers suspected that they were secretly ferrying troops to Central America. FEMA insisted the flights were part of its supersecret "continuity of government" (COG) program, and utterly refused to discuss the matter further.

FEMA made COG another of its obsessions. Under COG, FEMA has the last word in national eschatology. While mundane natural disaster plans gathered dust during the 1980s, FEMA beefed up its rather fanciful strategies for surviving a nuclear war, with emphasis on survival of the federal government. And the rest of us? Well, as Reagan's deputy undersecretary of defense put it: "Dig a hole, cover it with a couple of doors, and then throw three feet of dirt on top....If there are enough shovels to go around, everyone is going to make it."

Under the aegis of FEMA, top government brass have the benefit of rather more lavish excavations, with the crown jewel being a top-secret underground fortress built during the early 1950s (and predating the elaborate James Bond movie sets) at a cost of more than $1 billion. The Facility, as it is known, is a sort of nuclear winter White House situated beneath the solid granite of Mount Weather in Bluemont, Virginia, forty-five miles west of Washington. It has been described as an "underground city," complete with roads and a battery-powered

subway. It boasts office buildings and hospitals, private apart-
ments and dormitories, and a power plant and artificial lake
illuminated by fluorescent light. Rounding out the science
fiction furnishings are a color video phone system and one of
the world's most powerful supercomputers.

In the event of a major nuclear or other catastrophe, surviving feds would run the country from The Facility as well as
from FEMA's underground command center in Olney Maryland, and up to fifty regional bunkers salted throughout the
nation. There's even an underground Pentagon more than six
hundred feet below solid granite just north of Camp David.

Unfortunately, during a national catastrophe the feds administering the former United States might not be familiar names to
you. FEMA's COG scheme involves about three thousand
unelected, unaccountable people recruited and trained by
FEMA "to serve in executive positions in the federal government in time of national security emergency."

FEMA under Giuffrida never had a chance to retreat to its
mole-man cities, govern by remote control, or even demonstrate
the uses of "legitimate violence." Giuffrida resigned in 1985,
reportedly under pressure from Pentagon and FBI officials who
saw in the ambitious "general" a more imminent emergency:
their endangered fiefdoms.

MAJOR SOURCES

Chardy, Alfonso. "North Helped Revise Wartime Plans." *Miami
    Herald*, 9 July 1987.
Emerson, Steven. "America's Doomsday Project," *U.S. News & World
    Report*, 7 August 1989.
Goldberg, Donald, and Indy Badhwar. *Penthouse*, August, 1985.
Peck, Keenen. "The Take-Charge Gang." *The Progressive*, May 1985.
Poundstone, William. *Bigger Secrets*. Boston: Houghton Mifflin
    Company, 1986.
Sheehan, Daniel P. *Affidavit of Daniel P. Sheehan*. 12 December 1986.

5

The Sickening Secret

No one can be certain what genius first realized that disease could be turned from an uncontrollable killer into a weapon. Maybe some fourteenth-century Tartar. Perhaps the same one who got the bright idea, as he watched his comrades dropping from plague during their three-year siege of the Genoan-occupied Black Sea town of Caffa, to catapult cadavers over the city walls.

Nice move, if a little shortsighted. The Genoans fled the city all right. Then they dispersed, bacillus-ridden, throughout Europe.

Or perhaps it was whichever German surmised that anthrax might do quite nicely in cutting down Europe's livestock supply during World War I. It really doesn't matter who thought of it first, the fact is, biowar got its biggest boost from exactly the effort designed to curtail it: the 1925 Geneva Convention. On June 17, 1925, most of the global powers at the convention affixed their stamps to a protocol banning the use of biological weapons.

There were two important abstainees. The United States

didn't sign, which was slightly curious because at that point, America showed little interest in developing germ weapons. The other no-show was a different story. With the impetus of an ambitious and, in a twisted way, visionary young military doctor named Shiro Ishii, Japan had become infatuated with dreams of infecting its enemies. A decade later Japan occupied Manchuria and Ishii commanded his very own biowar empire, replete with the emperor's seal.

The sprawling operation was centered in a remote Manchurian town called Pingfan and was euphemistically named the Anti-Epidemic Water Supply Unit, Unit 731, now better known as the Ishii Corps.

Unit 731's research methods were scientifically sloppy and ethically, well, not quite right. Their test subjects were humans: Koreans, Chinese, and Russians at first. Then, after Japan went to war with the West, American, British, and Australian prisoners found themselves marched, shipped, and hauled to an encampment near the faraway Manchurian city of Mukden. There they were met by a masked welcoming committee of medical personnel who greeted them by spraying some indeterminate liquid in their faces, ramming glass probes in their rectums, and injecting them with mysterious serum.

Many of the soldiers, unsurprisingly, died. But their bodies were not disposed of according to orthodox disease-control techniques. To say the least. The creepy team of scientists came back and dissected the corpses.

These practices were a matter of routine for Ishii's Unit 731, whose vast kingdom of disease is thought to have traversed much of eastern Asia. The lab at Pingfan, alone, held germ factories that bred eight tons of toxins per month. It also contained an impressive flea farm useful in vectoring Ishii's personal favorite malady, bubonic plague. Ishii's unit pelted several Chinese cities with "flea bombs," igniting outbursts of plague.

Unit 731 infected thousands of human beings, American and British POWs among them, with plague, tetanus, anthrax, botulism, meningitis, tuberculosis, and a potpourri of similar noxious concoctions. Ishii's team of medical experts coolly charted their subjects' illnesses from infection to death. Prisoners who complained of crippling diarrhea were "tested" by being compelled to run laps around the camp until they dropped from exhaustion. Some were made to stand naked in 40-below weather until their limbs froze, ostensibly to study the effects of disease in cold climates. The details aren't really important.

At least not to the United States War Department and General Douglas MacArthur. In Ishii and his files, the military brass realized, they had a motherlode of data that the United States could never develop on its own due to—as two American biowarfare researchers eloquently put it upon returning from interviews with Ishii and his underlings in Tokyo—"scruples attached to human experimentation."

Taking a unique approach to supporting our boys in the field, MacArthur suggested a deal that would allow Ishii and the rest of Unit 731's mad scientists immunity from war-crimes prosecution if they would just share their test results with American researchers, an arrangement that suited Ishii just fine. Only the state department objected, on grounds that later revelation of the deal might "seriously embarrass" the U.S. government.

Ishii slipped into reclusive retirement, devoted, according to his daughter, to religious study—though rumors ran rampant that he made repeated visits to Korea helping the United States mount a biowarfare campaign there. Dr. Murray Sanders, the military physician who finally blew the whistle on the secret deal, believed that Ishii gave lectures at Fort Detrick, Maryland, where American scientists immersed themselves in a supersecret germ weapons project after the war.

Many of Ishii's top associates went on to illustrious and rewarding careers with Japanese universities, corporations, and the government. The doctor who oversaw the cold-weather experiments struck lucrative deals with commercial fisheries as a "freezing specialist." His contribution to the frozen fish industry can only be guessed at.

The extensive unpleasantness that was Unit 731 remains one of World War II's more obscure large-scale crimes against humanity, thanks to both a U.S. government coverup reflex and Japan's always intriguing compulsion to transform, ignore, or reinvent its own history.

Indeed, if a Tokyo graduate student in the early eighties hadn't stumbled across a shred of Ishii's scant remaining paper trail, the Japanese public might never have known about its existence.

But it seems Ishii's empire extended into Tokyo, where things become a little tougher to conceal, seeing as how there are fifteen million people there. In 1989, a construction crew hit on a chock-full stash of human remains beneath the pavement of Shinjuku, Tokyo's futuristic redevelopment zone. "The remains were found just steps from the site of the wartime laboratory of Lt. Gen. Shiro Ishii," reported the *Asahi Evening News*, which noted the belief of Kanagawa University Professor Keiichi Tsuneishi—Japan's leading 731 authority—that Ishii's unit had transported the bodies of its victims to Tokyo for further "study."

In August of 1993, several Chinese families, who think that bones of family members may be among the ghoulish heap, began demanding that Japan identify the skeletons. So far the government's approach to the unusual archaeological find has been ho-hum, declining to investigate where the bones came from or run any tests.

Not that the United States always provides a better example of openness, at least on the topic of biowarfare. For some reason, a chapter of Peter Williams and David Wallace's book *Unit 731: The Japanese Army's Secret of Secrets*, was omitted from the American edition. It appeared in England, Australia, Canada, and New Zealand.

The chapter was titled "Korean War" and it explored the still controversial evidence that the United States military employed Ishii's techniques against China and North Korea. The charges had been around since the fifties, and were either hushed up or brushed off as commie propaganda (REDS' PHOTOGRAPHS ON GERM WARFARE EXPOSED AS FAKES—EVIDENCE IS CONCLUSIVE, hollered a March 15, 1952, *New York Times* headline). Williams and Wallace base their account largely on the findings of the International Scientific Commission for the Facts Concerning Bacterial Warfare in Korea and China (ISC), the one source "generally accepted today as being of high quality," the authors say.

The ISC found that numerous Chinese and Korean sites suffered unexplained outbreaks of bubonic plague and other diseases that coincided with the appearance of nonindigenous or out-of-season insects in those areas. A Chinese plague expert who examined the Korean outbreak told the ISC that his results "explain the reasons why the Americans deliberately protected the Japanese bacteriological war criminals." The United States used Ishii's "flea bomb" method to spread the plagues, ISC evidence indicated.

Nor were fleas the only weapon deployed by American biowarriors. On an April night in 1952 an American F-82 fighter was spotted flying over a Chinese village near the Inner Mongolian border. With the break of day, residents were greeted by an infestation of more than seven hundred voles. Of the voles who survived both the night cold and ravaging cats, many "were sluggish or had fractured legs."

A test on one dead vole showed that it was infected with plague. At first, "the Commission was puzzled how the voles had been dropped from the air," write Williams and Wallace. "But Unit 731 had devised such methods."

In North Korea, the ISC learned of a bizarre clam bombing. In what the ISC determined was a failed attempt to contaminate a local water supply, American planes unloaded cholera-infested clams on a hillside near a water purification plant.

"Japanese research had shown that marine lamelli-branch mollusks were well suited as media for the growth of cholera vibrio," Williams and Wallace report.

Such were the rewards of MacArthur's secret deal. Several

Mukden survivors—who years later still suffered from unexplained outbreaks of fever and illness—tried to pry the truth from their own recalcitrant governments. As late as 1987, British and American Mukden vets were told "no evidence" existed that Allied prisoners were victimized by Ishii's brand of scientific inquiry. In fact, such evidence had existed for more than forty years, and was known to MacArthur when he conceived the secret deal.

It was through this covert pact, and the subsequent conspiracy to cover it up within the U.S. and British governments, that Shiro Ishii became the father of modern biological weapons. The U.S. biowarfare program was lackadaisical until 1942, when Chang Kai-shek wrote a letter to Winston Churchill filling him in on Ishii's machinations. The British had their own, quite minor research effort going, and the United States joined in. A year later, the Americans got their own project off the ground at a place called Camp—later Fort—Detrick in Maryland.

The quest for the "biological bomb" was conducted under the same air of paranoid self-importance as was its atomic counterpart. But unlike the Manhattan Project, which drew leading physicists of the day, biowarfare research repulsed the nation's top biologists who recoiled from the endeavor. Those darn scruples again.

The government announced the biowarfare project in 1946, but the public's horrified response prompted the army's chief of staff, Dwight Eisenhower, to slap a three-year gag order on the project—broken only by Defense Secretary James Forrestal's 1949 debunking of public concerns as "unduly spectacular."

In the meantime, Fort Detrick, now largely an outpost of the CIA, plugged away at such unspectacular enterprises as the search for toxins that could disguise assassinations as natural deaths and other spooky schemes that have since became the stuff of spy-buff legend.

U.S. researchers did test toxins on humans, albeit volunteers. Prison inmates and, weirdly, Seventh Day Adventists lined up to get shot up with psittacosis, equine encephalitis, and tularemia.

But it still wasn't enough. One of the biggest problems in deploying biological weapons is somehow ensuring that—oops!—the germs don't blow back in your own army's face. To check how germ clouds drifted under actual weather conditions, the military started dousing American cities with bacteria.

A 1950 "attack" on San Francisco, in which a navy minesweeper spewed rare serratia bacteria all over the City by the Bay, sent eleven people to the hospital. One person died. Researchers also unleashed toxins into the Pentagon air conditioning system and the New York subways.

A lawsuit against the government by the San Francisco victim's family revealed three hundred "open air" germ tests between 1950 and 1969. In 1972 the U.S. government officially renounced the development and use of biological weapons.

Even so, secret germ tests continue, though often under the aegis of universities and private research institutes. Today's experiments have an ominous twist—genetic engineering. In 1986 the Wistar Institute, a venerable research facility in Philadelphia, infected Argentinian cattle with genetically altered rabies virus, catching Argentinian cattle ranchers completely by surprise.

The University of Oregon embarked on similar experiments in New Zealand.

The military found the biology business a hard habit to break. Despite the 1972 ban, the Defense Department was allowed to clone a Shiga toxin gene. Shiga toxin causes dysentery. The military, public spirited as ever, asserted that it merely sought a vaccine against the terminally runny affliction. But if the history of germ warfare research proves anything, it's that in the wacky world of infectious disease, defense and offense are often interchangeable.

The foreboding epilogue, or perhaps epitaph, to this unfortunate account is spelled A-I-D-S. The thesis that this fin de siècle epidemic sprang from biowarfare genetic experiments, perhaps on purpose, is common currency among conspiracy traffickers. Needless to add, there's nothing on the record to confirm it.

But then, there was "no evidence" that American prisoners were subjects of Ishii's human experiments either.

MAJOR SOURCES

Harris, Robert, and Jeremy Paxman. *A Higher Form of Killing: The Secret Story of Chemical and Biological Warfare.* New York: Hill and Wang, 1982.

McDermott, Jeanne. *The Killing Winds: The Menace of Biological Warfare.* New York: Arbor House, 1987.

Piller, Charles, and Keith Yamamoto. *Gene Wars: Military Control Over the New Genetic Technologies.* New York: Beech Tree Books, 1988.

Williams, Peter, and David Wallace. *Unit 731: The Japanese Army's Secret of Secrets.* London: Hodder and Stoughton, 1989.

6

A Lovely Little War

Looking back on it, the Gulf War—if America's massive assault on Iraq with minimal resistance can really be called a "war"—seems like surreal theater. Few events have so keenly delineated the distance between reality and spectacle. Even more alarming, the war left little question which domain we inhabit. Other than the obvious—yes, Saddam Hussein did invade Kuwait and, yes, that was really, really bad—very little in the predominant government-media view of the situation intersected with anything verifiable.

The U.S. government's actions leading up to, during, and after the war suggest that the inaugural battle of the New World Order was some kind of a manufactured crisis with a hidden agenda.

"The shallow, Nintendo view of the war on TV was false," former Pentagon defense expert Pierre Sprey testified to Congress. "It was created by hand-picked videotapes and shamelessly doctored statistics." "Surgical" air strikes? "About as surgical as operating on a cornea with machetes," as one *Washington Post* columnist wrote just a month into the bombardment.

"Kuwait will once again be free," predicted George Bush,

announcing the start of bombing. "Long martial law hinted by
Kuwait," noted a *New York Times* headline as the war wound
down.

George Bush said that Saddam Hussein was in some ways
worse than Hitler. His point is arguable, but the fact is that the
very same George Bush signed a National Security Directive in
1989 ordering closer ties with Iraq and clearing the way for
$500 million in credits to Mr. "Worse-than-Hitler." This is not
surprising. Bush had spent nearly a decade in an administration
weirdly enamored with Iraq, despite occasional public denun-
ciations of Saddam Hussein's police-state governance.

"Saddam's military machine is partly a creation of the
Western powers," reported investigative journalist Murray
Waas. Throughout Iraq's eight-year war of attrition with Iran,
the governments of France, Britain, and Germany sold the Iraqi
strongman everything from fighter planes and Exocet missiles
to ingredients for brewing nerve gas. The United States—
technically—maintained an embargo on arms sales to Iraq, but
the Reagan administration let it be circumvented by encouraging third-party munitions sales as well as through direct sales of
"dual use" technology: computers, even helicopters, which the
Iraqis pledged to use only for "education" or "recreation."
Nudge, nudge, wink, wink. According to Waas, when Bush
took office as president, dual-use sales "shifted into a far more
alarming area—the prerequisites of weapons of mass
destruction."

After the brief Gulf War, inquiries into these arms transac-
tions erupted into a short-lived scandal dubbed Iraqgate. At the
center of the storm was a seemingly insignificant Atlanta
branch of a multinational Italian bank, Banca Nazionale del
Lavoro (BNL), which somehow spirited $5 billion to Iraq over
two years until raided by the FBI on August 4, 1989. Yet under
the Bush administration, the accused bank managers were not
indicted for more than a year. And then, by some coincidence,
the indictment was returned one day after Bush declared a cease
fire in the Gulf War.

Officials of the tiny BNL branch were portrayed as "rogue operators" by government prosecutors who didn't find it worth their time to ask how $5 billion (yes billion) could find its way from one bank to a "worse-than-Hitler" dictator without the knowledge of government officials or at least the bank's higher-ups in Italy.

The Reagan and Bush administrations shared not only money and matériel but also intelligence information with Saddam as Iraq battled the forces of the evil Ayatollah in Iran.

"In other words," said former Reagan National Security Council staffer Howard Teicher, "we advised the Iraqis on how to prepare for war with the United States."

Leading up to the invasion of Kuwait, the United States sent Saddam Hussein not only aid but also comfort. Just a week before the August 2, 1990, invasion, Saddam sat down with U.S. ambassador April Glaspie—the now-infamous "green light" meeting. Glaspie was unnervingly blasé given the impending crisis. She even made a point of noting that the United States had "no opinion on the Arab-Arab conflicts, like your border disagreement with Kuwait." She also told Saddam that none other than Secretary of State James Baker had passed on word that "the issue was not associated with America."

Saddam apparently took Glaspie's remarks as carte blanche, and maybe they were intended that way. Hard to believe, given the administration's later public position, but this laissez-faire attitude was wholly consistent with Bush administration policy. A few days after the Glaspie-Hussein confab, and just three days before the invasion, John Kelly, the assistant secretary of state in charge of the Middle East, testified before Congress, where he was asked if in the event of an Iraqi military action, "is it correct to say that we have no treaty, no commitment, which would oblige us to use American forces?"

"That's exactly right," Kelly replied. Another shining green light.

No one promised the United States would *not* use force. But if the Bush administration's aim was to prevent war, it was picking an odd way to go about it. If anything, Bush and his buddies were egging the Iraqis on.

The Kuwaiti al-Sabah monarchy, which stood to suffer the most, also exhibited bizarre behavioral symptoms. In a preinvasion summit Iraq demanded $10 billion from Kuwait as compensation for singlehandedly fending off the forces of Islamic fundamentalism for eight years by engaging Iran in a disastrous stalemate war. The demand was not altogether unreasonable, and, in fact, Kuwait agreed to pay. But the al-Sabahs offered only $9 billion—a deliberate slap in the face. Later, after other agreements were reached, Kuwait would alter their terms. At the time, Saddam's troops were massing on the Kuwaiti border. Courage on the al-Sabah's part? Not likely, since they were the first ones out of the country when the tanks rumbled south. They chilled out in a five-star Saudi hotel while Bush's "coalition" fought their battle.

"If Saddam comes across the border, let him come," said Kuwait's foreign minister, Sheikh Sabbah, to Jordan's King Hussein in the midst of the preinvasion non-negotiations. "The Americans will get him out."

He had reason for confidence. When Iraqi troops ransacked the Kuwaiti Foreign Ministry they found a November 22, 1989, memo recording the results of a meeting between Kuwaiti officials and officials of the CIA.

"We agreed with the American side that it was important to take advantage of the deteriorating economic situation in Iraq in order to put pressure on that country's government to delineate our common border. The Central Intelligence Agency gave us its view of appropriate means of pressure...."

The CIA denounced the document as bogus—but admitted that the meeting took place.

There was another interesting, if somewhat less sinister meeting—this one on April 12, 1990—with five U.S. senators powwowing with the "Butcher of Bagdhad." Republican Alan Simpson sucked up to ol' Butch, telling him that his problems "lie with the Western media and not with the U.S. government....And it is a haughty and pampered press; they all consider themselves political geniuses."

This sentiment was echoed later by Glaspie, who shared with Saddam her opinion that "if the American president had control of the media his job would be much easier."

Ah, but during the Gulf War the American president did have control of the media. As did the military. Herding reporters into "press pools" proved effective—helped along by the journalists' acquiescence.

"If you look at it from the outset, the press was reflecting the views of the government," said *Los Angeles Times* Washington Bureau chief Jack Nelson, "and it never really changed."

Robert Fisk, Middle East correspondent for the British *Independent* was one of the few reporters to ignore the pools. When he showed up at one scene where the pool reporters had clustered awaiting the official military handouts, he was met by an NBC reporter who greeted him by saying, "You asshole. You'll prevent us from working. You're not allowed here. Get out."

The vituperative press pooler was Brad Willis, whose version of the incident, as recounted in *Harper's* publisher, John MacArthur's, book about the Gulf War press, included an extra detail. Fisk, Willis claimed, *posed* as a pool member and Willis, displaced by Fisk, was then bounced from the scene as a result. If Fisk's gambit succeeded, not only Willis but the whole pool would have been deprived of coverage because the nature of pool reporting was not to compete for the best story but to share the military's prescrubbed version of the story.

"It was a textbook example of the probably deliberate divide-and-conquer strategy of the U.S. military," wrote MacArthur. "Fisk, of course, wanted an uncensored exclusive and would do whatever it took to get it; he didn't want to share. Willis, playing by the Pentagon rules, was angry at the prospect of getting beaten by another reporter who was breaking the rules."

Consequently, with Fisk one of the rare exceptions, war

reporting took on a quasi-Orwellian demeanor. The press-promulgated paradigm of the conflict was Yellow Ribbonsville, U.S.A. versus Satanic Saddam. American reporters, almost to the one, referred to the U.S. military as "we," obviating any remaining distinction between journalist and subject and casting time-honored "objectivity" to the desert winds. Iraqi Scud missiles became "terrorist weapons" and "horrifying machines of death," while U.S. bombs were "smart." When *Newsweek* put the Stealth bomber on its cover it asked, "How many lives can it save?"

"That was the spin," marvel media critics Martin Lee and Norman Solomon in their book, *Unreliable Sources.* "American weapons don't destroy lives; they save them!" After all, dead Iraqis did not count as "casualties." They were merely "collateral damage," which in *Time* magazine's definition meant "dead or wounded civilians who should have picked a safer neighborhood."

"Denial was the key to the psychological and political structures supporting the war," Lee and Solomon wrote.

As for the war's motives, the interests of Western-based multinational oil companies and perhaps more important, the Western banks where Kuwaiti and Saudi oil Sheiks stowed their profits were treated with silence.

While Bush administration propaganda was treated as fact, the U.S. media was quick to denounce Iraqi "propaganda," even when it wasn't propaganda—as in the infamous case of the Baby Milk Bombing. A week into the war, CNN's Peter Arnett, the only Western reporter in Bagdhad, drew global condemnation for reporting that an allied bombing raid had destroyed Iraq's only infant-formula factory, leaving the nation's newborns hungry.

The U.S. military pooh-poohed the Iraqi claim. "It was a biological weapons facility, of that we are sure," said Joint Chiefs chairman Colin Powell. But the French contractors who built the plant and the New Zealand dairy technicians who visited it regularly swore it was exactly what the Iraqis said it was.

The *MacNeil/Lehrer NewsHour* showed a short clip of wounded Iraqi civilians—with the commentary that the scenes were subject to "heavy-handed manipulation" by the Iraqi government. As Lee and Solomon point out, the barely subliminal message was that anyone concerned about Iraqi suffering was a Saddam Hussein dupe.

Late in 1991, former Bob Woodward collaborator Scott Armstrong reported another unstated motivation for the war—though his story in the left-wing *Mother Jones* magazine met with major media indifference. Armstrong wrote that the previous decade, and at an astronomical cost of $200 billion, the United States and Saudi Arabia had assembled a massive infrastructure of "superbases" in the desert. This was all done without public, or even congressional knowledge. The war protected those bases, and the bases were instrumental in fighting the war.

Bush's star burned bright in the Gulf War glow, but somehow he managed to fritter away his political capital and lose his reelection attempt. But even in defeat, Bush, or at least his kids and pals, got a boon from the Gulf War. According to reporter Seymour Hersh, Neil and Marvin Bush; family friend and Bush's secretary of state, James Baker; and once high-flying chief of staff John Sununu (among others) have all worked hard to strike war-spoils deals with the Kuwaiti government.

Baker represented Enron, America's biggest builder of natural gas pipelines. The Enron exec who dispatched Baker to Kuwait wondered aloud to Hersh: "Is there any reason American companies shouldn't profit from the war in Kuwait?"

American politicians continue to profit. Bush's successor, Bill Clinton, enjoyed a healthy boost in his then-pallid polls when on June 26, 1993—two and a half years after the Gulf War ended—he ordered another bombing raid on Bagdhad.

Why? The given rationale was that the Iraqis had attempted

to assassinate Bush when the ex-president had visited Kuwait a few months earlier. Kuwait arrested seventeen supposed low-level conspirators in the plot, but as Hersh reported, "The American government's case against Iraq—as it has been outlined in public, anyway—is seriously flawed."

The dread Iraqi terrorists hand-picked for the Bush job included a coffee shop owner and a male nurse—the latter was the only source of information about the supposed plot. Most of the aspiring assassins were whiskey smugglers. The Kuwaitis have been known to exaggerate, especially about Iraqi violations of their sovereignty. When a group of Iraqi fishermen unwisely landed on the Kuwaiti island of Bubiyan, the Kuwaiti press release said that an Iraqi naval force had attempted to invade the island only to be defeated by crack Kuwaiti troops.

None of the male nurse's evidence has proved conclusive, or even close. The most solid bit of evidence is the "signature" of an electronic remote control detonator found in the bomb allegedly sent to blow up Bush. But Hersh reports that the piece was a common scrap of circuit board whose signature was anything but distinctive.

It is doubtful whether the "real" reason why the United States went to war in the Persian Gulf will ever emerge—and even more doubtful whether there was a single, identifiable motive. Unlike in Vietnam, where the ambiguous outcome elicited natural suspicions, in the Gulf the decisiveness of victory has buried the reality deeper than any Iraqi or American soldier who went to a sandy grave.

MAJOR SOURCES

Armstrong, Scott. "Eye of the Storm." *Mother Jones*, November-December 1991.

Hersh, Seymour M. "A Case Not Closed." *New Yorker*, 1 November 1993.

Hersh, Seymour M. "The Spoils of the Gulf War." *New Yorker*, 6 September 1993.

Kamen, Al. "Was It a Milk Factory or a Weapons Plant?" *Washington Post* (in *San Jose Mercury News*), 8 February 1991.

Lee, Martin A., and Norman Solomon. *Unreliable Sources: A Guide to Detecting Bias in News Media.* New York: Lyle Stuart, 1991.

MacArthur, John R. *Second Front: Censorship and Propaganda in the Gulf War.* New York: Hill and Wang, 1992.

Royce, Knut. "A Trail of Distortion Against Iraq." *Newsday,* 21 January 1991.

Salinger, Pierre, and Eric Laurent. *Secret Dossier: The Hidden Agenda Behind the Gulf War.* New York: Penguin Books, 1991.

Sifry, Micah, and Christopher Cerf, eds. *The Gulf War Reader.* New York: Random House, 1991.

7

The Adventures of the Keystone Kommandos

The assault on an apocalyptic religious sect calling themselves the Branch Davidians, in the tumbleweed flatlands of Waco, Texas, on April 19, 1993, followed in the grand tradition of American law enforcement mayhem.

This proud heritage includes such landmarks as the incineration of the Symbionese Liberation Army house in Los Angeles; the aerial firebombing of the black-separatist MOVE organization's communal apartment complex in Philadelphia—still the only American city ever to have been bombed from the air; and the Chicago police's 4 A.M. assault on Fred Hampton, riddling the Black Panther boss with bullets while he was sleeping in his own bed.

The Waco massacre that claimed the lives of eighty-six sect members (and a handful of federal agents) at the Branch Davidians' compound was more than a tad paramilitary. But the incident may have had much in common with the slaughter at Jonestown, Guyana, fifteen years earlier. Either it was a mass suicide—or mass murder by the government, which then tried to blame the victims for their own deaths.

In the six-week staredown before the Bureau of Alcohol, Tobacco, and Firearms (ATF) and the FBI went gonzo on the "cultists," the media flooded the nation with imprecations, encouraged by the authorities, that the Branch Davidians—led by the "Wacko from Waco" David Koresh (née Vernon Howell)—were likely to commit mass suicide at any time, just like those Jonestown nuts. Of course, given the feds' aural assault on the Davidians, the Kool-Aid solution may have appeared a not unwelcome option. Replicating a technique used four years earlier to flush Manuel Noriega from his sanctuary, the feds blared an earsplitting mishmash of noise that included the sound of rabbits being slaughtered, chanting Tibetan monks, roaring jet engines, and the Nancy Sinatra hit, "These Boots Were Made For Walking."

As if that wasn't torture enough, floodlights blazed all night long into the two-story ranch house where Koresh's followers struggled to catch a little shut-eye while the fed/press mob swelled and swarmed outside. But worst of all, the agents cut off all utilities and food supplies to the commune, an embargo enforced even when Koresh pleaded for replenishment of the group's baby milk supply almost six weeks into the standoff.

The siege began February 28 when the ATF embarked on a "surprise" attack against the Mount Carmel commune. The operation was so surprising that three local TV crews were on hand to capture it on videotape and two reporters stationed themselves in a nearby tree to get a fifty-yard-line view of the excitement. The attack produced a stalemate, with the ATF force incurring a 20 percent casualty rate (four dead, sixteen wounded).

At least some, if not all of the fallen feds were victims of the ATF commandos' own gunfire. According to communications specialist Ken Fawcett, who authored an affidavit based on his analysis of unedited video of the initial raid, the first shot was accidental. An agent's assault rifle somehow discharged and killed another ATF agent, Stephen Willis.

The full-scale battle began when an agent accidentally shot himself in the leg. Thinking they were under attack, the rest of the ATF platoon unleashed a fusillade of machine-gun shells.

In a network TV interview, ATF director Stephen Higgins tried to pin the lost "element of surprise" on leaks by a person or persons unknown. When several ATF agents later sued a Waco newspaper, the public learned that the ATF itself leaked the raid. Testifying before the Senate Judiciary Committee, Higgins was prudent enough not to repeat his lie. But even if no one had been tipped, an ATF chopper buzzed the compound before the commandos attacked. Being not complete idiots, the sect members probably surmised that something was up.

On April 19, the feds—with the FBI now leading the charge ahead of a chastened ATF—attacked in earnest, replete with armored vehicle assaults and an eight-hour barrage of CS, an especially noxious and flammable tear gas, usually fortified with kerosene. The compound burst into flames, the conflagration helped along by shock waves from M-60 tanks bashing the house. The surviving Davidians claimed, not implausibly, that the tanks actually started the fire by knocking over kerosene lamps that the electricity-denied sect was using to light the place. The tanks punched holes in the compound walls. The ventilation may have contributed in accelerating the blaze.

Koresh perished along with most of his followers, including many children.

The FBI immediately announced that two survivors of the cremated cult had confessed to sparking the fires. The bureau later pulled back a bit, noting that the cult members had not actually confessed—but they might as well have, because FBI sharpshooters personally witnessed them "cupping their hands."

An "independent" investigation later incriminated the Davidians, apparently confirming the Jonestownesque mass-suicide tale. But the truth about the Waco fire remains murky. It is worth noting that the fire investigator was a former ATF agent. The fellow's wife still worked in the ATF's Houston office, which was directed by senior agent Phil Chojnacki. It was Chojnacki who reportedly hovered over the compound in a helicopter before the ATF's February "surprise" raid.

Another lingering mystery is why the feds carried out their dime-store Green Beret operation at all. Conspiracy theories abound. One lawyer who claimed to represent some Branch Davidian members and their families, warned that over the weeks of the standoff there were troop movements across the nation and trainloads of U.N. tanks sighted in Portland, Oregon. As Peter Jennings said on a special report in the aftermath of the Branch Davidian's destruction, "this is a warning of things to come."

A writer for the magazine *Soldier of Fortune* suggested that the ATF was motivated by nothing more than petty vindictiveness. On February 21 Koresh was interviewed by an ATF agent and, in an apparent fit of hubris, screened a pro-gun group's anti-ATF video for his interrogator's benefit. On February 25 the ATF applied for the search warrant that resulted in the crisis.

Speculation aside, the only on-the-record purpose for the initial attack was to serve that search warrant. There is no evidence that the ATF informed the Branch Davidians of their intent to serve the warrant (though an ATF agent is said to have shouted something about it as the assault got underway), or that the Davidians refused them entry. Under the law, both must take place before law enforcement may use force to serve a warrant. The ATF could have asked for a special "no knock" warrant, but did not.

In a taped phone call after the initial raid, a puzzled Koresh told an ATF negotiator, "It would've been better if you just called me up or talked to me. Then you all could have come in and done your work."

There are even doubts over whether the Branch Davidians

were engaged in anything illegal at all. It is true that they were well stocked with arms and explosives—but popular assumptions to the contrary, there is nothing against the law about either, as long as all the paperwork is in order. At least some of the explosives had been purchased to excavate a ditch for a swimming pool. The pool was still under construction when the commune found itself at war.

Midway through the stalemate, the ATF suddenly announced that the Branch Davidians were manufacturing methamphetamines in a secret commune laboratory. No one bothered to ask, first of all, where this information came from, and second, what it had to do with anything. The ATF has no jurisdiction to enforce laws against drugs. Nor does the ATF have any authority to nab child molesters, another charge that helped demonize Koresh in the national media.

It is likely the drug-lab story was concocted to explain the Big Brotherish black National Guard helicopters circling over the site in violation of a Texas law that forbids use of state helicopters by federal authorities except in drug cases.

The methamphetamine allegation, significantly, never appeared in any legal document. As one skeptical reporter noted, it's not a crime to lie to the press, but fudging before a judge carries a few consequences.

On the other hand, the ATF affidavit filed in applying for the February 28 search warrant was not a model of accuracy. In it, ATF agent Davy Aguilera claims—in what later served as evidence of Koresh's fanaticism—that on April 6, 1992, Koresh warned a Texas Human Services official that he was a "messenger from God" and that when he revealed his true nature, "the riots in Los Angeles would pale in comparison to what was going to happen in Waco, Texas."

Scary stuff, except that when Koresh issued this alleged threat the L.A. riots were still three weeks away.

The ATF also claimed that they had to bust up the Davidians because Koresh, Hitler-style, had been bunkered up in there for weeks. In fact, he ventured into town at least once a week. He had sauntered out to a Waco night spot just two nights before the February attack.

The ATF never officially charged Koresh et al. with anything worse than illegal weapons possession. Five years before, Koresh and six associates were arrested by local police on attempted murder charges. Yet they cooperated fully (and were later acquitted). And how did the Waco sheriffs manage to avert the bloodletting that the federal authorities found ineluctable?

"We treated them like human beings," said Waco D.A. Vic Feazell, "rather than storm-trooping the place."

MAJOR SOURCES

Dingell, John D. III. "Licensed to Slaughter." *Incite Information*, July-August 1993.

Fawcett, Ken. "Why Waco?" In *Secret and Suppressed*, edited by Jim Keith. Portland, OR: Feral House Press, 1993.

Pate, James L. "Waco's Defective Warrants: No Probable Cause for Raid on Ranch Apocalypse." *Soldier of Fortune*, August 1993.

Report of Linda Thompson, American Justice Federation. Published electronically. Copy in authors' possession.

This chapter owes a debt to research compiled by Kenn Thomas.

8

The Conspiracy Queen and the G-Men

On April 23, 1981, agents of the Federal Bureau of Investigation arrived at Mae Brussell's home in the rustic, seaside burg of Carmel, California, to find out what she knew about a conspiracy to assassinate President Ronald Reagan.

It was the first and only face-to-face encounter between Brussell and the FBI, which at that time had kept a file on her for more than thirteen years.

Mae Brussell died of cancer seven years later at the age of sixty-six, closing a seventeen-year career of discursive radio broadcasts—based out of Bay Area nonprofit stations—that all but invented an entire genre of political research that has yet to find a place in the mainstream even today.

Brussell did not invent conspiracy theory. That human obsession had been around for a long time. But she pioneered the theory that a fascist cabal—directly traceable to the Third Reich itself—was the ultimate source of power in the United States and the world. What made her both more fascinating and more threatening (depending on your point of view) than the garden-variety conspiracy buff was the fact that her ideas were not spun from the fabric of her imagination, but from her reading list. In 1964, while still a mild-mannered suburban housewife, she purchased, read, and—over the next several years—indexed and cross-referenced all twenty-six volumes of the Warren Commission's evidence in its investigation of President Kennedy's assassination.

By the time of her death, her home library alone held about six thousand books and twenty years' worth of newspaper clippings (she read seven papers a day) and magazine articles. In her lifetime, she generated hundreds of tape-recorded broadcasts and several published articles on topics as diverse as the CIA's connection to the kidnapping of Patricia Hearst, the Jonestown massacre, Watergate, satanism, and so on.

She had also accrued a worldwide following which, when she died, became certain that "the intelligence community" was responsible for the death of their spiritual leader.

The legends of Mae Brussell's conflict with the heat are legion. But the paper trail is not plentiful. The Secret Service kept a file on her, but it was generated mainly because Brussell was not content merely to spout her opinions over the air.

"More than half of the file's [144 pages] would not exist," wrote one researcher who read the file, "if she had simply refrained from sending letters to presidents, calling up various police agencies, or visiting Maureen Reagan." Much of the remainder of the Secret Service file arose from the fact that Brussell's father, Rabbi-to-the-Stars Edgar Magnin, was a personal friend of Richard Nixon, whom Brussell expended no small amount of energy excoriating.

But if a hint exists anywhere that "the man" treated Mae Brussell as someone worth snuffing (or at least worth having her privacy invaded), we figured it would come from that most paranoid of domestic police forces, J. Edgar Hoover's FBI.

The 1981 interview is the first Brussell-FBI meeting recorded in the thirty-eight pages of her file released under the Freedom of Information Act (FOIA). If there were others, perhaps on a less formal basis, they are not mentioned. The Bureau does note that sixteen pages of the file, comprising four documents, have been withheld because "the vast majority of information in these four documents pertains to other individuals."

The "other individuals" in Mae Brussell's life were a vast and varied lot. They ranged from her father, a leader of L.A.'s Jewish community, to Bruce Roberts, purported author of the Gemstone File (see page 225). One can only speculate on what those confidential pages contain. Maybe nothing.

The public pages mention a few references to "pretext inquiries" about Brussell. That's when an agent or informer gathers information by pretending to be someone else. Sneaky, sure, but they did it to Brussell—or, more accurately, to her father—as early as 1966, five years before she went on the air with her weekly all-conspiracy radio program.

An apparently apropos-of-nothing teletype memo tagged, "Assassination of President John Fitzgerald Kennedy. Miscellaneous Information," is dated September 17, 1967, even though it refers to incidents from the first two months of the previous year. The memo originated in the FBI's San Francisco bureau, and is directed to the director (Hoover) and the New Orleans and Dallas offices.

"San Francisco files reveal that on 1/20/66 [blacked out] private investigator, Carmel, Calif., reported that a client advised that May [sic] Magnin Brussell had expressed great alarm over fact that U.S. is becoming fascist and a fascist coup would occur within two years. Advised she is daughter of Rabbi Edgar F. Magnin, Wilshire Temple, Los Angeles. [Blacked out] advised she recently moved to Carmel Valley with several small children and it was rumored she has 'left wing' leanings and is not in good favor with her father."

The Teletype goes on to mention the "pretext inquiry" at Rabbi Magnin's residence, a check of Brussell's credit records (which seem to reveal nothing except the name and occupation of her husband), and a review of Monterey County sheriff's records on Brussell that proved "negative." The memo notes a letter to the editor Mae penned and an op-ed piece in which she "takes the view Lee Harvey Oswald was not a communist."

The Teletype's conclusion: "no further action being taken by SF."

Needless to say, The Teletype was, in fact, apropos of something, and the next document in the file, a memo from "Director, FBI" to Dallas sheds a little light on what prompted the sudden interest in the then-unknown Mrs. Brussell.

"Due to the fact that Mrs. Brussell has been in contact with James [sic] Garrison at New Orleans and has made public comments concerning the investigation, Dallas and San Francisco are to immediately incorporate the information received concerning her into an appropriate letterhead memoranda suitable for dissemination....This matter is to be handled immediately."

The FBI's more-than-idle curiosity about New Orleans district attorney Garrison's JFK assassination probe has been documented widely and well. By powwowing with Garrison, Mae got swept up in the Bureau's net. But there was more to it than that, though from the released documents it's hard to tell exactly what.

A note attached to the "director's" reply states without further elaboration that a September 17, 1967, Delta Airlines flight from Dallas to San Francisco received a bomb threat and that "Mrs. May [sic] Magnin Brussell who was boarding this flight for San Francisco made comments at Love Field, Dallas, she had conducted research on the Kennedy assassination and had been in conference with D.A. Jim Garrison, New Orleans, for three days."

The implication seems to be that Mae claimed she was the target of the bomb threat. The FBI's late-1967 interest in Brussell must have been prompted by the Delta Airlines incident, spurred on when the Bureau realized that she'd been hanging out with Garrison.

Nothing further appears in the thirty-eight pages regarding

the Delta bomb threat or Mae's possible relation to it. By the
time of the next entry in the file, Mae Brussell had embarked on
her public career as an innovator of American conspiracy
theories. She was planning to edit a publication called *Conspiracy Newsletter*. A single-page memorandum on U.S. Government letterhead (at the bottom of which appears a picture of a
Minuteman and the slogan "Buy U.S. Savings Bonds Regularly
on the Payroll Savings Plan") shows that the FBI was up to its
tricks again.

"On 12/19/72," says the memo from the San Francisco office,
"a pretext call was placed to [blacked out] by SA [blacked out]
under guise of a student desiring a copy of his new publication.
[blacked out] advised that publication of the *Conspiracy Newsletter* has been delayed indefinitely. He advised that both he and
MAE BRUSSELL, who would be editor of the publication,
currently do not have time to work on it.

"In view of the above, this matter is being closed; however,
San Francisco will remain alert for possible future publication
of *Conspiracy Newsletter*."

It is indeed comforting to know that the nation's top law
enforcement personnel remained "alert" against such threats to
public safety as "publication of *Conspiracy Newsletter*." But
again, there seems to be a piece missing from the FOIA file's
picture.

The single page in the file is headed "Re Bureau letter to San
Francisco, 8/25/72." Where's the letter? Not in the file. The
innocent explanation would be that Mae Brussell was not
mentioned by name in the letter, which given the extreme
literal-mindedness of the FBI's FOIA staff, of course, rules out
including the letter in her file.

The first three paragraphs of the "Re Bureau letter" memo
are blacked out, the largest single deletion in the released pages
of Mae Brussell's FBI file. Along with the absence of the earlier
letter, the blackout leaves the origin of the FBI's interest in
Conspiracy Newsletter a mystery.

The next document, dated November 6, 1975, is equally

intriguing, though for different reasons. By this time Mae was well known as, shall we say, an "alternative" radio personality. Week after week she took to the public-access airwaves to unleash almost incomprehensibly complicated monologues of conspiracy.

Mae notified an assistant U.S. attorney—who then passed on the info to the FBI—that she had received the following correspondence (the letter appeared to have been signed, but the name is blacked out):

"Mae, you are thinking yourself in a circle of madness. Charles Manson has been 28 years in prison and all that B.S. you are running is only a reflection of what the news and books have programmed your soul's mind brain to.

"You are looking for attention. It seems as if you are looking for your death wish in the Family."

An unrelated document dated five years later refers back to this incident and states flat out that "during October and November of 1975 she received threatening letters from [blacked out] member of the Manson family."

Now, true, the Mansonites dispensed death threats at about the same rate that meter maids hand out parking tickets. But they made good on plenty. If any organization deserves credibility when threatening to off someone, it's Charlie's kids. Yet according to the FBI document "Assistant U.S. Attorney F. Steele Langford stated that the contents of the extortion letter did not amount to a threat."

Pursuant to that sage assessment, the FBI ordered "no additional investigation." In a bold and decisive step, however, the FBI advised Mae to "change her telephone number to an unlisted number and to immediately contact the FBI upon receipt of any additional such communications."

Maybe they were too busy awaiting publication of *Conspiracy Newsletter* to worry about death threats from the Manson family, but the FBI's inaction must have seemed eerie when Mae died in 1988, just a few months after canceling her radio show—after almost two decades—in response to a death threat. (Though her terminal cancer was described as unremarkable by her doctor, Mae's followers have speculated vigorously that her enemies had the technology and motivation to deliberately transmit the dread disease.) Her topic of concern at the time was satanic cults in the military. She also held the view, oft-mentioned in the FBI documents, that the Manson gang was connected to a U.S. intelligence or military operation.

The file next compiles Mae's 1976 correspondence with the FBI's director Clarence Kelley regarding her insistence that the body buried in Howard Hughes's grave is not Howard Hughes ("Remember, you were appointed by Richard Nixon, who played around with the law in his own hands. Did he put you there to hide, à la Watergate, or are you going to name those agents, your employees, who MADE THE POSITIVE IDENTIFICATION?"). Then the final fourteen pages deal exclusively with Mae's claim, made in April of 1981, that John Hinckley had placed her house under surveillance, the claim that prompted FBI agents to drop in on her in person.

Coming less than a month after the assassination attempt on President Reagan, Mae's claim, which she duly reported to the authorities, that Hinckley paid her a visit in January of that year attracted understandable interest. The episode began when Rudy Guiliani, then a U.S. attorney, now mayor of New York City, brought Mae's call to the FBI's attention. On April 23 the FBI interviewed her at her home.

She told them how, on January 13, she noticed a white sedan parked across the street from her house. She immediately assumed that the occupants of the vehicle were spying on her. A man and a woman sat in the car and Mae confronted them. The man remained silent, for the most part. When Reagan was shot, Mae recognized photographs of the accused assailant as the same quiet young man she had seen parked in front of her home.

After Mae's death, many of her friends and followers soared to incredible levels of paranoia, stashing her voluminous clip files where the heat couldn't reach them, but when she had FBI agents in her living room, Mae practically begged them to explore her private library.

She went so far as to request that the FBI set up a "task force" solely to wade through the "thousands of newspaper clippings and hundreds of books she has collected," according to a May 4, 1981, FBI report of the visit.

"The Bureau should be advised that any further contact with Mrs. Brussell regarding her theories would not be considered a wise expenditure of investigative effort," concludes the uncharacteristically wry report.

Another memo about the Hinckley incident and Mae's exciting FBI houseguests contains the agents' assessment that "Mrs. Brussell is well known to be mentally unstable and is not taken seriously by the local community concerning her conspiracy theories."

Interestingly, the Secret Service file on the Hinckley incident, while ultimately dismissing Mae's report, notes that "the subject, Brussell, appears legitimate."

Mae Brussell's FBI encounter ends with the alleged Hinckley-sighting and subsequent agent interview, though Mae remained at large for seven more years. Did the FBI completely lose interest in her after fourteen years, finally writing her off as a harmless nut? Did she give up on contacting them, and consequently, on getting her name placed in FBI records? Or is there something else in the file's unreleased pages.

The file ends with the FBI's brief summary of its contact over the years with Mae Brussell. The final incident it describes, that last official mention of Mae in FBI records, comes from a phone call she placed to the Monterey Resident Agency in 1977. The story is a poignant one, in a bizarre way.

"She advised that she was concerned over a situation regarding one of her daughters. She noted that a young man who was appearing in a play with her daughter had shown a romantic interest in her. This individual appeared to have plenty of money although he had no visible means of support. Brussell thought this individual might be an 'agent provocateur' directed against her by the FBI via her daughter."

MAJOR SOURCES

Beebe, Greg. "Conspiracy Theorists Ponder the Mae Brussell Question." *Santa Cruz Sentinel*, 28 February 1992.

Despot, X. Sharks. "Mae Brussell: Secret Service Files on the Queen of Conspiracy Theorists." *Steamshovel Press,* no. 8 (Summer 1993).

Vankin, Jonathan. *Conspiracies, Cover-Ups, and Crimes.* New York: Dell, 1992.

Whalen, John. "All Things Conspired." San Jose *Metro*, 17 November 1988.

Mae Brussell's FBI file, in authors' possession.

9

Microfilm at 11

In 1977, Carl Bernstein—of Woodward/Bernstein fame—reported that "more than four hundred American journalists... in the past twenty-five years have secretly carried out assignments" for the CIA. The *New York Times*—one of the CIA's most valuable media collaborators, according to Bernstein's sources—subsequently spread the blame a bit by putting the figure at "more than eight hundred news and public information organizations and individuals."

It was an astonishing revelation. For more than two decades, scores of distinguished reporters had let the CIA peek at their notes. They had assisted in the recruitment of foreign spies. They acted as Agency messengers abroad. Some of them even drew a paycheck courtesy of a trench-coated Uncle Sam.

If the prospect of the fourth estate shilling for intelligence agencies wasn't troubling enough, many of the CIA's journalist-spooks had knowingly spread propaganda abroad. And more than a few times, disinformation sown overseas filtered back home, the "blowback" or "domestic fallout" roosting in American newspapers as the gospel truth. It is also clear that CIA "black," or unattributed, propaganda has at times been aimed squarely—and illegally—at Americans.

The Agency also managed to place its own operatives inside some of the most prestigious American news organizations. As *New York Times* and *Time* magazine "employees," CIA spies enjoyed the perfect cover. Masquerading as inquisitive reporters, Agency operatives could turn up anywhere and ask probing questions without arousing suspicion.

"One journalist is worth twenty agents," a high-level CIA official told Bernstein. The CIA's faux newsmen even underwent training to learn to act and talk like reporters. Meanwhile, bona fide reporters were schooled in the elite art of spycraft: secret writing, surveillance techniques, and other skills.

The CIA's media manipulation organ came to be known in Agency parlance as the Propaganda Assets Inventory. Frank G. Wisner, the Agency's first chief of covert action, immodestly called it Wisner's Wurlitzer, a way of orchestrating public opinion anywhere in the world. Though Wisner committed suicide in 1961, his tune carried on for several more decades. In addition to its journalist assets and agents, the CIA has subsidized or owned as many as fifty newspapers, news services, radio stations, and magazines—mostly abroad but also at home. For instance, the Agency operated proprietary papers like the *Rome Daily American*, the *Manila Times*, and the *Bangkok Post*.

We may never know the full scope of the CIA's media manipulations, thanks to the deft maneuvers of former Agency directors William Colby and George Bush, who managed to curtail a Senate probe into the matter. Stonewalled at every turn and cowed by warnings that it was embarking on a latter-day "witch-hunt," the Senate Select Intelligence Committee chaired by Frank Church "deliberately buried" the results of its inquiry into the CIA-journalist connection, wrote Bernstein.

But we do know that top news executives gave their blessing to the rental of reporters as spies, informants, and propagandists. As former CIA director William Colby put it, "Let's not pick on some poor reporters. Let's go to the managements. They were witting." In their quest to combat "global communism," Bernstein wrote, "America's leading publishers allowed themselves and their news services to become handmaidens to the intelligence services."

The list of print and broadcast news executives who collaborated with the CIA was a rarefied one, including former *New York Times* publisher Arthur Hayes Sulzberger, Columbia Broadcasting System president William Paley, *Time* and *Life* magazine founder Henry Luce, and James Copley of Copley News Service (which happily turned over information on antiwar and black protesters, published CIA-produced editorials, and loaned at least twenty-three employees to the Agency). Other media mastodons who lent themselves to the CIA included ABC TV (a well-known, unnamed correspondent was said to be a CIA asset), NBC, the Associated Press, United Press International, Reuters, *Newsweek* magazine, Scripps-Howard, Hearst Newspapers, and the *Miami Herald*.

According to Bernstein's CIA and Senate sources, the two most important Agency assets, by virtue of their vast foreign reporting resources, were the *New York Times* and CBS. At the *Times*, the late Arthur Hayes Sulzberger approved cover arrangements for more than a half dozen CIA employees posing as *Times* staffers in foreign bureaus. Even though Sulzberger was close to then-Agency director Allen Dulles, he agreed to sign a secrecy agreement, as did his nephew, C. L. Sulzberger. According to several CIA sources, C.L. Sulzberger, the *Times*'s late foreign affairs columnist, once slapped his byline on a CIA briefing paper and published it verbatim. (Sulzberger called this charge "a lot of baloney.") The *Times* submitted stories to Dulles and later to his replacement, John McCone, for vetting and approval. More than once, McCone "edited" out certain bits of information from the stories, in effect deciding for the *Times* which news was "fit to print."

Like CBS's Paley and the elder Sulzberger, *Time* and *Life* magazine founder Henry Luce was a close chum of Dulles, who often enlisted the aid of his arch-conservative publishing pal. Luce allowed staff members to work for the CIA and offered jobs and credentials to CIA officers. He even appointed a personal representative to deal with the CIA, *Life* magazine publisher C. D. Jackson, who cut his teeth as the CIA's "special consultant to the president for psychological warfare." (Given Jackson's prominence as an American media czar, one has to ask, *psychological war against whom?* Conspiracy researchers certainly see *Life*'s glomming onto the Zapruder film footage of the JFK assassination as suspicious. Not only did Jackson's magazine buy up the rights to the film and keep it vaulted for years, it published frames from the famous home movie footage out of sequence, giving the incorrect impression that Kennedy's head snapped forward, as the Warren Commission wrongly concluded in its efforts to convince the public that a lone assassin fired from behind.)

Henry Luce's wife, Claire Boothe Luce, reportedly also knew of some of the CIA's undercover employees. A right-wing socialite who traveled in spooky circles, Madame Luce sponsored anti-Castro activities based in Florida and later became a founding director of an organization with the evocative title, Association of Former Intelligence Officers.

Although information swapping with intelligence operatives was once considered part of the give and take between reporters and their sources, some of the CIA-media alliances went well beyond the pale. Noted columnist Stewart Alsop, who wrote for the *New York Herald Tribune*, the *Saturday Evening Post*, and *Newsweek*, "was a CIA agent," according to a high-ranking Agency official quoted by Bernstein. Alsop helped plant disinformation in foreign media and evaluate potential CIA assets abroad. Alsop's brother, Joseph, pooh-poohed the charge, but one-upped his sibling by telling Bernstein that he, *himself*, was closer to the CIA than brother Stew.

The distinction between reporting and propagandizing for the CIA grew hazier still in the case of Hal Hendrix, one of the Agency's most valuable assets during the 1960s. As the *Miami*

News's Latin America correspondent, Hendrix was at ground zero in the Agency's covert action hotbed. According to Bernstein, Agency files contain lengthy reports of Hendrix's activities on behalf of the CIA. Though Hendrix has denied having anything but a "normal journalistic relationship" with the CIA, his co-workers referred to him as "The Spook."

Hendrix later ditched his reporting job and went to work for the International Telephone and Telegraph Corporation (ITT) in Chile. He perjured himself before a Senate committee probing CIA and ITT involvement in the covert campaign to thwart the election in 1970 of leftist leader Salvador Allende. Asked about the provenance of a cable he sent to inform an ITT vice president that the Nixon administration had approved plans "to keep Allende from taking power," Hendrix claimed the source of his information had been a Chilean friend. Whoops. A CIA cable subsequently turned up disclosing that Hendrix's real source was an Agency officer.

According to Bernstein, journalists were used extensively in the CIA's attempts to undermine Allende. Reporters disbursed funds to Allende's foes. They wrote anti-Allende propaganda for CIA-controlled publications. When some of this propaganda burrowed its way into the American media, it was hardly accidental. A 1970 CIA assessment spoke of "continued replay of Chile theme materials" in the American press, including the *New York Times* and *Washington Post*. "Propaganda activities," the report went on, "continue to generate good coverage of Chile developments along our theme guidance."

After the revelations of the late 1970s, how many journalists continued to shill for the CIA is anyone's guess. Although the *New York Times* reported that the CIA had terminated its relationship with journalists, in fact, the Agency under George Bush had only banned *paid*, full-time relationships, while Bush left the door open to pro-bono and part-time collaboration. In 1980, a *Los Angeles Times* headline announced CIA 'MIGHTY WURLITZER' IS NOW SILENT.

End of story? Maybe not. Even though the rationale for the

earlier media-CIA partnership—Cold War-era "national security"—is presumably dead and buried, a classified CIA
report that surfaced in 1992 would suggest that the affair
continues. The report on CIA "openness" stated that the
Agency's public affairs office "now has relationships with
reporters from every major wire service, newspaper, news
weekly, and television network in the nation." Apparently these
relationships have been fruitful for the CIA, because they have
"helped us turn some 'intelligence failure' stories into 'intelligence success' stories...." In many cases, the report continued, "we have persuaded reporters to postpone, change,
hold, or even scrap stories that could have adversely affected
national security interests."

It sounds as if the Mighty Wurlitzer plays on.

MAJOR SOURCES

Bernstein, Carl. "The CIA and the Media." *Rolling Stone*, 20 October
    1977.
Crewdson, John M., and Joseph B. Treaster. "CIA: Secret Shaper of
    Public Opinion." *New York Times*, 25–27 December 1977.
Lee, Martin A., and Norman Solomon. *Unreliable Sources: A Guide
    to Detecting Bias in News Media*. New York: Lyle Stuart, 1991.

II

From Beyond

10

Classified Secrets of the Sky

W hat crashed in Roswell, New Mexico?

Something large and silvery wobbled through the air and plowed into the desert dirt with a tremendous ka-boom. That much, generally speaking, goes without dispute. The date was July 2, 1947.

It is also a fact-on-record that the government took an immediate interest in...well, whatever it was. The air force dispatched a team to scoop up the wreckage—one metallic chunk was about four feet long—and flew some back to Wright-Patterson Air Force Base in Dayton, Ohio, for scrutiny. General Roger Ramey, the officer in charge, ordered his men not to talk to the press. But before Ramey could clamp a lid on the affair, the base's public information officer issued a press release announcing government acquisition of a "flying disc." An Albuquerque radio station picked up a leak of the story. As it broadcast a report, a wire came through from the FBI.

"Attention Albuquerque: cease transmission. Repeat. Cease transmission. National security item. Do not transmit. Stand by…"

A day later, the air force held a press conference and announced that what crashed at Roswell was a balloon.

The UFO saga actually began a few days earlier when businessman and avocational aviator Kenneth Arnold chased a squadron of nine "bobbing and weaving" objects as he flew in his private plane. He described the objects as "saucer shaped." Some pithy wag at an AP bureau dropped the phrase "flying saucers" into a wire dispatch and, forever, into the English language. The air force said that Arnold had pursued "a mirage."

There have been innumerable UFO reports since 1947. Some have been captured on film, still and moving (the UFOs and the film). They pop up all over the world, even in outer space. NASA astronauts have reported seeing weird objects, and UFO scribe Sean Morton, coauthor of *The Millennium Factor*, says that NASA photos of the so-called "dark side" of the moon remain, for some reason, classified.

The myth that UFOs only reveal themselves to corn huskers and residents of trailer parks is easily dispelled. A quick scan of UFO history books shows the air corps of one nation or another pursuing unidentifiable "blips" on a regular basis.

On November 23, 1953, an F-89 interceptor was chasing a UFO over Lake Superior when, according to radar operators, the two blips on the screen seemed to merge into one which then blinked off the screen. The jet and its pilot, Lieutenant Felix Moncla, were gone without a trace. For some reason, the air force file on the vanishing contains just two pages. One of them is a page from a book debunking UFO theories.

Nevertheless, Roswell (which among the UFO-intrigued has achieved one-word status) remains the most important landmark in the UFO coverup because, apparently, it has actually been covered up. There is no mention of the crash in the air force's Project Blue Book files. Blue Book recorded all UFO reports that crossed an air force desk along with their various "scientific" explanations. Generally considered the Warren Report of the UFO phenomenon—a coverup posing as an investigation—Blue Book gives Roswell increased prominence by its omission.

Some might write the whole incident off as unlikely, noting that a spacecraft capable of navigating the firmament and engineered to endure the rigors of interstellar travel is unlikely to crash like so many Cessnas. But then there is Majestic 12 (MJ-12). Among many UFOlogists, there is strong belief in the existence of MJ-12.

A committee of twelve eminent military, intelligence, and academic personages, the group was allegedly chartered to manage and conceal the most important event in world history—contact with aliens. Albeit dead ones.

According to the MJ-12 "eyes only" briefing paper prepared for Dwight Eisenhower when he was still president-elect, four "Extraterrestrial biological entities," or EBEs, turned up two miles from the crash site. According to some accounts, two of the aliens were still alive at the time and one put up a struggle. The EBE carcasses are now allegedly kept on ice in Los Alamos, New Mexico.

The problem with the Majestic 12 document—the only hard evidence that MJ-12 ever took a meeting—is that it may well be a hoax. No one in a position to do so has ever authenticated it.

There is only one mention of MJ-12 in any other official paper, a November 1980 air force analysis of a UFO film that outlines in minute detail how the government is "still interested" in UFO sightings, which it investigates through "covert cover."

That document, like the original MJ-12 paper, somehow seems too good to be true—the smoking gun that every good conspiracy theory needs and lacks. It would be as if some researcher combing through CIA JFK files suddenly produced a memo reading, "Assassination of president scheduled for 11/22/63, Dallas. After consultation with FBI, director recommends triangulation of crossfire be utilized." It would kind of make you wonder.

Real or not, MJ-12 has spawned no shortage of legends and speculation, primarily that it still exists and is still administering the UFO coverup, coping with each alien abduction and saucer crash as it comes up. "Suicided" journalist Danny Casolaro included MJ-12 as a tentacle in his postulated secret government "Octopus." (See page 120.) In some versions of the tale, MJ-12 is in charge of cooperation and negotiation with the alien race among us.

Or should that be "races"? John Lear, a self-described former intelligence agent who is now one of the leading voices on the UFO circuit, charges that the government is aware of a veritable Rainbow Coalition of EBEs.

These range from three types of insecto-humanoid Grays, skinny and eggheaded enemies of all mankind, to the friendly Blonds, who look more like humans but who, despite their general good nature refuse to break the Star Trekkish "universal law of noninterference" to save us from the evil Grays. Also on the roster are the Hairy Dwarves (self-explanatory), the Very Tall Race (also self-explanatory), and the mysterious Men in Black.

The existence of the Robertson Panel, unlike that of MJ-12, is not dubious. Convened by the Central Intelligence Agency in January 1953, this board of scientists issued a report that was not fully declassified until 1975.

Chaired by one Dr. H. P. Robertson, the panel met secretly in the Pentagon for five days. They looked at the UFO cases that appeared to be the most credible—and dismissed every single one of them.

Merely denying the existence of unexplainable or extraterrestrial UFOs, as the Roberston panel did, hardly constitutes a coverup, except under the most circular logic. The panel, however, moved considerably beyond debunking. It recommended that the government take pains to squelch UFO reports, to the point of promulgating an anti-UFO "education" campaign.

"This education could be accomplished by mass media such as television, motion pictures, popular articles," the CIA panel's report said. It went on to suggest using "psychologists familiar with mass psychology" to help assemble the program and even wondered if Walt Disney Studios might be interested in producing anti-UFO cartoons.

The report went on to recommend that UFO enthusiast groups should be placed under surveillance due to "the possible use of such groups for subversive purposes."

None of the Robertson Panel's rather conspiratorial musings prove that the government really has something to hide; deep-frozen aliens, for example. On the other hand, they do give a depressing clue as to how institutions respond to ideas that they deem, in the words of the panel report, "a threat to the orderly functioning of the protective organs of the body politic."

MAJOR SOURCES

Andrews, George C. *Extra-Terrestrial Friends and Foes*. Lilburn, GA: IllumiNet Press, 1993.

Good, Timothy. *Above Top Secret: The Worldwide UFO Cover-up*. New York: Quill William Morrow, 1988.

Good, Timothy. *Alien Contact: Top Secret UFO Files Revealed*. New York: William Morrow, 1993.

Randle, Capt. Kevin D. *The UFO Casebook*. New York: Warner Books, 1989.

11

Apolloscam

On July 20, 1969, Neil Armstrong planted his left foot in the lunar dust and became the first human to walk on the moon. Unfortunately, that stellar moment in history may have been marred by one not-insignificant detail: If inquiring author Bill Kaysing has it right, Armstrong made his giant leap for mankind not 240,000 miles above Earth in the barren Sea of Tranquillity, but a mere 90 miles north of lusty Las Vegas on a top-secret movie soundstage. Yes, as Kaysing tells it, the nation was gulled into believing that Armstrong and Edwin E. "Buzz" Aldrin, Jr., were gamboling through a bona fide lunar landscape, when in fact the two "actors" were hamming it up in a sinister government production that qualifies as the greatest hoax of all time.

Sheer lunacy, you say? Not according to the millions of skeptics who watched the spectacle of men walking on the moon in disbelief. And not according to Kaysing, who outlined his highly evolved theory in a self-published exposé, *We Never Went to the Moon*. A former technical writer for Rockwell International (which contributed to the alleged "moon missions"), Kaysing claims no direct knowledge of NASA's she-nanigans. Rather, his certainty derives from the epistemological alignment of a "hunch," photographic "proof," and a gnawing feeling that "the government is a specialist in hoaxing the public."

If his thesis is, well, somewhat weightless in the hard evidence department, Kaysing more than compensates with copious enthusiasm. "America's 30 Billion Dollar Swindle!" he declares, played itself out over the course of five more sham moon landings and involved "well-faked photographs," phony moon rocks, and "programmed astronauts"—not to mention "the help of father-figure [Walter] Cronkite as the journalistic goat."

First and foremost, Kaysing has questions—questions that NASA and the former astronauts evade like a grifter dodges the "heat":

- In photographs of the lunar sky, why are no stars visible, and why are the astronauts "extremely evasive regarding stars"? With no blocking atmosphere, the celestial tableau would have been "the most magnificent available to mortal man," Kaysing writes. The answer, he posits, is that NASA's set decorators knew they couldn't dupe professional astronomers with an ersatz starry backdrop.
- If the moon's surface was powdery enough for deep footprints, why didn't the lunar lander's rocket thruster dig a gaping crater? And why in photographs is there no moon dust on the lander's legs?
- If the moon was proven to be "sterile" after the first Apollo mission, why were astronauts in later missions held in quarantine so long? Kaysing submits that they needed quality time in an airstream trailer to "1) eliminate guilt feelings; 2) study and memorize moon data; and 3) practice responding to questions."
- "Why did so many astronauts end up as executives in very large corporations?"

Kaysing provides answers to most of the questions, including the most obvious—why would NASA go to the trouble of faking the Apollo moon shots? It seems the space agency launched its elaborate ruse when, after years of technological screwups and bureaucratic snafus, NASA realized it would never put a man on the moon by the close of the 1960s.

To avoid international embarrassment, NASA and the military's stealth apparatus, the Defense Intelligence Agency (DIA), established a top-secret operation that Kaysing calls the Apollo Simulation Project (ASP). For their secret base of operations, the cold-blooded ASP team chose a site in Nevada adjacent to land used by the Atomic Energy Commission in nuclear bomb testing—the perfect deterrent to the overly curious. Of course, ASP's secret base also had the advantage of being less than an hour's drive from "a twenty-four-hour-a-day, seven-days-a-week, anything-goes resort boasting more than thirty large casinos." According to Kaysing, who presents his case in semiomniscient fashion, ASP quite naturally hooked up with the Vegas "Cosa Nostra," which patriotically provided the space program with expert "services," apparently in the lethal splashdown department, so to speak.

In its desert redoubt, ASP excavated an underground cavern and installed "a complete set of the moon." (Some word-of-mouth versions of the moonscam theory place the phony set in Arizona or New Mexico.) In fact—and in the absence of traditional journalistic sourcing, we must take Kaysing at his word on most "facts"—none other than film director Stanley Kubrick assisted in the plot, generously using his *2001: A Space Odyssey* to develop the Hollywood special effects required to foist the NASA hoax on an unsuspecting public. (It makes you wonder what *The Shining* was all about.)

According to Kaysing, ASP's modus operandi went something like this:

- An *empty* Saturn V rocket lifts off in Florida—in full public view, thereby lending the Apollo con a patina of authenticity. However, once out sight, the ghost rocket ditches into the South Polar Sea.
- The "astronauts" are jetted to ASP's Nevada complex where

they enjoy "every conceivable luxury, including a few of the shapeliest showgirls from Las Vegas, cleared for secret, of course." When Armstrong and his fellow playboy thespians aren't earning membership in the 240,000 Mile High Club, so to speak, they "are free to wander about and play the slots" and "sample the twenty-four-hour buffet from the Dunes" hotel. (In this moral vacuum, the well-informed Kaysing reports, one of the astronauts may have "socked an ASP official in a dispute over a showgirl named Peachy Keen.")

- When the curtain finally rises, the special-effects team, TV cameramen, and "ASP moon walk director" create a near-seamless piece of performance art, as Armstrong recites his scripted "one-small-step" line. Every aspect of the phony video feed is "meticulously" choreographed, down to the "boo-boos," jokes, "and seeming improvisations of the astronauts." Meanwhile, NASA cooks up counterfeit "moon rocks," the purported hard evidence of the journey, in a high-tech ceramics kiln.

- In time for their triumphal return to Earth, the astronauts are coaxed away from the Vegas vixens and whisked to a hidden air base south of the Hawaiian Islands (the "Tauramoto Archipelago," Kaysing obligingly specifies). There they are sealed inside a dummy space capsule and dropped from a C5-A transport plane into the roiling seas.

If the plot sounds a lot like the 1979 film *Capricorn One*, which dramatized a similar cabal involving a bogus mission to Mars, it is because, according to Kaysing, Hollywood borrowed the idea from the first edition of his book.

Like the O.J. Simpson-Telly Savalas film (or any conspiracy hypothesis worth its salt), Kaysing's theory has its martyrs, a whole cemetery full. There's Tom Baron, the aerospace technician who complained to Congress about dangerous corner-cutting in the Apollo program—and died in a train accident "just *four days* after he testified." There are also the three astronauts—including Gus "The Right Stuff" Grissom—who died on the launchpad in a 1967 "mishap" when fire swept through their capsule. Grissom had groused publicly about Apollo's safety troubles, leading Kaysing to postulate that perhaps the DIA arranged a little "accident" to silence the whistle-blower and impress other loud-mouth fly-boys.

And, as in many a postulated conspiracy, this one involves brainwashing. Kaysing suggests that the astronauts might have been subjected to state-of-the-art mind-control techniques and turned into "Manchurian Candidates," thus ensuring their obedient participation in the hoax. This, he postulates, might explain their subsequent reclusiveness and, in some cases, "severe mental problems."

What are they trying to hide, anyway? Kaysing wonders. Neil Armstrong "will not speak on the phone to me," our author complains in his book. Buzz Aldrin apparently won't appear on talk shows alongside Apollo's intractable critic. Despite their seeming aloofness, however, the space jockeys may in fact be *very* interested in the California researcher's doings: Kaysing intimates darkly that agents of Armstrong keep close tabs on his ongoing quest to defrock Apolloscam.

Alas, NASA's secrets remain as impenetrable as any Vegas vault. Barring unforeseen revelations, hectoring ex-astronauts may be the only way for Kaysing to get to the bottom of the conundrum. Like David flinging tiny Earth rocks at a space-suited Goliath, the intrepid investigator has issued a standing challenge: "I am willing," Kaysing pledges, "to debate any or all of the astronauts at any time on live TV or in person anywhere."

So far the Manchurian Spacemen have declined to take that one small step.

MAJOR SOURCE

Kaysing, Bill. *We Never Went to the Moon: America's Thirty Billion Dollar Swindle!* Soquel, CA: Holy Terra Books, 1991.

12

Saucer Blitz!

Sure, they lost World War II, but never underestimate the stick-to-itiveness of the Nazis. Second to none in sinister invention, the Third Reich's mad scientists were capable of attempting practically anything—so long as the project was ethically dubious or ambitiously screwy, on a Wagnerian scale. No wonder, then, that when it comes to the origin of flying saucers, some consider the Nazis at least as suspect as space-warping ETs.

There is at least a theoretical cornerstone for such speculation. During the war, Hitler's Dr. Strangeloves apparently dabbled with designs for flying disks. Whether they were successful isn't quite so indisputable, but in late 1944, Reuters news agency reported that the Germans had a "secret" air defense weapon that resembled "the glass balls that adorn Christmas trees. They have been seen hanging in the air over German territory, sometimes singly, sometimes in clusters. They are colored silver and are apparently transparent."

Allied pilots reported numerous sightings of these so-called Foo Fighters (from the French *feu*, for fire), which they encountered throughout Europe and even in Japan and Turkey. According to pilots' reports, the mysterious objects had the disquieting habit of pursuing squadrons, occasionally outrunning the speediest conventional aircraft. Allied intelligence agencies scrambled to get the goods on a possible Nazi secret weapon, thought to be something along the lines of "high altitude, high-velocity balloons." After the war, investigators sifted through German records, but ultimately ruled out the possibility of Jerry-built flying disks, fire balls, or swift, maneuverable balloons. In short order, the strange, unexplained phenomenon was all but forgotten.

All *but*, for theoreticians in the Nazi-centric wing of UFO-logy have exposed the sweeping (and highly speculative) post-war history of German achievement in saucer science. If you buy this premise, Foo Fighters were mere Model Ts in the march of German saucerology. In his magnum opus on world conquest by Nazi-connected bluebloods, *Casebook on Alternative 3*, conspiracy pathfinder Jim Keith relates the findings of one Renato Vesco. According to Vesco, author of a tome called *Intercept—But Don't Shoot*, Foo Fighters were forerunners of something called Kugelblitz, the Ball Lightning Fighter. Keith reports that the massive Kugelblitz conformed to "popular concepts of 'flying saucers.'" Though it seems unlikely that these giant craft advanced beyond the blueprint stage, if they got even that far, Keith relays various accounts of saucers launching from construction sites in Prague, Czechoslovakia, and Breslau, Germany, in early 1945.

Then there is the "confidential Italian document," supposedly liberated by an informant, which, according to Keith, described a rather one-sided dogfight between Allied planes and a mysterious vehicle: "A strange flying machine, hemispherical, or at any rate circular, in shape, attacked them at a fantastic speed, destroying them in a few seconds without using any guns." Of course, the problem with stunning and anonymous documents is that they also tend to be apocryphal.

But not even the formidable Kugelblitz could reverse the course of war for the doomed Third Reich. Did Nazi saucerology hunker down and die with the suicidal Führer, then, or did it merely latch on to a new sponsor, as did so many German rocket scientists and superspies? There's actually evidence to suggest the latter. According to a 1955 CIA memorandum dredged up by UFO researcher Timothy Good, aerospace engineer John Frost, who designed a disk-shaped aircraft for the U.S. military, "is reported to have obtained his original idea for the flying machine from a group of Germans just after World War II."

Good's well-documented reporting jibes with more speculative claims that German saucer scientists took their ambitious blueprints to the Soviet Union and to the United States. According to Keith, German scientist Rudolph Schriever maintained "that the various UFO reports since the end of the war showed that his Kugelblitz designs had been discovered and put into production."

Keith also submits that the German saucer scientist named Miethe moved to the United States after the war and worked on John Frost's experimental saucer, the famous "Avro flying disk." Manufactured by A. V. Roe Ltd. of Canada, and funded jointly by the U.S. Army and Air Force during the 1950s, the Avro VZ-9 was an operative flying saucer powered by a jet engine turbine and an array of exhaust nozzles that could propel the craft in any direction—except, unfortunately, up. Although Pentagon self-congratulation was typically over the top, film footage of test flights showed the Avro disk teetering awkwardly a few pathetic inches above the icy airport tarmac. In 1954 the Canadian Defense Ministry dropped the project altogether, reporting that "it served no purpose."

Was the U.S. saucer program a bust? Not according to witnesses who described glimpsing disks similar to the Avro prototype in hangers at military bases in California and Ohio during the 1960s. If we're to believe the anonymous testimony of "eyewitnesses," these late-model "zip craft" were capable of reaching supersonic speeds and lofty altitudes—a far cry from the wobbly Avro contraption.

In 1950, *U.S. News and World Report* jumped on the government UFO bandwagon and told its readers to sober up in an article titled, "Flying Saucers—The Real Story: U.S. Built First One in 1942." Calling the new aircraft a "revolutionary" hybrid of helicopter and jet plane, *U.S. News* knowingly informed its readers that "space ships" and "Martians" had nothing to do with the mysterious sightings. Anyone encountering a UFO was actually witnessing a secret military test flight.

If *U.S. News* aspired to be a voice of sobersided authority during the UFO craze of the 1950s, the government itself may have been spiking the celestial punch, according to some theorists. They maintain that for decades the government has discreetly encouraged speculation about extraterrestrial UFOs and little gray men as a cover for its ongoing development of very terrestrial saucer technology.

Other UFOlogists prefer to turn that theory on its head. They suggest that far from baiting the public with myths about extraterrestrial aliens, the government encourages articles like the *U.S. News* piece to direct attention away from the *real* source of saucer technology: actual extraterrestrial aliens.

Ideal's UFO Magazine exposed the *real* story when it quoted a "Lieutenant Colonel George Edwards (USAF-retired)," who purportedly worked on the Avro VZ-9 project: "Although we weren't cut in on it, we knew that the air force was secretly test-flying a real alien spacecraft. The VZ-9 was to be a 'cover,' so the Pentagon would have an explanation whenever people reported seeing a saucer in flight."

The theory goes that the U.S. government had come into possession of several alien-built saucers, beginning with the alleged 1947 crash in the desert outside of Roswell, New Mexico. By the late 1980s, "extraterrestrial biological entities" (EBEs) had recklessly ditched (or generously donated) as many as nine saucers, which were now in the clutches of the coverup-inclined U.S. government. Despite attempts by the best and brightest American scientists to "reverse engineer" the otherworldly craft, all efforts thus far have failed to recreate the eerily advanced alien technology. (Some enterprising re-searchers, however, theorize that the government did unlock the secrets of the saucers and used futuristic alien technology to send Americans to the moon—in the 1950s!)

The current hotbed of government UFO testing is supposedly a mysterious military enclosure in the desert north of Las Vegas known variously as Dreamland, Area 51, and S-4. By day, experimental stealth planes take wing in the base's restricted airspace, but at night the pulsing saucers are said to hover and zag in veritable celestial gridlock, as hotshot (earthling) test pilots give warp drive a go, or maneuver with genuine alien saucernauts.

Theories about alien saucers at Dreamland got their big break in 1989 when an engineer named Bob Lazar stepped forward to tell the world (or at least viewers of Vegas station KLAS-TV) that as a government employee at S-4, he had inspected a bona fide alien saucer. Lazar claimed that the craft, which he called the "sport model," was propelled by "gravity amplifiers" and powered by an "antimatter reactor"—inciden-tally, the state of the art in speculative UFO physics since the 1950s. Unfortunately, Lazar's story has remained controversial, not least because thus far no one has managed to unearth proof of his claimed MIT and Cal-Tech credentials (although his junior college attendance records are beyond dispute).

If other researchers are to be believed, the aliens at Dream-land have got nothing on the Aryans at the South Pole. UFOlogist Vladimir Terziski is partial to the theory that during the final days of World War II, a tattered Third Reich repaired to Antarctica aboard flying saucers and U-boats (perhaps with Wagner's *Ride of the Valkyries* thundering the background). Not surprisingly, some theorists place the Führer, himself, on board a sub or saucer high-tailing it to the South Polar cap.

Terziski reports that he has come into possession of a startling video documentary "by the secret German society" known as the Thule Gesellschaft, the occult Thule Society, which, before the appearance of Hitler, concocted much of the twisted ideology later adopted by the Nazis. If Terziski's updated information on the Thule Society is to be taken seriously, the Germans built "ten-meter diameter" saucers of the Vril series and giant dreadnought discs "for antishipping warfare." They also outfitted their interplanetary saucers—yes, you read right—with "electro-magneto-gravitic" drives (mass-produced like Volkswagens, no less) and colonized the moon as early as 1942! Lunar *lebensraum* was only the beginning. That same year, according to the Terziski, the Nazis speared the Antarctic ice with swastika flags and renamed the continent Neu-Schwabenland. Then they burrowed underground (an echo of Nazi hollow Earth theories?) and established the subterranean capital of New Berlin, which today sports a population of two million *sieg heilers*, terrorizes surface dwellers with fascist saucers, and, of course, secretly enjoys most-favored nation trading status with the U.S. government.

One final note on goose-stepping Saucer-Waffen: An interesting factoid overlooked by most Nazi-centric UFOlogists is the famous abduction story of Barney and Betty Hill. Betty, we should remember, described the offending saucer jockeys as wearing uniforms "similar to air force" and speaking with a "foreign" accent. Barney got right to the point, initially describing their leader as looking "like a German Nazi. He's a Nazi...."! Achtung! Today Poland, tomorrow the Milky Way!

MAJOR SOURCES

"Flying Saucers—The Real Story: U.S. Built First One in 1942." *U.S. News & World Report*, 7 April 1950.

Good, Timothy. *Alien Contact: Top Secret UFO Files Revealed.* New York: William Morrow and Company, 1993.

Keith, Jim. *Casebook on Alternative 3: UFOs, Secret Societies and World Control.* Lilburn, GA: IllumiNet Press, 1994.

Terziski, Vladimir. "Secret Research on Antigravity and Space Flight Organized by the German Secret Societies During World War II." *Steamshovel Press*, no. 9 (Fall 1993).

Vallee, Jacques and Janine. *Challenge to Science: The UFO: Enigma.* New York: Ballantine, 1975.

13

Saucer Therapy

Most debate between UFO believers and skeptics hovers around whether the phenomenon originates in outer space or with some explainable "scientific" source. But there is a third option. What if UFOs are some form of mysterious technology serving the purpose of mass psychological manipulation?

Could UFOs be the first step in a plan to establish a totalitarian government masquerading as a "star child" religion? Do those lights in the sky herald the coming of New Age Nazis from beyond? Perhaps Arthur C. Clarke's all-powerful *2001* monolith has already arrived—except this time it's pissed off!

"The main effect of UFOs on their witnesses is a conditioning process," says Jacques Vallee, a French astronomer whose renown has come primarily from his writings on UFOs. "Through exposure to its powerful imagery, man appears to be acquiring new forms of behavior and new models of his relationship to the world of nature."

Vallee quickly points out that "to conclude that UFOs are

nothing more than secret devices deployed by some intelligence agency would be wrong and simplistic." But he nonetheless asserts that there is some sort of genuine technology behind UFOs, and if that technology is not the product of human ingenuity (a possibility Vallee entertains) it is being manipulated by ingenious humans toward some cryptic end.

Jay Katz (a pseudonym for prolific conspiracist Jim Keith) notes numerous instances of verified spookery within the contactee community in his spiral-bound tract *Saucers of the Illuminati*. He points the finger at such suspicious characters as CIA psychological warfare specialist Nicholas de Rochefort and other named CIA "assets" who infiltrated and undermined the National Investigations Committee on Aerial Phenomena, an early civilian UFO group. He reserves particular scorn for John Lear, a former CIA pilot "who has done more than anyone… to convince the public that aliens are among us, living in huge underground bases and collaborating with the government to put us all in the vat-prepared soup." Then there is self-admitted government informer William Moore who helped publicize the famous MJ-12 documents.

"For the general public, I suspect the possibility that UFOs are controlled in some fashion by humans for some secret, conspiratorial purpose is almost unthinkable," writes Katz. "There is an almost total media blackout about the possibility that UFOs are anything other than an extraterrestrial phenomenon."

John Keel is another UFO researcher who dismisses the ET and "scientific" explanations as equally loony, choosing instead to log the "medical and psychological effects" of UFO contact on its victims. He sees UFOs as a "Trojan horse," infiltrating human society to deliver a probably unwelcome payload that has yet to be revealed. As for the human spirit's ability to overcome the sinister designs of the mind-controllers, Keel is not overly sanguine. "We are biochemical robots helplessly controlled by forces that can scramble our brains, destroy our memories, and use us in any way they see fit," he says.

Just as Keel has noted that "men in neat coveralls were seen monkeying with telephone and power lines" in the vicinity of a strange series of UFO incidents in Virginia, *Saucers of the Illuminati* questions the meaning of reports of "aliens" driving off from UFO landings in ordinary, motorized vans. Katz takes note of crowds that gather for "UFO watching parties" outside the army's "top secret" Area 51 in Nevada and remarks wryly, "the relatively common occurrence of garden variety humans being seen in the vicinity of, entering and leaving, and sometimes piloting UFOs may be a significant clue as to the meaning and origin of these craft."

While Keel has studied primarily the experiences of individuals, Vallee is concerned with contactee cults. These groups of hardcore UFO believers always center on some figure who claims direct relations with alien visitors. And in these groups that now exist on the fringes of society and politics Vallee sees the germ of a new "high demand" religion and political philosophy.

The idea seems absurd at first. But almost any idea powerful enough to win the slavish devotion of millions of humans must originate in the alleged contact between humans and a superior intelligence: numerous Olympian gods descending to meddle in the affairs of everyday Greeks; Moses and the burning bush; Jesus appearing to Paul on the road to Damascus.

Or more recently, the Mormon Church. Its founder, Joseph Smith, was visited by an "angel" who told him where to find the long-buried tablets inscribed with *the Book of Mormon*. In twentieth-century parlance, Smith had a "close encounter of the third kind."

On the more cynical end of the spectrum, note the Church of Scientology, created by pulp science fiction scribe L. Ron Hubbard, whose quasi-religious and very expensive techniques to recover the "Thetan" inside us all woos Tom Cruises and John Travoltas from far and wide.

There's a whole sub-genre of UFO literature devoted to the notion that mankind's most significant religious experiences may be misread incidents of extraterrestrial contact. The above-noted *2001* utilizes that theme. Erik Von Daniken's *Chariots of the Gods*—which unlike the Kubrick film, purported to be nonfiction—caused an early seventies sensation with its claims that various ancient wonders (the pyramids, the planes of Nazca) were constructed in tribute to, if not actually by, extraterrestrials.

But Vallee's hypothesis cuts the other way: "Close encounters" could just be misinterpretations of the religious experience.

Are "miracles," visions, angelic visitations, and UFO contacts all the same natural phenomenon whose explanation falls outside traditional concepts of nature and physics? This question takes Vallee into a digression about the nature of not merely UFOs but reality itself. To make his lengthy and not-entirely-comprehensible argument as concise as possible, Vallee feels that our modern understanding of the universe is based on a mistake. We assume "linear" causality: one thing leads to another. I punch you in the nose, you fall down. I explain Vallee's theories of reality, you become hopelessly confused.

Instead, Vallee postulates that we inhabit an "associative" universe where conventional "if A then B" logic does not apply. Rather, the logic of coincidence prevails.

His analogy is a computer database. Computers store information randomly and retrieve it using commands. When we enter keywords in a computer databank, we are attempting to produce coincidences. Where, in our conspiracy theory database, do the words "assassination" and "cancer" coincide? Just punch in the magic words and from the chaos of randomized digits come five articles about Mae Brussell.

The universe in which we live, breathe, and perceive, Vallee says, is in fact nothing more than a "process by which informational associations are retrieved and traversed."

In a universe of coincidence, weird phenomena would be "expected, even common," writes Vallee, "and UFOs would lose much of their alien quality." Anyone who understood even a little of this abstruse concept could figure out a way to manipulate those phenomena for their own presumably nefarious purposes. Vallee, like Katz, finds most contactee and UFO study groups rife with spies from the government and other quarters more difficult to discern. Their purpose is beyond investigation, almost as much so as that of the UFOs themselves.

"Contactee systems often include belief in higher races and in totalitarian systems that would eliminate democracy," Vallee notes. The cults he investigated are prone to theories of their own racial superiority based on presumed descent from the "star children." The social consequences of those beliefs are not cheerful to contemplate.

Katz concludes that the teleology of the UFO phenomenon could be the inauguration of a global monarchy. Vallee is less specific. "If the Manipulators do exist, I certainly salute their tenacity, but I am curious about their goals," he says. "One would like to know more, then, about the image of humanity such manipulators harbor in their own minds—and in their hearts. Assuming, of course, that they do have hearts."

MAJOR SOURCES

Katz, Jay. *Saucers of the Illuminati*. Lilburn, GA: IllumiNet Press, 1993.
Keel, John. *Disneyland of the Gods*. New York: Amok Press, 1988.
Vallee, Jacques. *Messengers of Deception*. New York: Bantam Books, 1980.

III

They Died Alone

14

The Sex Goddess Who Knew Too Much

The main question that comes out of the case history of Marilyn Monroe's death is not whether she was murdered or even by whom, but how the men who ran this country in 1962 ever found time to do their jobs. They were all too busy with Marilyn Monroe.

The Kennedy brothers, Jack and Bobby, president and attorney general respectively, were either in bed with her for hours at a time or talking dirty to her on the phone for even longer. Sam "Momo" Giancana—the Chicago/Vegas mob boss who, some say, *really* ran the country—was preoccupied with the sex icon to end all sex icons, and wiretapped her—as did Teamster leader and Kennedy-hater Jimmy Hoffa. Giancana saw her as a means to gain power over the Kennedys. He bedded her too. At one point Momo boasted to another gangster that he had one up on the Kennedys because he was the last to have sex with Marilyn before her death.

And, unsurprisingly, J. Edgar Hoover spent his time listening to recordings taken from bugs in every room in her house—or anyone else's house or hotel where she stayed.

The Marilyn tapes, according to Hollywood private eye Fred Otash, who recorded and retained many of them, are "probably the most interesting tapes ever made—with the exception of Watergate."

Come on. What's on the Watergate tapes but a bunch of old lawyers cussing, smoking cigarettes, and grumbling about politics? The Marilyn tapes are said to contain lengthy recordings of America's most glamorous movie star doing the nasty with America's most glamorous president. And other intriguing episodes. Private investigator Milo Speriglio, who had spent thirty years on the Monroe case, says that the tape recorders were rolling right through Marilyn's murder.

Among researchers, writers, and sleuths who claim either to have heard some of these tapes or know what's on them—or to have just done a lot of legwork—there is a dazzling spectrum of opinions on how the former Norma Jean Baker met her demise at age thirty-six, on August 4, 1962. And at whose hands. Most of the hypotheses involve the Kennedy brothers and Giancana, with Hoover in the wings, as always, watching.

Speriglio names none other than Jack Kennedy himself, in collusion with his morally bankrupt father Joe (by that time incapacitated by a stroke that diminished his physical and mental faculties but apparently left his capacity for evil unscathed), as ordering the hit. Marilyn had become too pesky. Her constant calls to the White House and the Justice Department had become a hot gossip item for Washington insiders. And there was the omnipresent threat of a press conference at which Marilyn would blow the lid off her relationship with the Kennedy brothers, an option Marilyn was apparently considering. Not only did she jeopardize the Kennedy dynasty, but national security. In some kind of weird attempt to impress his extramarital flame, Bobby blabbed secret info about the CIA-Mafia kill-Castro plots to Marilyn Monroe, of all people. Or so the story goes. The official version is that Marilyn committed suicide by barbiturate overdose.

But even *Goddess* author Anthony Summers, who believes that Marilyn did not intentionally kill herself and goes no further than to "leave open" the possibility of murder, seems in his book to have been persuaded that Bobby Kennedy was at Marilyn's bungalow the night of her death. The attorney general may have visited her on a humane "mission of mercy," that night, Summers, perhaps wishfully, speculates.

Marilyn was extremely distraught that day, attempting to call everyone she knew in a fit of despair over her broken relationships with the Kennedy brothers. Career minded as always, they rather cruelly led her on then cut her off. In most versions of the story, Bobby initiated his relationship with Marilyn mainly to protect the president. Jack saw Marilyn as a fling. She saw him as marrying material. She harbored delusions of First Ladydom and when Jack grew bored of her, she wouldn't let him go. In stepped Bobby, who made the tragic error of falling in love with her.

Some biographers have written that Marilyn Monroe carried a Kennedy child in 1962, though whether it was supposed to be Jack's or Bobby's is not clear.

According to Summers's recreation of events, Bobby Kennedy would have arrived to find Monroe already in the throes of overdose, but alive. He, or an aide, called an ambulance, which was to take Marilyn to the hospital, but she died en route. When the younger Kennedy brother saw that his paramour had passed, he switched immediately into coverup mode. No matter how she died, it would not look good for the aspiring next president to show up at a hospital towing the corpse of America's favorite sex symbol.

The ambulance, according to Summers, turned around and returned to the bungalow. The body that wet dreams were made of was laid out on the bed, the room straightened, and a call placed to Marilyn's confidant and psychiatrist Robert Greenson. It was Greenson who, officially, discovered the deceased Marilyn Monroe. By this time Bobby was safely out of L.A. Maybe. A police officer named Lynn Franklin tells of pulling over a car driven by Peter Lawford sometime after midnight— hours after Marilyn died. Bobby Kennedy was in the backseat.

Unlike some other writers on the topic, Summers admits that his scenario might be "wrong in certain details, but it is a fair construction from the information now available." He also says that, probably, "no serious crime was committed that night." But the death of Marilyn Monroe was, in Summers's view, Bobby Kennedy's Chappaquidick—a case of being in the wrong place at the wrong time with the wrong dead woman. But Bobby got away where his younger brother Ted got caught.

In the updated edition of his book, Summers interviews an unnamed source who claims to have heard tapes of Marilyn's final night. The tapes appear to have been edited. Bobby Kennedy, Peter Lawford, and Marilyn Monroe are on the tapes—the two ex-lovers screaming at each other while Lawford tries to calm them down. At one point, according to Summers's informant, there are sounds of a struggle. Bobby may have pushed Marilyn onto the bed.

The tapes leave the impression, according to Summers, that Marilyn was dead when Bobby left the house after his second visit of the evening and that later there was a phone call placed to Marilyn Monroe's home. On the tapes, someone picks up the phone, but says nothing. When Marilyn's body was found, she clutched a phone in her hand. The implication, according to Summers, is that it was placed there—the call was intended to establish a phone record that Marilyn was alive and answering the phone at a time when she was, in fact, far too dead to chat.

Conspiracy theorists and medical examiners alike have long been bothered by the absence of pill residue in Marilyn's stomach and the lack of any glass of water in her apartment with which she could have swallowed the massive overdose required to kill her. And medical examiners never found any signs of injected drugs either. Summers was the first to publicly postulate the one method of ingestion that would leave no trace, unless checked for. It wasn't.

Peter Lawford, the debauched actor and Kennedy in-law who arranged Jack's West Coast trysts, knew something about Marilyn's death, but took his secrets to his drug-and-booze induced grave. When one of his former wives asked him if he knew how Marilyn died, he made an odd remark.

"Marilyn took her last big enema."

The starlet "complained of chronic constipation," Summers wrote. "Enemas relieve that complaint. Their use was also a common fad, particularly among show business people in those days, as an aid to instant weight loss." Marilyn Monroe had been taking enemas for years.

The rectal ingestion theory is now a common one. *Double Cross,* written by the late Sam Giancana's godson also named Sam Giancana, and his brother, Chuck, says that Marilyn's killers listened to Giancana's wiretaps as they lurked near her home, waiting for the opportune moment to strike. They overheard Bobby Kennedy and another man in the house irate at Marilyn. Finally, Bobby ordered Marilyn sedated and left. The hit men sneaked in and, as Marilyn lay in a drugged stupor, admistered a lethal "suppository."

The latest Marilyn book at the time of this writing, Speriglio's *Crypt 33* (titled for the compartment where Monroe's body was stored at the L.A. County morgue), describes how gangland superstar Johnny Roselli—a Giancana associate who is better known for his involvment in the CIA-Mafia plots to kill Castro and, by some accounts, JFK—showed up at Marilyn's house to distract her (they knew each other; Roselli traveled in show biz circles) while two hit men sneaked in the back. One knocked her out with a chloroform-soaked cloth, then the other administered the killer enema. It is unclear from the rather choppily written *Crypt 33* whether Speriglio bases his scenario on evidence from the actual Marilyn tapes, though he seems to imply that he does.

Crypt 33 includes Speriglio's assertion that Joe and Jack

Kennedy beseeched Giancana to rub Marilyn out and that the gangster, always looking for leverage with the Kennedys, happily obliged. The book revises Speriglio's earlier theory, spelled out in *The Marilyn Conspiracy*. Namely, that Giancana and Hoffa, under pressure from Bobby Kennedy and aware, through wiretaps, of his affair with Monroe, set him up for scandal. Slaying his sex-queen-on-the-side was part of the plot. But the Kennedy coverup worked. Neither Bobby nor Jack suffered destruction. Until later. And then by somewhat different methods.

The coverup continues. On that point all the Marilyn writers concur. Whether she was murdered, committed suicide, or died by accidentally misjudging her capacity to tolerate downers (Summers's preferred hypothesis), there is no question that the Kennedy brothers got involved with her in some way that grew too dangerous. In 1985, possibly for this reason, ABC killed a story on its *20/20* news magazine that independently corroborated the information in Summers's book *Goddess*. The half-hour segment included information about several of Jack Kennedy's other affairs, including liaisons with mob moll Judith Campbell Exner and suspected Nazi spy Inga Arvad.

ABC's higher-ups were skittish and ordered the segement trimmed. Finally it was down to thirteen minutes when ABC News president Roone Arledge, a close friend of Robert Kennedy's wife Ethel, killed it altogether. He denied that his friendship had any bearing on his decision, condemning his own reporters' story as "sleazy." According to Hugh Downs, one of the network's more staid on-air personalities, the "sleazy piece" was "more carefully documented than anything any network did during Watergate."

One biography recounts that more than a decade after Marilyn Monroe's death, a TV actress named Veronica Hamel, later well-known on the show *Hill Street Blues*, purchased the house where Marilyn lived and died. During redecorating, she discovered a thicket of aged wires sticking out of the roof. The actress hired a private contractor to destroy the cables that had transmitted the sounds of Marilyn Monroe's anguished life and eerie death to a place in history where they have never been found.

MAJOR SOURCES

Brown, Peter Harry, and Patte B. Barham. *Marilyn: The Last Take.* New York: Signet Books, 1993.

Gregory, Adela, and Milo Speriglio. *Crypt 33, the Saga of Marilyn Monroe: The Final Word.* New York: Birch Lane Press, 1993.

Speriglio, Milo. *The Marilyn Conspiracy.* New York: Pocket Books, 1986.

Summers, Anthony. *Goddess: The Secret Lives of Marilyn Monroe.* New York: Onyx Books, 1986.

15

Lizard King Lives!

In all likelihood, rock and roll legend Jim Morrison is buried in Paris's Père-Lachaise cemetery. That fact, of course, hasn't inhibited numerous "sightings" of the Doors' lead singer since his would-be death in 1971. Chalk it up, if you will, to the rock icon's prodigious mythology—like Dead Elvis's perpetual loitering or the Virgin Mary's fondness for making cameo appearances on tortillas.

Still, the circumstances of Morrison's death were quite mysterious and confusing. It's not surprising that a crop of postmortem rumors sprang up insinuating that by the good graces of assorted conspiracies—from the political to the supernatural—the Lizard King lives. Indeed, the official version of Morrison's death is in some respects even less believable than the surreal myths.

Officially, Morrison died at about 5 A.M. on July 3, 1971, of a heart attack, a rather improbable fate for a twenty-seven-year-old man—although somewhat less so for a rock star prematurely weathered by a decade of gut-flushing bacchanalia. As his longtime girlfriend, Pamela Courson, told the story, Morrison decided to take a bath in their Parisian flat one evening. Courson went to bed and the next morning discovered Morrison's corpse in the tub.

Bizarre rumors began to surface almost immediately, undoubtedly nursed along by Courson's puzzling attempts to screw a lid on the news. Courson initially told reporters that Morrison was "not dead but very tired and resting in a hospital." Nonetheless, word began to wend through Paris that Morrison had died of a heroin overdose in the sleazy underground nightclub, Rock 'n' Roll Circus. (Another popular rumor had it that Morrison OD'd on cocaine, a drug that he was known to binge on.) Rumor had it that Morrison was hustled home and deposited in the bathtub in an attempted revival. Of course, there were no witnesses.

Although Courson was claiming that Morrison was still alive days after his demise, in fact, a Parisian doctor had already signed the death certificate, listing the deceased as "James Morrison, Poet." The coffin was sealed before either the American Embassy or Morrison's family had been notified. No autopsy was performed. Only a full six days later, after Morrison's quiet burial at Père-Lachaise, did Doors manager Bill Siddons hold a press conference announcing the news that the "Young Lion" had died of a heart attack brought on by a blood clot and possibly a lung infection.

The *Los Angeles Times* stirred doubts when it headlined a story, WHY MORRISON DEATH NEWS DELAY? Inevitably, there was talk of a coverup. After all, only Courson, a couple of French medical examiners, and unknown police officers had actually *seen* Morrison's corpse. Not even Siddons (who jetted to Paris after Courson denied Morrison's death over the phone and then broke down crying) thought to open the casket when he arrived at the flat.

There were other improbable details in the official scenario, which subsequently fueled bizarre lore: How had an American rock star like Morrison finagled his way into Père-Lachaise, the historic French cemetery where luminaries like Balzac, Chopin,

Molière, and Oscar Wilde are entombed? For some unexplained—ergo, suspicious—reason, the headstone didn't appear for several months, and the grave remained unmarked.
When Doors drummer John Densmore later visited the cemetery, he announced, "...the grave is too short!"

In addition to the unsubstantiated theory of the nightclub
heroin OD, which was favored by Parisians, an assortment of
alternate scenarios began to circulate.

One political conspiracy theory had it that Morrison was
assassinated in a plot masterminded by those crew-cut reaction-
aries at the FBI. In a scheme to snuff the radical New Left and
hippie movements, J. Edgar Hoover's boys had iced not only
Morrison, whose popularity, antiauthoritarian bent, and native
smarts made him a threat to the American Way, but Janis Joplin
and Jimi Hendrix, who had "allegedly" died of drug ODs
earlier. (The theory was docu-dramatized in the low-rent film,
Down on Us, later retitled *Beyond the Doors*.)

It wasn't as farfetched a scenario as it now seems, given the
government's very real plots to undermine the New Left and the
FBI's attempts to discredit Martin Luther King, Jr. (not to
mention troubling government links to King's assassination).
And after Morrison's infamous Miami arrest (for allegedly
waving his wand onstage) the FBI did launch an investigation
into his past. Of course, aside from a total lack of evidence, the
theory just doesn't gel because Morrison refused to rent himself
to any political causes. So why would "the man" hassle with a
political hit?

The occult theories about Morrison's death sprout from his
well-known dabbling in the esoteric arts (he was "married" in a
Wiccan ceremony and believed that an Indian spirit inhabited
his body). One had it that he died when someone plucked his
eyes out with a knife to "free his soul." Another supernatural
theory proposed that a jilted mistress in New York killed
Morrison via transatlantic witchcraft. Some chose to think that
Jim's spirit had sloughed off its mortal coil (as Courson claimed

he had often done during trances), but this time canceled the return trip.

The most popular theories have it that Morrison, the martyred artist in a *Jesus Christ, Superstar* sense, somehow defied death, either metaphysically or literally. Morrison gets out alive!

As James Riordan and Jerry Prochnicky wrote in their Morrison biography, *Break on Through*, his "bizarre lifestyle inspired such thinking." Morrison's notorious disappearances had sparked death rumors before, and the confusion surrounding his apparently authentic death only egged on speculation. He had often talked about scrapping the burdens of super-celebrity by faking his own death and vanishing into the heart of Africa or some other suitably mysterious place. He told intimates that he would use the nom de guerre Mr. Mojo Risin' (the famous anagram of *Jim Morrison* in the song, "L.A. Woman") to contact them after he had "split to Africa." And Morrison was fascinated with conspiratorial scenarios that had the Disciples stealing the body of Christ from the crypt in what he jokingly called "the Easter heist."

Not surprisingly, then, the sightings began soon after his "death," at first in Paris, and then in Los Angeles, where a black-leather-bedecked Morrison reportedly hung out in underground gay nightclubs. A Bank of America employee in San Francisco claimed to be handling the account of someone calling himself and resembling Jim Morrison, although the clerk, later contacted by journalists, admitted he wasn't certain it was the Doors singer. In 1974, the rumor mill shifted into overdrive when Capitol Records released an album called *Phantom's Divine Comedy*, with a band identified as drummer X, bassist Y, and keyboardist Z—and with a lead singer who sounded eerily like Morrison. (A recent account has it that the Morrison sound-alike was actually proto-punk rocker Iggy Pop.)

One legend, described in *Break on Through*, had it that "at an obscure radio station in the Midwest Jim supposedly showed up in the dead of night and did a lengthy interview that explained it all." Of course, after the interview the mystery dude vanished again, and "no recordings of the interview exist."

Other rumors placed Morrison in Louisiana, where he was said to be living a secret life. In what looks like a connection to the Bank of America sightings, the incognito Morrison purportedly wrote and published a 1975 book called *The Bank of America of Louisiana*, under the auspices of the Zeppelin Publishing Company. The book's disclaimer, which states that names in this fiction "based on fact" had to be changed or "I would find myself back in the courts," is signed "Jim Morrison." The final line in the book is cryptically hoaky, just as we'd expect from an immortal sixties rocker: "B of A & Company, USA...where monkey business is big business."

But these sorts of rumors were inspiring, at least to a group of fans who, armed with Morrison's dental records, attempted to exhume the peregrinating corpse's casket—without success. Eventually, though, even Doors keyboardist Ray Manzarek was moved to remark, "If there's one guy who would have been capable of staging his own death—getting a phony death certificate or paying off some French doctor... and putting a hundred and fifty pounds of sand into a coffin and splitting to some point on this planet—Africa, who knows where—Jim Morrison would have been the guy to pull it off."

The speculation only gets funkier and, of course, foggier.

Thanks to the fact that Morrison's father, Steven Morrison, had been an admiral in the U.S. Navy, and was therefore "privy to intelligence and counterintelligence information," theories of an espionage role in Jim's death inevitably sprouted. According to conspiratologist Thomas Lyttle, a Scandinavian magazine published an article "detailing French intelligence efforts to assassinate Jim Morrison in Paris."

In his mondo Morrison essay in the anthology, *Secret and Suppressed*, not only does Lyttle fuse the espionage and spooky mystical theories, he mounts that double-header to the Louisiana doppelgänger, breeding a full-tilt conspiracy Cerberus.

Lyttle begins with the theory that crass commercial interests intervened in Morrison's spiritual transmigration (just as record execs compromised his earthly artistry). How Lyttle gets from A to B to C is a bit confusing, but boiled down to basics: he contends that Morrison dabbled in voodoo/voudon mysticism, which holds that the soul or aura needs a few months' quality time in which to successfully split to the beyond. Voodoo high priests, according to this tradition, have been known to intercept astral-bound souls, collecting their prize in a clay jar called a *canari*. This raises the question: Was Morrison's aura "bought and sold and then collected on that fateful day in Paris when he 'died'?"

According to Lyttle, the *canari* that captured Morrison's elemental identity was none other than Zeppelin Publishing Company, the same Louisiana outfit behind the aforementioned Jim Morrison/B of A book. (Lyttle states, but doesn't exactly prove, that the original Jim Morrison founded the Zeppelin organization himself, which seems to suggest that Morrison 1 approved the sale of his soul.) And the "high priest"? Again, according to Lyttle it was the mysterious proprietor of "B of A Company," who "owns an active passport and IDs under the name of James Douglas Morrison and claims to actually be the not-so-dead rock star!"

What this means is that the soul of Morrison 1 possesses the physical body of the mysterious Morrison 2, to whom Lyttle assigns the shorthand, JM2. And apparently JM2 was into more than just sex, drugs, and morose poetry. According to Lyttle, JM2 "claimed to be operating as an intelligence agent for a number of domestic and international groups including the CIA, NSA, Interpol, Swedish Intelligence, and others." Lyttle reports that he has seen documents, presumably provided by JM2, purporting to chronicle JM2's CIA work and "rogue financial activities with the Bank of America" on behalf of intelligence agencies, including "experiments to destabilize foreign currencies." Lyttle warns that he can't authenticate these papers, "but everything looked extremely official and very elaborate," he reassures.

Appropriately so, for JM2's plot is wonderfully elaborate. As Lyttle reports, JM2 has claimed publicly that there are "numerous" Morrison doubles doing yeoman's work in an obscure espionage cabal involving CIA sociological experiments. What's more, all the James Douglas Morrisons "knew one another and met from time to time to work it all out."

Whew. It makes you wonder whether that "Paul McCartney is Dead" hoax was in fact orchestrated by James Bond's archnemesis, Ernst Stavro Blofeld.

JM2's astral projections notwithstanding, a more mundane explanation for the suspicious secrecy surrounding the original Morrison's death emerged in the 1991 biography, *Break on Through*. Although Pamela Courson took her secret to the grave in 1974 after overdosing on heroin, authors Riordan and Prochnicky interviewed close friends to whom she had confided.

They reported that a despondent Morrison found Courson's heroin stash and overdosed—perhaps snorting it, for he was afraid of needles—in the Parisian flat. The next morning Courson discovered the corpse, and with the help of a close friend, attempted to prevent the sort of media circus that paraded around the drug-related deaths of Hendrix and Joplin. Somehow, Courson and company managed to persuade a French doctor to certify the death as a heart attack, thereby precluding an official autopsy. Meanwhile, they inveigled permission to lay Morrison to rest quietly in Père-Lachaise, days before informing the world, hardly knowing that they'd also laid the foundation for Morrison's mythological resurrection.

MAJOR SOURCES

Hopkins, Jerry, and Danny Sugerman. *No One Here Gets Out Alive*. New York: Warner Books, 1980.

Lyttle, Thomas. "Rumors, Myths and Urban Legends Surrounding the Death of Jim Morrison." In *Secret and Suppressed*, edited by Jim Keith. Portland, OR: Feral House, 1993.

Riordan, James, and Jerry Prochnicky. *Break on Through: The Life and Death of Jim Morrison*. New York: William Morrow and Company, 1991.

16

The Godfather Part III: The Real Story

As spiritual leader to the world's 800-million-strong Catholic population, the Pope is hardly an isolated figure. But Alberto Luciani, Pope John Paul I, who led those 800 million for just thirty-three days, died all alone one autumn night in 1978.

David Yallop, an English investigative journalist, has made the best case that the pope was poisoned. His book *In God's Name* argues that despite the brevity of his papacy, Luciani was bent on reform. Highest on Luciani's list of things that needed setting right: the Vatican Bank and related church financial institutions—the real Roman Empire.

By Luciani's time, following the reign of Giovanni Montini, Pope Paul VI, the Vatican Bank had mutated into a multinational high-finance hydra, diversified into regions not likely to have been frequented by the Holy Spirit. The transformation had begun five decades earlier when the Vatican struck a lucrative deal with Benito Mussolini's fascist government and followed up by inking a similar pact with Hitler.

Luciani desired nothing less than to undo the previous 50 years of history. Speaking to the Vatican diplomatic corps, his first official words as pope—prior even to his inaugural Mass—were: "We have no temporal goods to offer, no economic interests to discuss."

Quite a statement for the inheritor of a banking and real estate conglomerate with combined assets topping $3 billion; a force so unstoppable that a decade earlier it nearly demolished the Italian economy. When the Italian government displayed the gall to request a few taxes be paid on the Vatican's corpulent stock portfolio, the Holy See threatened to dump all of its holdings onto the Italian stock exchange, an exercise that would have strangled Italy's economy. Vatican Inc. remained tax exempt.

Perhaps the nastiest of the Vatican Bank's unsavory affiliations tied it to the penumbral P2, a mysterious Masonic-lodge-cum-criminal-syndicate with members in the highest reaches of government, the Mafia, and the Vatican itself.

Not incidentally, P2 was also a neo-fascist political cadre (at least Vatican financiers have kept consistent company over the years) responsible for assorted terrorist actions including a disastrous train station bombing in Bologna.

For P2 founder Licio Gelli—business partner of Klaus Barbie, financial backer of Juan Peron, paid CIA contact, and honored guest at Ronald Reagan's 1980 inauguration—finance and fascism are symbiotic. One Gellian aphorism holds, "the doors to all bank vaults open to the right."

The Vatican Bank was operated by an American bishop named Paul Marcinkus, who, for reasons never explained, was strolling through the Vatican village at dawn the very morning the Pope was discovered deceased. Marcinkus, not previously known for 6 A.M. power walks, had entered into numerous agreements on the bank's behalf with P2 members Michele Sindona and Roberto Calvi.

Sindona, now in prison, was an international speculator and mafioso who engineered frauds that led to the largest bank failures in American and Italian history. Marcinkus alternately claimed an ongoing business partnership with Sindona and denied ever meeting him.

Of the other P2 financier, Marcinkus once said, "Calvi merits our trust. This I have no reason to doubt."

"His comments are particularly illuminating," notes Yallop with a certain dry bemusement, "coming as they did just eight months after Calvi had been fined $13.7 million and sentenced to four years imprisonment, and only seven months after the Vatican and Marcinkus discovered (if we believe the Vatican version) that Calvi had stolen over $1 billion and left the Vatican to pay the bill."

Roberto Calvi was corrupt beyond comprehension, an Italian banker who pilfered millions upon millions in his career of white-collar crime. He liked to instruct his buddies to read Mario Puzo's novel, *The Godfather*, a copy of which was always on or near his person. "Then you will understand the ways of the world," advised this deeply immoral man.

How amusingly ironic, then, that Calvi's own death and the Byzantine scandals leading up to it formed the basis for *The Godfather Part III*, the second sequel to the film version of Puzo's gangster epic.

Calvi met his timely demise at the end of a noose affixed to the underside of London's Blackfriar's Bridge. Tough luck for Calvi, who though his hanging was ruled suicide by a coroner, seems certain to have met his picturesque doom courtesy of his P2 comrades. He must have been feeling acrobatic to scale the underside of the bridge and string himself up from beneath, rather than over the side the quick and easy way. For that matter, he could have just jumped, which would have been far more convenient considering his pockets were loaded with bricks.

Four hours before Calvi's death, his secretary fatally defenestrated in Italy.

Under the direction of Marcinkus, the Vatican Bank fronted for Calvi's complex and illegal stock deals. The Vatican Bank nominally owned numerous companies controlled in reality by Calvi. The setup scratched both backs. The Vatican and Calvi each raked in millions. Calvi was also P2's financial manager. Whenever P2 "puppetmaster" Gelli phoned the banker, he used the code name *Luciani*.

The uncommonly principled papacy of Alberto Luciani placed this gnarly net in grave jeopardy. Luciani intended nothing less than divesting the Vatican of both its vast wealth—the church, like Jesus, should be poor, the new pope believed—and of Bishop Paul Marcinkus.

If indeed Luciani died on September 28, 1978, of "natural causes," it was a phenomenal break for Gelli, Calvi, Sindona, and Marcinkus, as well as for the Mafia and P2. The first three men on that list had already demonstrated more than the mere capacity to plot and order murders. In addition to rival crooks, they'd killed various investigators for seeking a peek inside their dirty deals.

Marcinkus may not have had a history of murder but his motive for doing away with Pope John Paul I was no less powerful than that of his colleagues in chicanery. If Gelli, Sindona, or Calvi—most likely all three in concert—overlooked the opportunity to arrange for the pope's death they must have been careless crooks, and, after the pontiff keeled over, the luckiest men then alive.

Pope John Paul I, the world's most powerful and influential religious leader, conducted his daily business under security about as tight as that provided for the guy who delivered his morning papers. That is to say, none.

Not only was Luciani unguarded and unattended the eve he expired, but some sources say that when his fatal distress set in, whatever and whenever it was, he pushed a special bedside alarm button. The flashing alarm light went ignored and the guard in charge of what passed for the night's security detail was in bed. No one asked why the light in the papal apartment, clearly visible from outside, burned throughout the night though the pope stuck to a regular regimen of 9:30 bedtimes.

No autopsy was performed on Pope John Paul I, to the great consternation of Italian journalists, who—understandably, given Italian political history—are much quicker to suspect conspiracy than their American counterparts. The Vatican tried to pacify the protesting press, falsely stating that church law prohibited autopsies on popes (there was never any such edict).

The death was ruled the result of acute myocardial infarction, though no death certificate was issued to that, or any other effect.

According to Yallop, in the absence of an autopsy, a fatal dose of the drug digitalis would be indistinguishable from a heart attack. The same could be said for a multitude of other toxins. But Yallop focuses on digitalis because Gelli instructed all P2 members to commit suicide with a dose of that drug, provided by their benevolent lodge, if pressured to reveal secrets of the quasi-Masonic crypto-fascist group.

Yallop's sources tell him that when the pope was found, his stiffening fingers were clutching a set of notes detailing many of the changes he proposed in Vatican operations. The Vatican announced that he held a copy of *The Imitation of Christ*. The first reporters who heard that claim broke out in guffaws.

"It's difficult to believe that the death was natural," said a top aide to the French archbishop Marcel Lefebvre, "considering all the creatures of the devil who inhabit the Vatican."

When Karol Wojtyla, John Paul II, won election as Luciani's successor he received an immediate briefing on the radical plans of Pope John Paul I. He implemented not a single one.

MAJOR SOURCE

Yallop, David. *In God's Name*. New York: Bantam Books, 1984.

17

The Man Who Got Too Close

Just after 12:30 in the afternoon on August 10, 1991, chambermaids at the Sheraton Inn in Martinsburg, West Virginia, stumbled upon a grisly sight. In room 517, a nude man lay in the bathtub, his white knees protruding from a pool of bloody water. Blood was everywhere, spattered on the wall above the tub and smeared on the bathroom's tile floor.

The dead man was Danny Casolaro, a forty-four-year-old freelance journalist and would-be novelist from Fairfax, Virginia. His wrists were deeply slashed in twelve places. Under the body, paramedics found a straight-edge razor blade, an empty beer can, a paper coaster and two white plastic garbage bags. Nearby was a scrawled note that read in part, "Please forgive me for the worst possible thing I could have done."

It certainly looked like a garden-variety suicide. Which, apparently, is why the county coroner decided against an autopsy and released the body to a local mortician. The undertaker embalmed the corpse that same evening, before next of kin had been notified, a move that was not only hasty, but also illegal.

Had Martinsburg's finest immediately contacted Casolaro's family, they might have handled the case a bit more gingerly. For when notified of his brother's death two days after the fact, Anthony Casolaro, a physician, instantly recalled Danny's warning to him the previous week: "I have been getting some very threatening phone calls. If anything happens to me, don't believe it was accidental." On top of that, the day before and on the day of his death, someone had made a series of threatening phone calls to Casolaro's home. And according to Danny's housekeeper, who picked up the phone, the threats were hardly subtle. "You son of bitch," went one. "You're dead."

An ardent if somewhat unseasoned journalist, Danny Casolaro had claimed to family and friends that he was on the verge of exposing a tangled cabal he called "the Octopus," a sprawling conspiracy theory. Casolaro believed that an international klatch of seven or eight men had masterminded a host of scandals with tentacles extending to the controversial October Surprise, the alleged 1980 deal between the Reagan-Bush campaign and Iran to keep U.S. hostages on ice; the Inslaw affair, which revolves around charges that the Reagan Department of Justice stole computer software from a private firm; Iran-Contra; and the BCCI banking scandal, believed by Casolaro to be the funding arm (or tentacle) of many a national security conspiracy. In a book proposal, Casolaro had described, in his typically enthusiastic prose style, a "web of thugs and thieves who roam the earth with their weapons and their murders, trading dope and dirty money for the secrets of the temple."

The fatal trip to Martinsburg seemed extremely significant to Casolaro's family and friends because, as Casolaro had boasted to just about everyone he bumped into, there he planned to rendezvous with a supersource who would lock the final pieces of the Octopus puzzle into place.

Chagrined by national media coverage of their negligence

(and improbable rumors that the town was in cahoots with the Octopus combine), Martinsburg authorities quickly opened a belated investigation, including a full-blown autopsy by the state medical examiner. Although the chain of evidence had been broken, and rather drastically at that, local and state officials came back with findings that vindicated the original conclusion: Casolaro had killed himself, they confidently stated. There was supposedly no evidence of a struggle, and the wounds appeared to be self-inflicted, according to the local authorities. There was also the straightforward suicide note—in Casolaro's own handwriting.

Nonetheless, critics argued, the local police overlooked or underplayed other evidence that at least *suggested* more sinister possibilities:

- Before the emergency crews had arrived on the scene, Barbara Bittinger, the assistant head housekeeper at the Sheraton, saw two bloody towels under the sink. As she later told investigative journalist John Connolly, "It looked like someone threw the towels on the floor"—and it wasn't the maids—"and tried to wipe the blood up with their foot, but they didn't get the blood, they just smeared the floor." The police only briefly questioned Bittinger. Yet her account of the towels was corroborated by the professional cleaner who later scoured the room—and threw the towels away.

- According to a George Washington University physician who reviewed the autopsy, Casolaro's deep wrist gashes didn't have the usual "hesitation marks" of the aspiring suicide who tests his pain threshold. In Casolaro's case, this apparent gusto was all the more peculiar, for, according to friends and family, he was exceedingly squeamish. FBI special agent Thomas Gates, whom Casolaro had used as a sounding board for his theories, later told a congressional committee that Martinsburg police described the wounds to him as "hacking" lacerations, which sounds much more violent than the official "no struggle" line.

- Local police were unable to account for Casolaro's missing notes, which he reportedly trundled to Martinsburg in a briefcase. Both notes and briefcase had vanished without a trace.
- A waitress in the Sheraton cocktail lounge recalled that Casolaro had entered the bar with a man she described as "maybe Arab or Iranian." Police were never able to locate that man.
- And Casolaro's family and many friends found it hard to believe that he had taken his own life. Described as outgoing, upbeat, and boyishly exuberant, Casolaro seemed an unlikely candidate for suicide.

Danny Casolaro, without a doubt, had mixed with a cast of strange and possibly dangerous characters. Like many a conspiracy researcher who bites into that rotten apple, Casolaro found himself in a beguiling world of intrigue where the right knowledge, if you can only amass enough of it, promises to unlock America's encrypted history. Unfortunately, the spooks, thugs, and con artists who populate that David Lynchian landscape often embroider fact with outright fantasy—for reasons that remain, to say the least, obscure.

The character who nudged Casolaro into the conspiracy abyss was an oddball genius named Michael Riconosciuto. Described as a "mad scientist" and a "pathological liar" who expertly weaves fact and fantasy, Riconosciuto claims involvement in just about every national security scandal of the last decade.

In notes and conversation Casolaro dubbed his mad scientist source "Danger Man." Riconosciuto vaulted into Casolaro's universe during the spring of 1990. The introduction was made by a mutual acquaintance, Bill Hamiltion, who was mired in his own private conspiracy, the notorious Inslaw scandal.

Riconosciuto had been feeding information to Hamilton, the proprietor of Inslaw, Inc., about the alleged theft of Hamilton's proprietary computer software by officials in the Reagan administration's Department of Justice. Hamilton had won some early battles in his pitched war with cronies of Attorney General Edwin Meese III. The bone of contention, Hamilton's PROMIS software, was a powerful and potentially Orwellian computer program designed to integrate law enforcement databases nationwide, enabling government authorities to keep tabs on court cases, defendants, criminals, attorneys, cops, judges, and just about anyone else who appears on the radar screens of the criminal justice system.

Hamilton and his high-profile lawyer, former U.S. attorney general Elliot Richardson, charged that Meese's crew had violated a contractual agreement to use a more primitive version of PROMIS and had plundered an advanced, proprietary version of the computer program. Two federal judges sided with Hamilton, ruling that the Meese Department of Justice "took, converted, and stole" Hamilton's PROMIS "by trickery, fraud, and deceit."

Typically, after the scenery-chewing Riconosciuto made his grand entrance, the Inslaw affair got even weirder, bouncing to distant points on the globe like an overheated spy novel. Casolaro found himself in a seductive world of intrigue.

Riconosciuto told Hamilton and Casolaro that he had modified the PROMIS software for sale to foreign countries. The man fencing the stolen computer program, according to Riconosciuto, was an Ed Meese pal named Dr. Earl Brian. It got even better: Riconosciuto claimed that profits from the stolen merchandise were Brian's reward for helping to broker the October Surprise deal for the 1980 Reagan-Bush campaign. As Danger Man told it, he and Brian had personally delivered a $40 million payoff to the Iranians at an alleged October 1980 rendezvous in Paris, purportedly attended by Iranian mullahs, George Bush, and future CIA Director Bill Casey. Brian, of course, has denied any association with Riconosciuto, the Inslaw affair, or the October Surprise.

It might have been easy to dismiss Riconosciuto as a complete crank, except that certain aspects of his story checked out. Hamilton *had* discovered that the Canadian Mounties were

using the stolen PROMIS software. Witnesses claimed to have
seen Riconosciuto and Brian together on the Cabazon Indian
reservation in Indio, California, where Riconosciuto said he
had modified PROMIS and developed high-tech weapons for
the Nicaraguan Contras. Other sources acknowledged that
Riconosciuto and Brian were indeed involved in a joint venture
between the Cabazon Indians and the Wackenhut Corporation,
a private security firm known as the CIA's favorite dirty job
contractor. The venture used the Cabazon tribe's quasi-sov-
ereign status to skirt restrictions on manufacturing and selling
arms. According to a report by the Riverside County district
attorney, local cops hired for security at the reservation referred
to Brian as "being with the CIA."

And the Machiavellian purpose of Riconosciuto's software
modifications? To turn PROMIS into a tool of international
espionage, a high-tech bugging device that would be distributed
to "scores" of foreign intelligence and police agencies. Unbe-
knownst to the hapless foreigners, CIA computer hackers
would then have an electronic "trap door" giving them secret
access to foreign intelligence data.

After Hamilton introduced Casolaro to Danger Man,
Riconosciuto proceeded to drop additional bombshells. He
claimed to have sabotaged the CIA-connected, money-laundering Nugan Hand Bank; to have designed "fuel-air explosives"
for the Contras; and to have helped develop the cannon-like
Super Gun produced for Iraq by Gerald Bull, who was murdered in Brussels. Each of these angles Casolaro dutifully
recorded in his book proposal. According to Casolaro's notes,
Riconosciuto also ushered the journalist into the outer limits of
conspiratorial UFOlogy, claiming knowledge of the government's secret dealings in the Nevada desert with space aliens.

Like many a semiomniscient Deep Throat, though,
Riconosciuto promised but never delivered evidence buttressing
his loftiest claims, including tape recordings that were to have
proved he had hobnobbed with Reagan's CIA director, Bill
Casey.

But Riconosciuto did direct Casolaro to some very dangerous characters, indeed. Shortly before his death, Casolaro made plans to visit Riconosciuto's old stomping ground, the Cabazon reservation—hardly hospitable territory for whistle-blowers. During the early 1980s one tribe member's attempts to oust the reservation's white administrator, John Philip Nichols, came to a dramatic halt when someone fired a bullet into the malcontent's forehead, execution style. A former bodyguard of Nichols claimed, before emigrating hastily to South America, that his boss had hired the killers and ordered him to pay them off.

Nichols, a globetrotting "social worker," liked to brag about having worked on CIA plots to assassinate Fidel Castro and overthrow Chilean President Salvador Allende (who was eventually assassinated). During the mid-1980s, Nichols was convicted for soliciting the murder of five people. He got a generously light sentence and was back on the reservation eighteen months later.

Casolaro also became chummy with an entrepreneur whom he would have been wise to christen *Extreme* Danger Man. Apparently Robert Booth Nichols (no family relation to John Philip Nichols) had worked on the Cabazon-Wackenhut joint venture. He soon replaced Riconosciuto as Casolaro's most important contact in the conspiratorial funhouse. At first Casolaro was drawn to this suave figure, who has been described as "Clark Gable without the ears." Later Casolaro would refer to him as "a thug who acted like a gentleman."

Casolaro eventually learned that the FBI had identified Robert Booth Nichols as a drug trafficker and money launderer with ties to the Gambino organized crime family and the Japanese mob, the Yakuza. (Nichols unsuccessfully sued the government for slander.) Three days before his death, Casolaro told a special agent of the FBI that Nichols had warned him, "If you continue this investigation, you will die." Casolaro wasn't sure if it was a threat or a show of concern.

Investigative journalist John Connolly has suggested that while it might not have been the Octopus that killed Casolaro, perhaps he was done in by some rogue element encountered during his investigation. In a well-researched *SPY* magazine article, Connolly wrote that Casolaro had discovered from a former special prosecutor in the Department of Justice that Nichols had once offered to become a mob informant—a snitch. That knowledge, Connolly speculated, might have placed Casolaro in extreme danger. As Connolly put it, "If John Gotti, for example, had ever found out what Danny Casolaro had found out, Nichols would be a dead man."

To be fair, though, Nichols had quite an alibi. The day before Casolaro's death, Nichols told Bill Hamilton that he was leaving for Europe that same evening. Days later, when he called Casolaro's brother to offer his condolences, Nichols mentioned that he had just returned from London.

Other journalists have guessed at alternatives to foul play, including the possibility that Casolaro grew suicidally despondent over his inability to get published or his failure to get to the bottom of the Octopus cabal. The fact that the autopsy revealed trace amounts of an antidepressant drug helped fuel such speculation. The autopsy also revealed that Casolaro had early symptoms of multiple sclerosis, and suicide theorists have suggested that he took his life rather than develop full-fledged MS. Of course, these are all just guesses.

Just as Casolaro's surviving notes shed little light on his demise, they are equally vague about the precise shape of the conspiracy he claimed to be on the verge of exposing. We know that he planned to interview "renegade" CIA agent Edwin Wilson, then languishing in a federal prison on charges of supplying explosives to Libyan leader Mu'ammar Qaddafi. Along with a number of other veteran CIA operatives, Wilson figures in the Christic Institute's theory of the "secret team" (see page 310) a coven of spooks purportedly responsible for two decades' worth of national security scandals, from the JFK hit to drug trafficking in Southeast Asia to Iran-Contra and beyond. Although the Christic theory has been widely ridiculed (and its related civil suit tossed out of court), the fingerprints of

Wilson and other CIA operatives have indeed turned up in a number of "off-the-books" operations.

While the Octopus as unified-field conspiracy theory may sound a bit farfetched, Casolaro certainly was loping through some very ominous terrain. A House committee looking into the Inslaw affair thought as much and recommended that Casolaro's death be investigated further.

In early 1994, the Clinton Department of Justice decided to open a nationwide probe into the Casolaro case. As Casolaro's phone pal, FBI special agent Gates, told the House committee: "There is cause for suspicions."

MAJOR SOURCES

Casolaro, Danny. "Behold, a Pale Horse: A True Crime Narrative." In *Secret and Suppressed*. Portland, OR: Feral House, 1993.
Connolly, John, and Eric Reguly. "Badlands." *SPY*, April 1992.
Connolly, John. "Dead Right." *SPY*, January 1993.
Connolly, John. "Inside the Shadow CIA." *SPY*, September 1992.
Corn, David. "The Dark World of Danny Casolaro." *The Nation*, 28 October 1991.
Fricker, Richard L. "The Inslaw Octopus." *Wired*, 1.1 (1993).
Ridgeway, James, and Doug Vaughan. "The Last Days of Danny Casolaro." *Village Voice*, 15 October 1991.
"The Inslaw Affair: Investigative Report by the Committee on the Judiciary." Washington: U.S. Government Printing Office, 1992.

18

The Cloud Buster

Like his famous "cloud-buster," an exotic contraption of metal pipes and snaking tubes designed to make rain *and* disperse clouds, Wilhelm Reich provoked extreme reactions. To devoted Reichians, he was and is a martyred genius, a man whose revolutionary scientific discoveries drove his spiteful enemies—the government, the medical establishment, the communists—to destroy him.

But to his detractors, Reich was various other things, few of them flattering. Take your pick: mad scientist, medical "quack," eccentric sexologist, paranoid schizophrenic, haywire conspiracy theorist. Sure, he had once been a pioneering psychoanalyst and a student of Freud, a genius even, but somewhere along the line he went off the deep end.

The truth, of course, may fall short of both extremes. But there's no doubt that Wilhelm Reich, who died in prison in 1957, *was* a latter-day heretic. His spectacular, far-ranging theories about orgastic inhibition, cancer, nuclear radiation, weather modification, cosmic "orgone" energy, and UFOs (to name only a few) were, shall we say, radical departures from the orthodoxy of his day—or any day, for that matter.

Even if Reich was delusional when he claimed to be the victim of an overt conspiracy by "HIGs" (hoodlums in government) and "Red Fascists"—as he named his tormentors in later years—there's also no doubt that he was plagued by a far subtler kind of "conspiracy." As a stubborn, unrelenting iconoclast, Reich was fated to butt heads with the scientific establishment and the political order. For their part, disdainful of what could only be way-out pseudoscience, the orthodoxies did what orthodoxies do when faced with the radically unconventional: They marginalized the oddball by rejection, ridicule, innuendo, and, ultimately, legal action.

Given that level of hostility to his work, it's easy to see how Reich eventually grew into the role of "conspiracy theorist." And also why many Reichians continue to believe he was deliberately murdered.

But we're way ahead of the story.

It begins in the Vienna of Sigmund Freud, where young Willy Reich embarks on a life-long quest for what would become his Holy Grail (and ultimately his undoing): the "life-fulfilling" energy of sexual potency. As a rising star in the psychoanalysis movement, Reich refashioned Freud's early libido theory into what he now called his theory of "orgastic potency." Where Freud hypothesized that unconscious sexual repression led to neurosis, Reich took the theory to its logical, literal extreme, asserting that all neurosis is caused by blocked up orgastic energy. In other words, she's gotta have it, and so does he.

Needless to say, Reich's ideas about sexual healing didn't thaw frigid Austria of the 1920s. Reich was just too radical for Vienna and too much the renegade even for psychoanalysis. Once referred to as "Freud's pet," Reich increasingly found himself in the doghouse. For one thing, Reich was bedding some of his fraulein patients and prescribing masturbation to others—not exactly what Freud had in mind when he institutionalized the couch. But it was Freud's decision to scrap the libido theory altogether (partly in response to this young wild man who had taken Freud's sexual metaphor to literal extremes) that finally put Reich on frosty terms with psychoanalysis.

By the mid-1930s, after an equally parabolic career in the Communist Party of Berlin (they loved his critique of Hitler's "sex-politics," but sex education for *der jugend*, ages eight to twelve? *Nein!*), Reich had moved to Scandinavia, on the outs with sexually hung-up Marxists and one step ahead of the sado-masochistic Nazis. In Norway, Reich made the first of his unrelenting scientific discoveries vindicating his theory of orgastic energy: the "bions."

Reich found that rotting matter—even when sterilized—broke down into microscopic blue "vesicles" that were in some sense "alive." Reich dubbed these particles "bions" and believed them to be quasi-life forms somewhere between inanimate and animate matter. Some bions pulsed with a kind of radioactive energy that caused Reich's skin to welt when he placed them on a slide over his hand.

Reich decided that this radiation, which fueled the bions, was the "life force" energy he would later christen "orgone," so-named because it was, he said, identical to the sexual energy of orgasm. As far as Reich was concerned, he had bridged the gap between psychology and biology, isolating the energy that charges both mind and body.

Of course, the scientific establishment had another opinion: Reich was an unhinged dilettante whose hat was obviously too tight. Though Reich never claimed to have "created" life (he had merely tapped its source, he said), the Dr. Frankenstein label stuck, encouraged no doubt by the Austrian's peculiar experiments measuring the bioelectrical orgastic energy of kissing couples.

As the skeptical biologists saw it, Reich's throbbing bion vesicles were garden-variety microbes, or else he was misinterpreting some other mundane phenomenon. But Reich's careful replications of the experiment, taking into account those criticisms, always produced the same results. And though mainstream science has yet to systematically recreate the experiment, various modern researchers claim to have reproduced Reich's uncanny, hard-to-explain micro-critters.

Whatever the significance of his discovery, Reich's unconventionality proved to be of far greater interest to Norway's popular press: Who was this foreign shrink seeing patients in their underwear, advising them to touch themselves, conducting bioelectrical smooching experiments, and now causing vesicles to *throb*, for God sakes? Provincial Oslo was scandalized, and as the 1930s drew to a close, Reich, cursing his professional and political enemies, packed his bags for the seemingly hospitable climes of America.

Reich's research took off in New York and at Orgonon, as he dubbed his summer home in Rangeley, Maine, after the orgone energy. (Reich loved inventing technical neologisms, which lent an aura of authority to his unaccepted theories. The science of orgone energy? Orgonomy. Radium enriched with concentrated orgone? Orur.)

In 1940, Reich formulated his orgone energy theory, announcing that the cosmic life force not only streamed through the sexually healthy individual and between the pulsing bions, indeed it was "everywhere." (In sexually repressed people, however, orgone energy was stopped up, creating emotional and physical tension, or "armoring.") Reich believed he could see the bluish orgone charge crackling between the stars in the night sky and in a darkened room.

He managed to contain the orgone field emitted from bions in a specially built box lined on the inside with sheet metal and insulated on the outside by wood and other organic materials. Reich believed that the metal reflected the radiation inward. This unlikely invention Reich dubbed the "orgone energy accumulator." It would later bring the wrath of the Food and Drug Administration (FDA), the American Medical Association, and the psychiatric establishment down upon him.

The accumulator seemed to amplify the bion radiation, and

looking through the contraption's porthole, Reich got an eyeful of some sci-fi special effects: bluish vapors and flickering yellow lines and dots. But even when there were no bions in the box, Reich saw the same effect, albeit in a diminished form. As Reich explained it, the omnipresent atmospheric orgone was passing through the box and accumulating inside.

Reich racked up some interesting results with his orgone accumulators. When he put his hand inside an empty accumulator, he reported a warm tingling sensation. When he measured the temperature inside the box, it was on average a half degree warmer than room temperature, apparently evidence of the energy accumulation.

To establish his amazing find, Reich wasted little time arranging "a meeting of minds," as he described it, with Albert Einstein. Cordially, Einstein agreed to see him. Reich spent five hours in the famous physicist's Princeton home explaining his theories and urging Einstein to look through a hollow tube to view the orgone energy in the darkened room. We can only guess what Einstein really thought, but he graciously listened. Reich later delivered an accumulator, and Einstein conducted the temperature experiment, but concluded that the phenomenon was probably due to convection currents cooling the room.

Einstein's biographer, Ronald Clark, depicted the physicist as humoring the misguided psychoanalyst, "this eccentric, distraught figure [who] seems already to have slipped down the slope toward charlatanry or madness."

But Reich biographer Myron Sharaf reports that there have been at least twenty "positive replications" of Reich's temperature experiment since the 1950s, some with precise controls to eliminate the "convection" effect.

The Einsteinian rebuff didn't discourage the indomitable Reich from making further discoveries. "We're not playing for peanuts, here," he liked to say in stentorian Austrian tones.

Reich branched out into cancer research. He discovered

another kind of microscopic bion that grew from decaying matter: a black, rod-like organism that could immobilize the bluish, amoeba-like bion. He called these new organisms T-bacilli. When he injected mice with T-bacilli, the rodents died, many of them after developing cancer. Reich learned that he could cultivate many T-bacilli from the blood of cancer patients, but few from the blood of healthy persons. Were the bions a key to understanding cancer?

Reich found that cancerous mice "treated" in the orgone accumulator lived on average seven weeks longer than the sick rodents deprived of such therapy. Not surprisingly, Reich and his colleagues soon began building phone-booth-size accumulators for themselves—and for cancer patients.

Of the fifteen terminal cancer patients Reich saw in the early 1940s, six lived five to twelve months longer than expected, but then died. Six others were still alive when Reich published his findings two years later. Reich maintained that the orgone treatment reduced their pain and the size of their tumors. But he never claimed, as the FDA would later erroneously charge, that the accumulators could cure cancer. In fact, Reich believed that the accumulator alone couldn't treat the underlying cause of cancer: that clogged up libido, again. (Reich's emphasis on holistic health and the connection between mental and physical well-being was far ahead of its time.)

Then there was the orgone-powered engine, which has given Reich's numerous critics something to nosh on. It certainly *sounds* like that quintessential American swindle, the perpetual motion machine. Actually, according to Sharaf, who was a student and colleague of Reich's, the motor ran on a combination of orgone energy, concentrated in an attached accumulator, and electricity, but in "an amount insufficient to rotate the wheel without the accumulator."

When the student who built the motor deserted Orgonon—with the device—an increasingly paranoid Reich suspected that his engineering whiz kid was being coerced by the Atomic

Energy Commission, the communists, or some other malefactor. (Reich never published details about the contraption, giving rise to more doubts about its authenticity.)

As Sharaf reports about Reich's conspiratorial thinking, "He had always been capable of such erroneous pattern-finding, but this tendency increased sharply in his last years." If Reich's preferred villains seem a tad grandiose, we should remember that in the double-barreled tunnel of the nuclear age and the Cold War, paranoia was a bumper American crop.

In 1950, with the Korean War stoking up fears of global nuclear scrimmage, Reich hoped that his orgone accumulator might help treat radiation sickness. Thus began the dramatic Oranur Experiment, which many Reichians cite as a watershed—for science *and* conspiracy.

The orgone hit the fan, so to speak, when Reich placed one milligram of radium inside a series of nested accumulators. Almost immediately, Geiger counters went haywire, off the scale. Laboratory workers became dizzy and nauseated. The atmosphere was described as "oppressive" and "charged." But when removed from the room and tested outside, the radium registered normal Geiger counter readings.

Nonetheless the radiation in the room wouldn't dissipate. Reich, who had awakened the next day with a full-body tan, continued the experiment anyway. When he returned the radium to the accumulator, a bluish cloud could be seen through the windows of the room. People as far as ninety feet away from the building claimed to feel the sickening effects, which lasted for weeks. Later, when Reich's grown daughter, Eva, placed her head inside the empty accumulator, she lapsed into a near-comatose state and only revived several hours later.

So what was the Oranur Effect (Reichspeak for "orgone antinuclear") all about? Reich concluded that nuclear radiation had transformed the atmospheric orgone energy into a malignant force, just as healthy bions could decay into T-bacilli. Reich called this negatively amplified energy Deadly Orgone Radiation, or DOR. Backing up Reich's belief that orgone had "run amok" was an article in the *New York Times* of February 3, 1951—three weeks after the experiment. The *Times* reported that unusually potent levels of radioactivity had been detected in a three hundred- to six hundred-mile radius, centered near... Rangeley, Maine!

Conspiracy researcher Jim Martin believes that Reich's subsequent legal traumas were linked to his accidental discovery of the Oranur Effect. "Wilhelm Reich was imprisoned," writes Martin, "because he stumbled onto frightening facts about nuclear radiation during the early 1950s, a critical point in that newly developed industry." The dirty secret uncovered by Reich? "That there is *no shielding possible* against the biological effects of nuclear radiation," says Martin.

Nuclear goons not withstanding, at the time of Oranur, Reich was already in hot water with HIGs from the Food and Drug Administration. The FDA's antennae began twitching after two negative magazine articles about Reich appeared in *Harper's* and *New Republic*. Written by a freelance journalist named Mildred Brady, who privately called Reich's cancer theories "crackpot," the articles drew sly comparisons between sexologist Reich and the bohemian sex scene. Brady also drew subtle parallels between Reich and that always-alarming American phenomenon, the cult prophet. Brady's prophetic inference was clear: "the growing Reich cult," if not regulated, might wind up "disciplined by the state." Most damaging, however, Brady gave the erroneous impression that Reich claimed his accumulators would give patients "orgastic potency" and would cure cancer.

Once again, Reich found himself in need of a good press agent. Other journals picked up the scent and amplified Brady's distortions, as in *Collier's* claim that "the accumulator can lick everything from the common cold to cancer, according to Dr. Reich." *True* magazine just called it "the Marvelous Sex Box," which makes Reich's low-tech accumulator sound like Woody Allen's "orgasmatron" from the movie *Sleeper*. The message was clear: Reich was a dangerous quack. And maybe even some kinda *pre*vert. Spurious rumors began to circulate that

Orgonon was a sex racket or "nudist camp" that was "fed" children from a nearby summer camp. In between "orgies," female patients were said to have been... "masturbated" on the premises.

Reich, the one-time-communist-turned-Republican was convinced that his old foes, the Stalinists (Red Fascists), were behind the *New Republic* assault: After all, as every right-winger in the nation knew, the magazine's managing editor, Henry A. Wallace, was indeed connected to American communists, via his 1948 run for the presidency on the Progressive Party ticket.

Reichian writer Jim Martin also suspects a Stalinist connection. Martin points out that *New Republic* owner, Oxford wag Michael Straight, had not only jump-started Wallace's presidential campaign, he was a confessed (but reluctant) Soviet spy. More than that, *New Republic* was connected to Wall Street billionaires linked to the Rockefellers and British internationalists. Quoting from that group's sympathetic chronicler, the late Professor Carroll Quigley: *New Republic*'s "original purpose," as envisioned by Wall Street bankers, "was to provide an outlet for the progressive left and guide it quietly in an Anglophile direction." Given the fact that many right-wingers saw the Brit-inflected Wall Streeters as pawns of the Soviets, maybe Reich had a point when he later blurted to prison psychologists that the Rockefeller Foundation "made me a tool of its socioeconomic interpersonal relations." Or maybe not.

Reich hit upon a less complicated explanation when he formulated his somewhat self-serving, albeit perceptive, concept of the "emotional plague." Basically, what Reich meant by the phrase was the kind of intolerance that drives certain people to "persecute" those they deem "immoral" or otherwise unconventional. In other words, a witch-hunt, or at least the kind of superior ridicule that banishes unusual thinkers to the fringes.

There's no doubt that Brady's negative press helped set the stage for the FDA campaign against Reich, which was egged on by the American Medical Association and the psychiatric establishment. The investigation dogged Reich for years, as the FDA attempted without success to find a dissatisfied accumulator owner—for Reich had been shipping the "devices" (as the FDA always called them) to eager customers throughout the East Coast. All the while, the quack-baiting continued.

Shaken but not stirred, Reich continued his research into the Deadly Orgon Radiation (DOR), which he now saw as a global threat in the age of nuclear testing. After the Oranur Experiment, he had noticed "black" smog-like clouds hovering oppressively over the landscape. Convinced that these were DOR vapors, Reich invented his cloud-buster, which acted like a lightening rod, draining the DOR from the sky. Reich also used the machine—the hardware had a futuristic low-tech look, like something out of the movie, *Mad Max*—to make rain. At any rate, he convinced local farmers that he could modify the weather. They paid him to successfully reverse a drought. Later, Reich mounted the cloud-buster on the back of a truck and took it into the Arizona desert, looking like the Road Warrior, himself. He was convinced that DOR was causing the deserts to expand, and he set out to see if he could reverse the trend.

In the meantime, the FDA threw down the gauntlet. In 1954, at the FDA's request, Maine's attorney general filed a complaint against Reich, asking for an injunction. The complaint suggested that Reich was a charlatan, and it shamelessly distorted many of Reich's careful disclaimers about the accumulators. Reich stubbornly refused to appear in court, perhaps not fully understanding the American legal system, perhaps starting to buckle under the pressure. The FDA won its injunction, which was frightfully sweeping: Reich was ordered to destroy not only his accumulators, but also all literature "promoting" both the accumulators *and* his theories about orgone energy. That covered just about everything he had ever written, and Reich was one prolific author.

Furious, Reich shot off a telegram to the offending HIGs, threatening a deluge courtesy of his cloud-buster: "We are flooding the East as you are drying out the Southwest. You do not play with serious natural-scientific research." As biographer Sharaf writes, "Snow in Rangeley and rain along the New England coast came after Reich's weather operations; it had not been predicted." Thrilled, Reich slam-dunked a telegram to J. Edgar Hoover, trumpeting his ominous achievement.

By now Reich was convinced that President Eisenhower was secretly watching over him, grateful for Reich's anti-UFO "space gun." Whenever air force jets zoomed overhead, Reich took it as the presidential equivalent of a wink.

For Reich had taken up a lonely battle. In his book, *Contact With Space*, he speculated that the drivers of UFOs—"CORE men" (Cosmic ORgone Energy)—possibly had malevolent designs on the planet. "There was no escape from the fact that we were at war with a power unknown to man," he wrote. UFOs were causing the desertification of the earth, their "slag" exhaust spreading oppressive DOR through the atmosphere. Reich tied this theory to his idea of the "emotional plague": Man's "emotional desert" was abetting the UFOs in their scheme to smother the planet with DOR.

Back on Earth, the FDA and the state "Red Fascist HIGs, under Moskau [sic]" initiated contempt of court proceedings after one of Reich's colleagues shipped orgone accumulators across state lines. Reich represented himself at the trial and tried to make the case for conspiracy, but the judge rightly pointed out that the place for that had been the first trial. Still, Reich aroused the judge's interest when he pointed out that the chief prosecutor had been a former colleague at Orgonon, which raised all sorts of unsavory possibilities, from conflict of interest to entrapment.

But it was water over the dam. Reich was convicted on May 7, 1956, and sentenced to two years in prison, an especially harsh sentence for an ailing fifty-nine-year-old. That summer, FDA agents supervised the destruction of fifty-three accumulators. After an unsuccessful eleventh-hour intervention by the ACLU, the FDA oversaw the burning of more than six tons of books and other publications, including Reich's classics, *The Sexual*

Revolution and *The Mass Psychology of Fascism,* which were written long before he built his first accumulator. Despite the ugly specter of a bonfire of books—which Reich had seen before in Germany—the popular press made not a peep.

Reich died in prison, of "heart complications," on November 3, 1957, just two months before his parole.

Reichians see several details about his death as being suspicious: A manuscript he claimed to be writing never turned up. Reich had mentioned to his wife that when he asked for aspirin, he had gotten two pink pills instead; when she sent a letter requesting to see the hospital dispensary record, the warden penciled in its margin, "NO." And according to Jim Martin, Reich's daughter, Eva, now suspects foul play.

But a deus ex machina isn't really necessary to explain Reich's end. The doctor's radical ideas, his brilliant but often flawed pattern-finding, and his domineering will always brought the "emotional plague" crashing down on top of him. It still hangs like a DOR cloud, obscuring Reich's numerous contributions to psychology and therapy, sociology, child-rearing, and, who knows?—maybe even to biology and physics.

MAJOR SOURCES

Martin, Jim. "Who Killed Wilhelm Reich?" In *Apocalypse Culture* (expanded and revised edition), edited by Adam Parfrey. Los Angeles: Feral House, 1990.

Martin, Jim. "Quigley, Clinton, Straight, and Reich." *Steamshovel Press,* no. 8 (Summer 1993).

Sharaf, Myron. *Fury on Earth: A Biography of Wilhelm Reich.* New York: St. Martin's Press, 1983.

Wilson, Colin. *The Quest for Wilhelm Reich.* Garden City, NY: Anchor Press/Doubleday, 1981.

Thanks to Jim Martin of *Flatland* for compiling research used in this chapter.

IV

Mondo Politics

19

Votescam

No political act requires quite the same leap of faith as voting. Sure, the average citizen's one chance to participate in democracy comes at the ballot box. But what happens to your vote once you've pulled the lever, punched the computer card, or placed an X through the appropriate box?

Ken and Jim Collier "discovered" that at least on national election nights—the only time the ballot count really counts— the votes are all processed through a central corporation. A private corporation. The owners of this entity are the same media that report the results of the elections. When the News Election Service (NES) was incorporated back in 1964 by ABC, CBS, NBC, the Associated Press, and United Press International, it either put the vote count under the aegis of a responsible media organization concerned about reporting accurate and timely election returns, or in the clutches of a power-mad cabal.

The Colliers elect to see it as the latter, which is not surprising, because, as the authors of the book *Votescam*, the Collier brothers are the nation's self-styled leading advocates of the theory that all national elections, presidential and congressional, are rigged.

The News Election Service provides an ideal mechanism for chicanery—especially in the cyber-epoch of computerized voting. A little monkey-wrenching with a single, central, and private vote-tabulating computer—well, it's much cleaner than taking reams of paper ballots out into the West Texas outback and incinerating them as Lyndon Johnson did in an early congressional race. And it's more civilized than digging up the dead, or at least their voter registration cards.

The Collier hypothesis is as follows: The major media corporations use their direct and discreet access to NES to fix election results in advance. This not only enables them to make incredibly accurate projections, but, more significantly, to pick the president and the Congress. Not surprisingly, these politicians turn out to be slaves to corporate interests.

The actual vote totals are verified by county registrars—the only public officials responsible for counting votes. But that process doesn't wind up until months later. By that time everyone's lost interest, the media doesn't report those official results anyway, and if they did, there is ample time to tamper with those counts as well.

The media companies whelped NES when they realized that their prior practice of assembling returns individually led to occasionally embarrassing discrepancies in their reporting. These days, however, the actual returns have become irrelevant. Media election reporting derives almost exclusively from exit polls, in which a representative from a polling group hired by an individual media company asks voters leaving the polls a simple question: "Who'dja vote fer?"

Exit polling has been widely (and rightly) criticized for removing the electoral process from the hands of voters and transferring it to the statisticians. But at least it represented a small step toward decentralized election reporting. News organizations were, once again, actually competing—thus mitigating the chance of the next chief exec being selected by a coffee klatch somewhere in the bowels of Rockefeller Plaza.

In 1990, that hope withered.

"The three major television networks and Cable News Network," reported the *New York Times* on February 26, 1990, "have agreed to create a single election day exit poll of voters that would provide the same information at the same time to each organization."

The new unified group has operated since the 1990 congressional elections. Votescam becomes Pollscam.

Vote fraud in America is as old as American democracy. The Colliers simply posit its existence on a rather more expansive scale than the seemingly infinite number of well-documented local riggings. Computer technology only makes altering vote totals easier. The most popular election software, EL-80, has been found by independent computer experts to have switched the names of candidates, failed to record some votes, and failed to print out error reports. El-80 is also easily accessible to anyone with a basic knowledge of computer language. It is written in COBOL, and anyone who knows that language— and by the early eighties any college student who wanted to could learn it—can break into the program.

Taken together, say the Colliers, centralization of election reporting, vulnerability of high-tech voting, and corporate power adds up to one grim finality:

"It is the prescription for the covert stealing of America."

MAJOR SOURCE

Collier, James M. *Votescam: The Stealing of America*. New York: Victoria House, 1993.

20

The Mother of All "Gates"

Watergate, the mother of all scandals branded some-thing *gate*, may be America's most famous conspiracy. Most of us are familiar with at least the outlines of the scandal: a "third-rate burglary"; Richard Nixon's attempts to cover up that crime and countless others; the eighteen-and-a-half-minute gap in the White House tapes; Nixon's manipulation of the CIA and FBI in the furtherance of said coverup; "I am not a crook," yet, inexorably, Nixon's near-impeachment and resignation.

But stop and think for a moment about how little we actually know about the specific conspiracy that got the whole dirty snowball rolling. For starters, who ordered the break-ins at the Democratic National Committee (DNC) headquarters in the Watergate office complex, and why? Just whose phone was bugged? And when the coverup began, exactly who was covering up for whom?

Ah, into that yawning gap of knowledge leap the Watergate revisionists. Armed to the teeth with explosive counter-theories

147

and ostensible smoking guns, some are diehard soldiers in the struggle to rehabilitate Richard Nixon. Others really have unearthed compelling evidence that casts doubt on conventional assumptions about the scandal.

Regardless of the angle, all interpretations of the Watergate saga inevitably begin during the shifty hours of June 17, 1972. Responding to an early-morning call by a Watergate complex security guard, plainclothes cops stumbled upon five overdressed burglars cowering behind furniture in the Democratic National Committee's sixth-floor offices. The second-story men included CIA-trained Cuban exiles and "ex"-CIA wire man James McCord. They were carrying cameras, bugging devices, and lock-picking tools. Running the "black-bag" job from a nearby hotel room were "former" CIA operative E. Howard Hunt and White House "Plumber" G. Gordon Liddy. Hunt had recruited the anti-Castro Cubans, loyal to the super-spook since their nostalgic Bay of Pigs days. Hunt, Liddy, and McCord were the hands-on henchmen in Nixon's dirty tricks squad.

As conventional history tells it, the burglars were either attempting to plant an electronic bug in a telephone belonging to the liberal Democrats, or they were trying to remove/replace a malfunctioning bug positioned during an earlier break-in.

Yet there have always been problems with this theory—and despite its popularity, it remains just that: an unproven "theory." For starters, the burglars have told conflicting stories about what they were after: Was it dirt that DNC Chairman Larry O'Brien kept on Nixon, as Liddy earnestly suggested, or was it intelligence from another area of the office, as Hunt and two of the Cubans later claimed? If so, why risk so much for apparently so little? As Nixon's director of congressional relations later noted, "You take some damn chances if they're worthwhile, but that was crap."

Not surprisingly, the "unindicted co-conspirator" himself wholeheartedly agreed: "The whole thing was so senseless and bungled that it almost looked like some kind of a setup," Nixon announced in his memoir, typically giving himself the benefit of the doubt and flipping the story upside down to cast himself as the victim. The actual culprits? His supernumerary enemies, of course. Shortly before he was crowbarred from office, Nixon discovered "new information that the Democrats had prior knowledge and that the [Howard] Hughes organization might be involved....And there were stories of strange alliances."

Which brings us to the Democratic Trap theory, popular among diehard Nixon loyalists. Trap-gate has a factual anchor in seven volumes of executive-session testimony taken during the Senate Watergate investigation. The Senate testimony reveals that in April 1972, a New York private eye named A. J. Woolsten-Smith tipped off Larry O'Brien's deputy and also journalist Jack Anderson to a brewing spy operation against the DNC. Woolsten-Smith described the inchoate operation in some detail, from the Watergate office target to the Cuban personnel on the GOP team.

Armed with this information, Nixon-friendly theorists use twisted Nixonian logic to deflect blame for the resulting scandal: The donkey party *knew* the Republican burglars were going to break into the Watergate building, *so the Dems set us up!*

Theorists as disparate as the late H. R. Haldeman (Nixon's chief of staff) and left-wing critic Carl Oglesby have endorsed another version of the Trap theory. They suggest that Carl Shoffler, the police officer who made the Watergate arrests, was tipped off to the burglary in advance—either by the Democrats or by one of the burglars.

The evidence aligned "against" Shoffler? He had already finished his shift, but signed up for an additional eight hours of late-night work—on his birthday. When the call from the dispatcher came, Shoffler and his fellow officers were only a few blocks away from the Watergate, as if "awaiting the dispatcher's summons." And not least, an acquaintance of Shoffler, Edmund Chung, testified that in a subsequent dinner conversation, he got the "impression that Shoffler had advance knowledge of the break-in."

Shoffler denied making that statement and claimed that Chung had attempted to "bribe" him with a $50,000 "loan" if only Shoffler would "confess" to prior knowledge. Shoffler also suggested to the Senate that maybe Chung was a CIA agent, although that was never proven, nor did it even seem likely. Shoffler denied having any foreknowledge of the break-in and said of his decision to work overtime, "I just felt like it." And there the Cop Trap theory dead-ends.

Other entrapment theories posit a constellation of alternative villains, including those ubiquitous Howard Hughes operatives, Jack Anderson, and the CIA. The late Gary Allen, the cabal-sniffing John Birch Society author, titled a chapter in his book on the Rockefellers, "Was Nixon Watergated?" After all, Allen noted, the rise of Gerald Ford also brought zillionaire Nelson Rockefeller a proverbial heartbeat away from his much-coveted Oval Office.

The strongest revisionist theories arrived relatively late in the post-Watergate era, to a hissy fit of media disapproval. Finally, a critical mass of new evidence had coalesced to challenge the official story, the tale that had lionized a generation of aging journalists.

Secret Agenda, by Jim Hougan, and *Silent Coup*, by Len Colodny and Robert Gettlin, make a compelling case for the theory that Watergate didn't necessarily proceed from the top of the organization chart down.

According to *Silent Coup*, the key to the Watergate mystery was presidential counsel John Dean, a sort of conspiracy of one. This is a controversial recasting of Dean, whom history records as a peripheral player who turned whistle-blower and fingered the ostensible ringmasters in the scandal: ex-attorney general John Mitchell, chief of staff H. R. Haldeman, domestic affairs adviser John Erlichman and, of course, Nixon.

So what was Dean's agenda? Nothing so dull as tapping phones or scouring files for political dirt. For, according to *Silent Coup* and *Secret Agenda*, the Holy Grail of Watergate was sex! In *Secret Agenda*, Hougan suggests that the real target of the break-ins was a secret file featuring names, phone numbers, and perhaps even glossy pictures of prostitutes. At the time of the break-ins, a high-priced call-girl ring had been operating out of the posh Columbia Plaza apartment building a few blocks away from the Watergate complex.

According to Phillip Bailley, a young lawyer-pimp connected to that prostitution ring, a staffer at DNC headquarters had been arranging liaisons between the prostitutes and Democratic bigwigs. Apparently, at the DNC offices there was a file containing pictures and vital stats of the prostitutes, for marketing purposes.

It may have been Bailley's arrest for sexual pandering that triggered the fateful second Watergate break-in. As Colodny and Gettlin reveal, John Dean took a special interest in Bailley's well-publicized arrest. In a highly irregular and apparently unauthorized move, the presidential counsel took it upon himself to summon the federal prosecutor on the Bailley case to his office for a personal debriefing. It was then that Dean got a peek at important evidence: Bailley's address books.

According to Colodny and Gettlin, who build on Hougan's case, Dean's then-fiancée, Maureen Biner, was a friend and roommate of the prostitution ring's madam. What's more, Colodny and Gettlin confirmed that Maureen "Mo" Biner's name, phone number, and nickname, "Clout" (after all, she was about to marry the president's counsel), appeared in Bailley's confiscated address books. But Bailley's little black books also listed the girls from the Columbia Plaza ring.

Silent Coup's hypothesis? That with the press and FBI sniffing at the exposed call-girl ring, Dean had his own embarrassing, albeit tangential, connection to the D.C. strumpets. Consequently, he took it upon himself to dispatch the burglars to the Watergate on a fishing expedition. (*Silent Coup* is oddly silent on whether or not the DNC kept a dossier on "Clout.")

According to Colodny and Gettlin, then, the *real* motive behind the Watergate break-ins was considerably less conspiratorial (but a lot more steamy) than presidentially authorized blackmail or political counterintelligence. Dean wanted to know what was in the DNC's secret hooker files.

In detail too complicated to go into here, *Silent Coup* presents compelling evidence to suggest that Dean micromanaged a coverup immediately following the Watergate arrests—not to shield Nixon, but to cover his own exposed posterior. In this theory, Nixon really is a bit of a dupe, certainly responsible for many other high crimes and misdemeanors, but genuinely bewildered by news of the "third-rate burglary" (yet, being Nixon, reflexively jumping in to cover up a specific crime he knew next to nothing about).

But Dean's agenda (or Nixon's, if you prefer the traditional top-down theory) may not have been the only one operating in the murky waters of Watergate.

As investigative author Jim Hougan proferred on the twentieth anniversary of the break-in, "If one tries to understand Watergate in terms of a single monolithic operation conducted by a team of spooks with a unified goal, it will defy understanding."

Secret Agenda lays out fascinating evidence that suggests the burglars, themselves, may have had competing motives. Hougan singles out Bible-thumping wireman James McCord, an "ex"-CIA officer who ran Nixon's campaign security and joined Liddy's team of White House Plumbers. McCord's activities during the two break-ins were peculiar, to say the least, and perhaps even counterproductive.

An early attempt to penetrate the Watergate building was scuttled when McCord informed his fellow burglars that an alarm system prevented entry—an alarm that, Hougan discovered, didn't exist. Moreover, McCord made himself scarce at key moments during the break-ins and handled the job so sloppily that he must have been the most incompetent CIA officer since the guy who dreamed up the plot to make Castro's hair fall out. Unless, that is, McCord had designs of his own.

Was McCord trying to sabotage the operation? Hougan

theorizes that McCord was keeping tabs on the White House operation for his erstwhile employer, the CIA. Perhaps, Hougan suggests, McCord was protecting a CIA operation that snooping White House operatives were about to expose: DNC Chairman O'Brien, a Howard Hughes asset, may have had knowledge of the Agency's top-secret joint venture with the Hughes organization to raise a sunken Soviet submarine in the Pacific. Or, speculates Hougan, perhaps the call-girl ring was part or parcel of an illegal CIA operation. The Agency's illegal experimentation with mind control and drugs often involved prostitutes. Another possibility is that the CIA was spying on the prostitutes' clients—Democratic apparatchicks—for sexual blackmail purposes.

Which brings us, in a roundabout way, to Deep Throat. If McCord was under deep cover, and Dean was in deep doodoo, who was Deep Throat, the mysterious government source who fed *Washington Post* scribe Bob Woodward a steady stream of Watergate information?

In the Deep Throat wing of Watergate theory, there are enough candidates to fill an underground parking garage. High on the list is Robert Bennett, who was Howard Hughes's public relations flack and E. Howard Hunt's boss at a D.C. public relations firm that routinely provided cover for CIA operatives. (Bennett is currently a U.S. senator from Utah.) What really set alarms off about Bennett was that, per Hougan, he bragged about being a key source to Woodward and said that Woodward was "suitably grateful."

Other suspects on the Throat short list include Mark Felt, then-deputy FBI director; Ken Clawson, onetime-*Post*-reporter-turned-White-House-aide (author Ron Rosenbaum's fave candidate); David Gergen (John Dean's onetime choice, and now doing quite nicely as an aide to President Bill Clinton); and in Hougan's book, Admiral Bobby Ray Inman, the intelligence veteran and multidiscipline conspiracist (UFOlogists claim he's confessed to government knowledge of alien saucers, and Inman—himself no slouch as a conspiracy theorist—recently denounced a supposed cabal involving *New York Times* columnist Bill Safire, Senator Bob Dole, and the Israel lobby, which was out to submarine his short-lived nomination as Bill Clinton's defense secretary).

Silent Coup's nominee for Deep Throat is the most popular choice of all, however: General Alexander Haig. It was Hougan who first uncovered Bob Woodward's little-known connections to the Pentagon and, yes, to Al Haig. Before becoming a reporter, Hougan revealed, Woodward was a naval officer with a high-level assignment as military briefer to the chairman of the Joint Chiefs of Staff, Admiral Thomas H. Moorer. Moorer and other military sources have acknowledged that Woodward regularly briefed Henry Kissinger aide Al Haig in the White House basement.

Woodward admitted to Hougan that he had, in fact, been a military briefer, but denied having briefed Haig. However, several years later, when Colodny and Gettlin followed up on Hougan's reporting, Woodward denied that he had *ever* been a military briefer—*period*. As Colodny and Gettlin see it, Woodward has sought to obscure his naval career in an effort to cover his relationship with Deep Throat/Al Haig.

According to *Silent Coup*, Haig had his own secret agenda— and again the hapless Nixon comes off as a victim of his underlings' perfidy. Colodny and Gettlin allege that Haig fed Woodward a stream of self-serving information and *dis*information, in an effort to keep the Watergate spotlight on Nixon.

Why? According to *Silent Coup*, the Watergate scandal threatened to expose skeletons in Haig's own closet: In the early days of Nixon's administration, before the Watergate burglaries, write Colodny and Gettlin, Haig had been involved in a Pentagon spy ring that purloined secret foreign policy documents from National Security Adviser Henry Kissinger. Hardliners at the Pentagon, including Admiral Moorer, had worried that Nixon was too dovish on Vietnam and Communist China. According to *Silent Coup*, Haig was a ringer for the hawks.

The ambitious Haig had managed to cover his own tracks in

that affair, allege Colodny and Gettlin. That is, until Watergate began to expose other crimes and misdemeanors revolving around the Nixon administration. It was then, argue Colodny and Gettlin, that the president's new chief of staff began to manipulate the Watergate coverup in an effort to keep investigators from learning about the Pentagon spy ring. Consequently, Haig made Nixon look even more guilty—perhaps intentionally forcing the purported peacenick out of office. Hence the "silent coup."

Obviously Watergate is the conspiracy that keeps on giving. In fact, that scandal and the JFK assassination comprise the two foci in modern American conspiracy theory. There were even connections made between the Dallas hit and Watergate, an apparent nexus that opened the eyes of many budding conspiratologists to the possiblity that a black web of corruption lay just beneath the glossy surface of American politics. For starters, CIA-trained Watergate burglar Frank Sturgis had played a suspicious role as disinformationist in the wake of the Kennedy slaying, in an effort to pin the blame on Fidel Castro. Hunt and the Cubans had also been key players in the CIA's anti-Castro operations of the early 1960s, a touchstone of Cuban enmity for JFK. And according to some conspiracy theorists, Hunt and Sturgis bear an uncanny resemblance to two of the well-groomed "three tramps" arrested in Dealey Plaza and later released.

Nixon, himself, the man who gained so much from the death of his rival, just happened to be in Dallas on the day of the assassination, as a lawyer working for Pepsi. Much later when he began to flounder in the currents of Watergate, Nixon would issue bizarre, frantic warnings to CIA director Richard Helms that if the Agency didn't hop on the coverup bandwagon, Watergate would expose "the whole Bay of Pigs thing." This prompted H. R. Haldeman to write in his book, *The Ends of Power*, "It seems that in all of those Nixon references to the Bay of Pigs, he was actually referring to the Kennedy assassination....In a chilling parallel to their coverup at Watergate, the

CIA literally erased any connection between Kennedy's assassination and the CIA."

An entire tributary in Watergate speculation sluices around Haldeman's vague, evocative comment. Was *Bay of Pigs* Nixon's code phrase for a CIA role in the Kennedy assassination, and was he attempting to blackmail Helms into cooperating? Or was Nixon referring to the CIA's then-unexposed plots to bump off Castro—using Cubans trained by the CIA at the time of the Bay of Pigs invasion, Cubans who later resurfaced as Watergate burglars?

Helms, "the man who kept the secrets," isn't talking. And Nixon, publicly rehabilitated in his death, took the secret to his grave, where "strange alliances" of enemies will have a difficult time setting him up to spill the beans.

MAJOR SOURCES

Colodny, Len, and Robert Gettlin. *Silent Coup: The Removal of a President.* New York: St. Martin's Press, 1991.

Haldeman, H.R. *The Ends of Power.* New York: Times Books, 1978.

Hougan, Jim. *Secret Agenda: Watergate, Deep Throat and the CIA.* New York: Random House, 1984.

Rosenbaum, Ron. *Travels with Dr. Death and Other Unusual Investigations.* New York: Penguin Books, 1991.

21

Libido-gate

Judging from Washington's perennial sex scandals, power truly is the ultimate aphrodisiac—to paraphrase that seventies-epoch Casanova, Henry Kissinger, in a slightly different context. For young wonks and old goats alike, political prowess tends to breed hubris and hormones.

Not surprisingly, then, in the nation's pulsing capital, the fine art of sexual blackmail has what you might call "a history."

The pioneering figure of Washington "sexmail" was that creepiest of peeping G-men, J. Edgar Hoover. Thanks to his infamous sex files, which contained dirt on just about everyone in Washington short of his shoeshine boy, Hoover managed to dominate the capital (and eight presidents) for nearly half a century.

Not surprisingly, Hoover's busiest period came while John F. Kennedy occupied the White House and its many bedrooms. By several accounts, when rumors were rampant that Kennedy was going to pinkslip the aging, annoying FBI chief, Hoover put his plenary Kennedy files to work, thereby saving his own hide. With an obsession more than verging on the pathological,

Hoover had bugged JFK's legion love nests and tapped the princess phones of assorted Kennedy playmates, including mob moll Judith Campbell Exner and superstarlet Marilyn Monroe—whose bedroom was purportedly heavily trafficked by both Kennedy brothers.

The bug-eyed Hoover also glommed onto in-flight tapes of Jack and actress Angie Dickinson summiting in the boudoir of a chartered aircraft. Typically playing both sides against the middle, Hoover leaked info to the tabloid press about an old Kennedy affair with a senate secretary and about Kennedy's rumored former marriage, and then "put Kennedy in his debt by supplying background for the *Newsweek* rebuttal," according to journalist Anthony Summers.

When it came to recording Jack's and Bobby's compromising positions, Hoover had company. The Mafia and Jimmy Hoffa also managed to plant electronic bedroom ears in Marilyn Monroe's inner sanctum, especially at roué actor and Kennedy in-law Peter Lawford's beach house.

Hoover used the same tactics in his vendetta against Martin Luther King, Jr., bugging the civil rights leader's tryst spots with assorted paramours, spreading untrue gossip that King was a "switch-hitter," even marshaling surveillance photographs of King in the same room as a known—gasp—homosexual. Transcripts were leaked to the press, but the media didn't bite.

Hoover even had a bimbo file on Richard Nixon, of all the unlikely party animals. As Anthony Summers reports in his revisionist Hoover biography, *Official and Confidential*, while Nixon was vice president, he met a young Hong Kong travel guide named Marianna Liu. Convinced that Liu was a spy for communist China (a "Chicom"), the CIA had British intelligence train its infrared camera lenses on Nixon's bedroom window during his visits to Hong Kong. Liu and Nixon swore to Summers that there was never any sex, but Hoover was described as reading the Nixon-Chicom file "gleefully" and showing it to Dick before he became president.

Never one to let "evidence" get in the way of salacious innuendo, Hoover later came up with a report claiming that future Watergate boys H. R. Haldeman, John Ehrlichman, and Dwight Chapin were homosexual lovers. This was in 1969, before Watergate, and Hoover's source, an unidentified bartender, was claiming that the three were whooping it up at homosexual parties in the Watergate hotel. Of course, it wasn't true, and as Ehrlichman told Summers, "I came to think that Hoover did this to show his claws, or ingratiate himself to Nixon—probably both."

In Washington, what goes around comes around, and Hoover's actual homosexuality was hardly a well-kept secret among his numerous enemies. Mob boss Meyer Lansky liked to boast that he "fixed that son of a bitch" Hoover, purportedly by acquiring graphic photos of Hoover fellating his lifelong companion, Clyde Tolson. According to Summers, by the late 1940s there were also pictures of Hoover vamping as a closet drag queen. Even that quintessential CIA garbologist, counterspy catcher James Jesus Angleton was in on the act, purportedly having his mits on incriminating Hoover sex pics.

Blackmail or not, the mob's sway over Hoover *was* enormous: Publicly, the all-American, morally unimpeachable lingerie-wearing FBI director refused to admit that the Mafia even existed.

Hoover went to his grave more than two decades ago, taking his voluminous "personal and confidential" sex files with him. Of course they mysteriously vanished, giving rise to assorted conspiracy theories, including the possibility that Hoover loyalists destroyed them, that the CIA snatched them up, and even that Nixon's Watergate Plumbers made a bungled attempt to get their hot little mits on the explosive cache.

So, with Hoover out of the picture, is sexual extortion in Washington merely a historical idiosyncrasy, like Hoover, and the Kennedys, the product of a more reckless era?

Well, sexual blackmail may have a more enduring place in Washington politics than we tend to suspect. More than one vice investigator in Washington believes that mob-controlled call girls, intelligence operatives, and even Washington lobbyists have long run an underground racket aimed at sexually compromising Congress and the administration.

Conspiracy researcher Peter Dale Scott calls it "an ongoing, highly organized, and protected operation." Scott, a former Canadian diplomat and professor of English at the University of California, Berkeley, goes so far as to suggest that Washington's sex syndicate, exploited by intelligence spooks and the mob, has "driven the major scandals of Washington since at least the beginning of the Cold War."

Apparently, behind every good political scandal is a prostitute. Scott isn't alone in this thinking. According to Scott, "a retired Washington detective, one who played a small but important role in Watergate," believes that mob pimps and bigwig lobbyists use pricey call girls to put the squeeze on key officials. This is apparently a reference to Carl Shoffler, incidentally the arresting police officer who slapped cuffs on the Watergate burglars.

During a 1982 investigation into the use of "drugs and sexual activity to lobby congressmen," Shoffler did indeed advise congressional investigators to look into a male prostitution ring that serviced Capitol Hill. The veteran police detective believed that the sex ring might be linked to a high-flying Washington lobbyist, Robert Keith Gray, who had more than a few connections to CIA folk. According to Peter Dale Scott, some Washington investigators also suspected that the gay sex ring was connected to D.C. crime boss Joe "the Possum" Nesline.

Unfortunately, the congressional probe petered out before it got anywhere. Summing up the untested Libido-gate hypothesis, however, one of the congressional investigators put it this way to author Susan Trento: "If a lobbyist wants to use hookers to influence legislation, there's a pool of talent he draws from. There are certain madams in town that they make connections with. By simple logic, if you're in the business of influencing people with male prostitutes or kids, there has to be that supply chain.... [If] we start to identify some of the clients, it's possible we could find the suppliers for intelligence, organized crime, and lobbyists." In other words, follow the honey.

Former (and fugitive) CIA officer Frank Terpil had no compunction about identifying one such client, his former employer. Terpil told investigative author Jim Hougan that CIA-run sexual blackmail setups were common in Washington during the Watergate years. Terpil fingered his former partner, Ed Wilson, as the facilitator of one such CIA operation. Terpil claimed that Wilson ran the CIA mantrap from Korean agent Tong Sun Park's George Town Club, the Korean intelligence front that figured in the 1970s Koreagate scandal.

"Historically," Terpil explained, "one of Wilson's agency jobs was to subvert members of both houses [of Congress] by any means necessary.... Certain people could be easily coerced by living out their sexual fantasy in the flesh.... A remembrance of these occasions [was] permanently recorded via selected cameras."

Of course, we should note that Terpil hasn't offered any proof to back up that claim, and ex-CIA officers—not least of all, ones who have been convicted in absentia for terrorist activities—aren't celebrated for their candor. On the other hand, sexual blackmail was indeed a favorite CIA method of "turning" foreign agents or otherwise compromising them to do Uncle Sam's bidding. Considering all of the Agency's illegal doings on domestic soil during the last four decades, Terpil's story certainly seems plausible.

Interestingly, Robert Keith Gray, the omnipresent superlobbyist whose name came up during the 1982 gay sex ring investigation, also pops into the George Town Club-Terpil milieu. Gray, who (coincidentally or not) gravitates toward spy nests, was the club's first overseer and also a director at Terpil's firm, Consultants International, a notorious CIA proprietary front.

And speaking of strange coincidences, it might be nothing more than evidence that networking is key in D.C., but Terpil's and Korean lobbyist Park's names turned up a few years earlier in the trick book of a cathouse madam linked to yet another famous scandal, the biggest scandal of all: Watergate.

The theory that the Watergate affair sprang, unintentionally, from the bosom of a political sex ring was first proposed by journalist Jim Hougan in his fascinating book, *Secret Agenda.*

The madam, Heidi Rikan, worked out of Washington's posh Columbia Plaza apartment building, located across the street from the Watergate office complex. Hougan suggests that Rikan's call-girl ring may have been "either a CIA operation or the target of a CIA operation."

Briefly, Hougan's hypothesis is this: The Columbia Plaza girls were servicing a very interesting political clientele: Democratic muckamucks who placed their orders for companionship from a phone inside the Democratic National Committee headquarters in the Watergate building. Discovering this fruitful setup, Nixon's henchmen decided to target the Democratic fornicators. But in doing so, they stood a good chance of exposing the heavy breather already bugging the phone lines: the CIA. Ergo, the CIA's moles in the White House (allegedly superpatriotic conspirators James McCord and E. Howard Hunt) were forced to sabotage the Watergate break-ins in order to protect the CIA's highly illegal sex sting from Nixon's overeager burglars.

An illegal CIA sexpionage gambit unintentionally triggering the downfall of Richard Nixon? Say it ain't so!

Does the sexpionage industry go back even further in history than the babes of Watergate? Conspiracy theorist-emeritus Peter Dale Scott is game enough to hazard an affirmative. Employing the semiotics of conspiracy research—wherein names connect to other names, dates, and misdeeds, creating a tableau of suspicion that is usually intriguing, if not always conclusive—Scott has connected the dots.

Most interestingly, the Watergate madam, Heidi Rikan, was a girlfriend of mobster Joe "the Possum" Nesline, whose alleged connection to the Capitol Hill gay sex scandal a decade later aroused the suspicions of Washington detectives.

Assorted boyfriends and former husbands of both Rikan and

her sometime roommate, Mo Biner (who married key Watergate figure John Dean, which makes Mo a pivotal character, according to scandal revisionists), were associated with the Quorum, an early 1960s "swingles" club run by Bobby Baker, a former aide to Lyndon Johnson. Scott surmises that all roads led to Baker's club for a reason: the Quorum functioned a lot like the mob-and-intelligence-infested sex traps of the 1970s.

It was Bobby Baker who introduced President Kennedy to an East German bombshell named Ellen Rometsch, whom JFK, true to form, promptly bedded. Scott speculates that J. Edgar Hoover leaked word of this international indiscretion to the press. Whether or not Hoover was behind the leaks, they nearly ignited a global scandal. That's because JFK's nubile Valkyrie also happened to be sleeping with a Soviet diplomat, a coincidence that, if revealed, wouldn't have served Kennedy well at the height of the Cold War. The threat of a "bimbo eruption" with international implications forced Bobby Kennedy into scandal-kibosh mode.

Scott notes that the JFK-Rometsch peccadillo paralleled the scandalous 1962 affair that toppled British war minister John Profumo. Profumo publicly confessed to romping with Christine Keeler, a party doll/prostitute working for sexual procurer Stephen Ward. That scandal proved doubly damaging to Profumo because Keeler was simultaneously servicing, yes, a Soviet diplomat. And more recent revelations have disclosed that the British intelligence agency MI5 "had been using the Stephen Ward sex ring for some time to compromise the Soviet agent." Scott wonders, Did MI5 set out to compromise Profumo as well? Did the hyperlibidinous JFK blunder into a similar sex trap?

Interestingly, there is a more direct connection between JFK's peccadilloes and the MI5-manipulated Profumo affair. During the summer of 1963, Hoover's porous sex files began leaking again, resulting in press reports that a high U.S. official had slept with two members of Britain's Ward-Keeler sex ring, the very ring that toppled Profumo. That high U.S. official, no

7 the

surprise, was the prodigious JFK. Scott observes that "MI5, as Britain's counterintelligence agency, maintained direct relations with both Hoover in the FBI" and the CIA. Did the Brits help Hoover set up Kennedy for a fall?

Bobby Baker, catalyst of the JFK-Rometsch affair, later boasted that he had in his possession letters from the East German woman that could prove embarrassing to the Kennedys, which per Scott, "strengthens the impression of an ongoing, sophisticated blackmail operation" in this nation's carnal capital.

Perhaps. Or maybe it just proves that in Washington eventually everyone gets screwed.

MAJOR SOURCES

Hougan, Jim. *Secret Agenda: Watergate, Deep Throat, and the CIA.* New York: Random House, 1984.

Scott, Peter Dale. *Deep Politics and the Death of JFK.* Berkeley, CA: University of California Press, 1993.

Summers, Anthony. *Official and Confidential: The Secret Life of J. Edgar Hoover.* New York: Pocket Books, 1994.

Trento, Susan B. *The Power House: Robert Keith Gray and the Selling of Access and Influence in Washington.* New York: St. Martin's Press, 1992.

22

October Surprise

Few conspiracy theories have galled Washington more than the so-called October Surprise. Little wonder. Controversial speculation that the 1980 Reagan-Bush presidential campaign cut a treasonous deal with Iran to forestall the release of American hostages indicts not only a political party and two presidents, it also tends to confirm our worst suspicions about cynical political manipulation, casting doubt on the validity of the democratic process itself.

As far as official Washington is concerned, however, the October Surprise is pure bunkum. During the final days of the Bush administration, two congressional probes jettisoned the charges as a historical canard. As they say in the conspiracy-debunking business, case closed!

Or is it? Like the official investigations into the assassination of President Kennedy, the October Surprise probes raised almost as many questions as they purported to answer. We'll return to those questions presently.

First, the case for conspiracy.

High noon, January 20, 1980. In his inaugural address

President Ronald Reagan stares down the camera and promises Americans "an era of national renewal." Like slick crosscutting in a Hollywood thriller, his timing is impeccable: Twenty minutes later, as if by the force of his words alone, fifty-two American hostages are suddenly liberated after more than a year of humiliating captivity in Iranian clutches. As Reagan rides tall in the saddle and a diminished Jimmy Carter shuffles back to Georgia, few comment on the curious timing.

Two months earlier, however, Reagan had crowed about a "secret plan" involving the hostages. "My ideas require quiet diplomacy," he had boasted, "where you don't have to say what it is you're thinking of doing." Campaign bluster or a revealing admission?

An agglomeration of fact, rumor, and, curiously, elements of misdirection began to grow. Yet it wasn't until 1988, during Vice President George Bush's own bid for the presidency, that the October Surprise theory had its public coming out. The theory's proponents accused the Reagan-Bush campaign of plotting to steal the 1980 election by striking a deal with the Ayatollah Khomeini to keep the American hostages on ice until after the November elections. By sabotaging the legitimate U.S. government's attempts to free the hostages, the theory went, the Republicans would prevent a Carter-engineered "October Surprise" that might give the flagging Democrat an eleventh-hour political boost.

Certain facts were suggestive: A 1981 congressional probe into the Reagan campaign's theft of White House briefing books on the eve of a presidential debate disclosed that the Republicans had set up an espionage network that gathered intelligence on the Carter campaign and the president's efforts to liberate the hostages.

Reagan campaign manager William Casey, who would later become CIA chief, was receiving highly classified reports on closely held Carter administration secrets. A pedigreed spook who delighted in cloak and dagger work, Casey had served as a spy master in the OSS, the CIA's World War II precursor. But he remained an intelligence zealot even after his official break with spy central; as a Wall Street lawyer, he offered tax consulting to CIA front companies. Even his mumbling inflection, which sounded like he carried a mouth full of pebbles, suggested a propensity for the sub rosa.

But did Casey's machinations go further than campaign espionage? Did he conduct secret negotiations with Iranian hostage takers—and perhaps even strike a pact to keep the Americans captive in Iran? In short, did the Republicans pull their own October Surprise?

In this swampy terrain, the evidence grows murkier. In 1988, former Iranian president Abolhassan Bani-Sadr claimed to have secondhand knowledge that such a deal had occurred. Then living in exile outside Paris, Bani-Sadr claimed his sources in Iran informed him that George Bush had flown to meetings in Paris to seal the deal in mid-October 1980.

Soon a motley collection of arms dealers, convicts, con men, and errant spooks chimed in, signing onto the growing October Surprise witness list. Several claimed to have seen Bush glad-handing Iranian mullahs at a Paris hotel or flapping across French airport tarmac on or about the weekend of October 18. Most of the "witnesses" reported Casey sightings at the Paris tryst as well. Soon the list of attendees was bulging, like the roster at a Shriners' convention. Everyone and his CIA handler had been at the Paris rendezvous, it seemed. Most claimed that French and Israeli intelligence operatives were also on hand to shepherd the clandestine deal and presumably enjoy a buffet-style luncheon.

According to several other sources, Casey also attended a series of earlier meetings with a Khomeini emissary in Spain. According to Iranian arms dealer Jamshid Hashemi, he and his late brother, Cyrus, brought Casey and Iranian mullah Mehdi Karrubi together at Madrid's Ritz Hotel for two sets of meetings, in July and August 1980. As Hashemi told it, Casey proposed a quid pro quo: If Iran would hold the hostages until after the election, the incoming Reagan administration (which had yet to go through the formality of getting elected) would release Iranian funds and assets that had been frozen after Khomeini toppled the Shah of Iran and seized the American Embassy. The Reaganites would also emancipate $150 million in military hardware that the shah had already purchased— equipment desperately needed as Iran's war with Iraq heated up. At the second Madrid meeting, Karrubi returned to announce that Khomeini had approved the deal.

According to Jamshid Hashemi, the Republicans managed to slip the ol' payola to Iran even before the election—thanks to the connivance of Israel, which donated the necessary military hardware. If the October Surprise scenario was accurate, then it seems the secret arms-for-hostages deals later exposed during the Iran-Contra scandal could be backdated to 1980.

Although Casey had died of a brain tumor in 1987 and wasn't available to mumble a response, Bush and his campaign operatives denied the charges.

Unfortunately, the more loquacious sources claiming involvement in the secret deal were, by and large, denizens of the shady international arms bazaar. Some seemed to mingle verifiable fact with seedy fantasy. Chief among the semi-omniscient sources in this category was Ari Ben-Menashe, an ex-Israeli intelligence officer who claimed to have seen Bush at the Paris meetings. Ben-Menashe also claimed to know of the earlier Madrid meetings. As a military intelligence liaison with Iran in 1979 and 1980, Ben-Menashe helped broker the Reagan-Iran deals, he claimed. He also reported that Israel made shipments of light artillery and military hardware to Iran in 1980, in defiance of President Carter's arms embargo, to grease the October Surprise deal.

But journalists caught Ben-Menashe gilding his story, and Israeli officials claimed he wasn't who he said he was. On this latter point, though, Israel's intelligence honchos were even less reliable than Ben-Menashe. At first, they denied he had worked for them. But when Ben-Menashe produced letters of reference from Israeli intelligence brass, they changed their story, insisting now that he had merely been a peon translator—and an unreliable, exaggerating, damnable peon at that.

Yet other Israeli officials acknowledged Ben-Menashe's access to the top echelons of military intelligence; one called him "our Ollie North." Ben-Menashe clearly had access to very inside information. It was he who exposed the Reagan administration's arms-for-hostages schemes of the mid-1980s, tipping off the Lebanese newspaper that broke the story (only after *Time* magazine rebuffed his overtures).

If Ben-Menashe was maddeningly evasive, several sources, including Richard Brenneke, turned out to be unconditional frauds. A self-professed arms dealer from Portland, Oregon, the nerdy, cigar-sucking Brenneke had gained currency as a central October Surprise figure after he beat a perjury rap in federal court. Justice Department prosecutors failed to persuade a jury that Brenneke had lied when he testified in court that he had seen Bush and former Bush aide Donald Gregg at the Paris parley. (Brenneke, grandiloquent in the manner of Churchill's butler, also claimed to have ordered refreshments for the event.) Brenneke later went on to feather his nest in the conspiracy theory, making the absurd claim that he had also attended the Madrid meetings.

But Brenneke's tales imploded—rather suspiciously—when he hired a ghost writer to help him craft a memoir of his October Surprise peregrinations. When his coauthor/sometime paramour Peggy Robohm stumbled upon the obvious inconsistencies in Brenneke's tales, he invited her to check his story against his voluminous files, which contained personal desk calendars, credit card receipts, and other arcana from 1980. What Robohm found was irrefutable evidence showing that Brenneke had gone nowhere near Europe in the fall of 1980, but, rather, had left a paper trail placing him in greasy spoon cafes and cheesy motels in the Pacific Northwest.

His book deal blown, his budding celebrity crushed, his credibility zilch, how naive was this man who, in the paper-shredding age, did essentially the opposite, offering up his own impeachment papers? His timing was certainly interesting. Brenneke unraveled his own credibility as pressure was mounting for a congressional investigation into the October Surprise. Was Brenneke a disinformation time bomb awaiting an opportune moment to explode the October Surprise charges? Lending credence to such a possibility was another false prophet in the October Surprise rogue's gallery.

Soon after Brenneke injected himself into the October Surprise affair, a source calling himself "Razine" began calling journalists and making similar boasts. Speaking in a bogus southern drawl, Razine described himself as a retired CIA officer who had read a report at spook HQ in Langley, Virginia, placing Bush at the Paris meetings. Razine confirmed that Brenneke had also attended the meetings. But Razine was eventually unmasked as a one-time literature professor named Oswald LeWinter, who had once been convicted on drug smuggling charges.

When confronted by journalists, LeWinter claimed: "I was asked by some people to mount a disinformation campaign." He was paid $100,000, he submitted, by employers connected with U.S. intelligence, to make "sure that the media lost interest, that the story was discredited."

Brenneke and LeWinter had exchanged phone calls during their fifteen minutes of media fame, raising the possibility of a coordinated effort.

But LeWinter subsequently undercut his confession with the *new* claim that he had actually been dispatched to Paris in October 1980 to help expunge evidence of the clandestine assignation. Later, under oath to the House of Representatives' October Surprise task force, he doubled back *yet again*, this time declaring that he had fabricated all previous claims about the October Surprise as revenge against Uncle Sam for his drug bust. (LeWinter told the House task force that he improvised the alias *Razine* when a conspiracy tracker called him "just after he had finished eating a bowl of raisin bran.")

However pathological his lying, LeWinter was on the mark

when he gloated to journalists from PBS's *Frontline* program that "the October Surprise story did not break before the [1988] election, and, to my knowledge, it hasn't broken yet. The promised critical mass never came to be."

Debunkers in the media and Congress zeroed in on the errant sources, bagging them all with the likes of Brenneke and LeWinter. Yet the debunkers spun an equally improbable counterconspiracy tale in which a cabal of international grifters concocted the entire October Surprise opera, exchanging notes and embellishing their stories along the way. Why? The motive, according to the debunkers, had something to do with a vendetta by arms dealers against Reagan-Bushies following a U.S. sting operation that netted a gaggle of these "merchants of death." No matter how you look at it, the October Surprise orbits a bizarro world of conspiracy.

While Senate investigators concluded that there probably wasn't a secret deal between Reaganites and Iranian mullahs, they conceded that Casey was "fishing in troubled waters," having "conducted informal, clandestine, and potentially dangerous efforts on behalf of the Reagan campaign to gather intelligence" on Carter's hostage negotiations with Iran. The House task force, however, utterly dismissed both possibilities.

But several key findings of the House task force—dominated by Republican investigators hostile to the October Surprise charges—were either demonstrably false or inconclusive.

Casey's supposedly bulletproof alibi exonerating him from charges that he attended the Madrid meetings was actually full of holes. All agreed that Casey had been in London for several days following the date of the alleged Madrid meeting. Yet his whereabouts on the two days in question were unaccounted for, giving him ample time to have attended a covert colloquy in Madrid. But a former Reagan campaign staffer emerged to claim that Casey couldn't have been in Madrid before he jetted to London, because on those disputed dates, Casey had been his guest at the elite, male-only Bohemian Grove retreat in Northern California. Others recalled seeing Casey at the Grove, but couldn't pin down which weekend. In endorsing this alibi, the task force chose to ignore or downplay receipts, the diary entry of another Bohemian Grove camper, Casey's own desk calendar, and other solid evidence that made a more persuasive argument for Casey hunkering down at the Grove on the weekend *following* his European junket.

When Casey's family finally produced documents from the old spook's files, passports and calendar pages from the disputed dates were curiously missing and unaccounted for.

There were other flaws in the congressional probes, including the casual dismissal of sources unfairly lumped in with the likes of Brenneke and LeWinter. In addition to former President Bani-Sadr, there were two other Iranian officials who claimed to have had heard of the Republican-Iranian contacts of 1980: foreign minister Sadegh Ghotbzadeh, who told the French press in September 1980 that the Republicans were "trying to block a solution" to the hostage crisis, and former defense minister Ahmad Madani, who reported that Cyrus Hashemi had informed him in 1980 of Casey's efforts to negotiate covertly with Iran.

Perhaps the most reliable sources to surface were Claude Angeli, chief editor for *Canard Enchaine*, a French newspaper, and David Andelman, a former *New York Times* and CBS News reporter. Angeli told the task force that French intelligence officials, who refused to go on the record, claimed that their organization provided "cover" for meetings between the Reagan camp and Iranian officials on October 18 and 19, 1980. Andelman, who ghost wrote the autobiography of Alexandre de Marenches, the former head of French intelligence, testified that "de Marenches acknowledged setting up a meeting in Paris between Casey and some Iranians in late October 1980." By the time Andelman dropped his bombshell, the House task force had already interviewed de Marenches, who denied any knowledge of such meetings. Unable to reach de Marenches for further questioning after Andelman made his claim, the task force decided to take the French clandestine services veteran at his previous word.

Granted, the congressional probes did dispel a number of rumors and false leads. But they also left too many key questions dangling, like those mentioned above, for their reports to constitute the final word on the theory.

One last remark, from the inimitable figure in whose name the October Surprise deal—if it isn't a fantastic hoax—was carried out. In 1991, while playing golf with George Bush in Palm Springs, Ronald Reagan gave reporters a sound bite. In 1980, he had "tried some things the other way," that is, to *free* the hostages. What things? He refused to say, because "some of these things are still classified." Classified? How did an unelected political campaign manage to classify *anything*? Later, in a letter responding to congressional inquiries about the comment, Reagan had a *partial* memory recovery. On the golf course, he had been referring to his public support of "things" President Carter had been doing. As for what he meant by "classified" information, well, memory lane was not a through street. "I cannot recall what I may have had in mind when I made that statement."

MAJOR SOURCES

"Joint Report of the Task Force to Investigate Certain Allegations Concerning the Holding of American Hostages by Iran in 1980." Washington: U.S. House of Representatives, 3 January 1993.

"The 'October Surprise' Allegations and the Circumstances Surrounding the Release of the Hostages Held in Iran: Report of the Special Counsel." Washington: U. S. Senate, 19 November 1992.

Parry, Robert. *Trick or Treason: The October Surprise Mystery*. New York: Sheridan Square Press, 1993.

Sick, Gary. *October Surprise: America's Hostages in Iran and the Election of Ronald Reagan*. New York: Times Books, 1991.

Snepp, Frank. "October Surmise." *Village Voice*, 25 February 1992.

V

Blood 'n' Guts

23

The Royal Ripper

The definitive Jack the Ripper conspiracy theory became a major motion picture in the apocryphal Sherlock Holmes flick *Murder By Decree*, but it originated in a book called *Jack the Ripper: The Final Solution* by a British journalist, Stephen Knight, who postulated a cabal of Freemasons extending into the highest reaches of British government as the entity responsible for the Whitechapel murders. Knight harbored a particular fixation on Freemasons. He authored another, more general exposé titled *The Brotherhood* and was working on a sequel when he, abruptly, died.

Not even the monarchy came off clean in Knight's ripping yarn, which unfolded thusly:

Amidst an atmosphere of political upheaval and working-class resentment toward the aristocracy in general and the royal family in particular—with seven assassination attempts against Queen Victoria—one wayward but highly placed royal committed a slight indiscretion. He married a commoner. Secretly. And to make matters worse, he got her pregnant first. And, in the crowning gross-out to Victorian sensibilities, she was a Catholic.

177

The offender was Eddy, the sensitive and bisexual duke of Clarence, second in line to the throne. And considering that his father, the Prince of Wales, was endlessly enmeshed in scandals created by his own ribaldry, to the extent that his ascension to the throne seemed less than a sure thing, Eddy's gaffe posed a palpable threat to the monarchy itself. It was ripe for exploitation by republican rabble rousers, if ever the marriage became public knowledge.

Lord Robert Salisbury, England's prime minister and one of the country's highest-ranking Freemasons, resolved that it would not.

Salisbury acted not simply from patriotism, although he surely adored the British royal tradition, but from self-preservation. He owed his existence, or at least his importance (same thing) to Masonry. And in Britain, Masonry was inextricable from the crown, with none other than the blackguard Prince of Wales sitting as Most Worshipful Grand Master of England. Indeed, the Freemasons were the "power behind the scenes" that an earlier prime minister, Benjamin Disraeli warned about. Freemasonry and the crown could not endure without each other.

Salisbury entrusted the job to one of his dearest Masonic brethren, the royal family's physician and abortionist, Sir William Gull.

With the background set, the specifics of Knight's scenario— with the exception, as it turned out, of one important detail— germinated in a tale spun by Walter Sickert, a British impressionist painter and bohemian about town who moved with ease among East End unfortunates.

But Sickert also, according to his own account, befriended the duke of Clarence. In fact the Heir Presumptive passed as Sickert's fictional brother to facilitate frequent sojourns to the forbidden side of town where he led a parallel life.

While gallivanting in the guise of his alter ego, according to Sickert, Eddy fell in love with, sired a daughter by, and covertly wed a shop clerk named Annie Elizabeth Crook. Eddy's royal relatives would have none of it, of course. They swiftly grounded the young duke and, at the good doctor Gull's directive, shipped his unauthorized bride to an asylum. Or more likely, Knight found, to a "workhouse," i.e., something like a halfway house, but much more lax in recording the comings and goings of inmates.

There were two witnesses to the extraroyal nuptials: Sickert and a gal who worked in the same shop as Annie named Marie Kelly. Once Eddy's elders busted up the unlikely couple, Kelly fled in fear to her Irish home, where by her silence she ensured her safety.

A few years later Kelly returned to the East End, predictably down on her luck. With her only source of income concealed within her knickers, Marie found herself falling in with the wrong crowd.

In no time at all, a few of her comrades-in-harlotry to whom she had unwisely divulged her history—with visions of pound signs dancing in their not-entirely-sober heads—devised and enacted a thoroughly half-assed blackmail scheme, thus committing suicide.

After all, let's not forget the high stakes that Freemasons play for. As one excitable conspiratorialist, extrapolating from Knight's evidence, phrased it, "little did they know that their scheme was standing in the way of World Domination!!!"

Be that as it may, Salisbury certainly felt his Freemasonic job security was again in question and again he delegated authority for continuing the coverup to Gull. The physician carried out the killings in his carriage, driven by one John Netley, who had previously chauffeured Eddy to the East End during those halcyon days of pre-Ripperdom. A third accomplice, identified by Sickert as assistant police commissioner Sir Robert Anderson (another Masonic bigwig), helped lure the victims into the death buggy.

All this according to the painter Walter Sickert, whose son

Joseph relayed the knowledge to Knight. Joseph himself is progeny of the duke—his mother was Annie Crook's daughter Alice, who grew up to become the elder Sickert's paramour.

As for the finer details of the crimes and their coverup, Knight does an admirable job of tracking down and verifying, or at least corroborating, Sickert's scenario. This would mean that the Jack the Ripper murders were no more than routine government skullduggery—no different than silencing witnesses to the JFK assassination (you know, routine stuff). That is, if it were not for the elaborate Masonic symbolism and concordance with Masonic rite under which the slashings were carried out.

While peppering his explication with disclaimers to the effect that most ordinary Masons have no idea what the brethren at the pinnacle of their order are up to, Knight goes to great lengths detailing how the Masonic doctrine binding high-level initiates permits and even encourages them to perform acts of unadulterated evil. While on the one hand he indicts those Masons prone to act upon such doctrine as a "lunatic fringe," he names Gull, Anderson, and even Salisbury as adherents. Very elite lunatics.

The wall-scrawl at one crime scene blaming "Juwes" for the murders—improperly erased by police commissioner (and, of course, Freemason) Sir Charles Warren who claimed to fear an outbreak of anti-Semitic violence—referred not to Jews, Knight says, but to the three Juwes—motley hit men named Jubela, Jubelo, and Jubelum—who snuffed Solomonic architect Hiram Abiff, the prime martyr of Masonic myth. Similarly, the way the killers draped number four victim Catherine Eddowes's displaced digestive tract over her shoulder recalled Hiram's grotesque injuries. Eddowes's body was dumped in Mitre Square, which Knight calls "the most Masonic of all places in London," not least of all because the mitre and the square are basic Masonic implements. Mitre Square was, to boot, the location of several Masonic meeting halls, including Mitre Tavern where Gull's enclave sometimes gathered.

Gull for some reason mistook Eddowes for Kelly and that's why her murder bore the heaviest Masonic symbolism. It was supposed to be the capper. The one that says, "We're the Freemasons and you're not." When they realized they'd hacked up the wrong gal, the killers waited thirty-nine days—that's the Masonic "perfect" number, three times the "favorite" number thirteen, Knight points out—to do the Kelly hit.

The lavish mutilations to Kelly's person apparently conform to same arcane Masonic prescription for how to mutilate people. One supposes that the very presence of guidelines for such activity indicates something amiss in Mason-land. But most important, the murders themselves, their shock value and the panic that erupted during the ten-week reign of Jack the Ripper (be he one or three) represented a reassertion of Masonic supremacy then threatened by working-class unrest.

The principles of advanced Freemasonry, in fact, require such terrorism to counter challenges to the brotherhood's authority, Knight reports. In Sickert's story, Lord Salisbury himself, while somewhat disquieted by the murders, is "pleased" by their public display of Masonic dominance.

Perhaps questionably, Knight relies on *The Protocols of the Elders of Zion* as his source for Masonry's secret agenda, offering but a brief caveat that "the *Protocols* have been the subject of debate since they first appeared in print." He states that their use by anti-Semites twists their true significance and that "they had been in existence for a long time before they were finally published." As such, Knight asserts, "it seems inescapable that they exerted an influence." In particular, he writes, without offering any verification beyond the "it sure looks that way" mode of argument, the *Protocols* exerted an influence on the "fanatical mind" of Sir William Gull.

While Knight's research is persuasive, sometimes ground breaking, he has a tendency to rely on the "what else could it be?" substitute for actual evidence beloved of so many harder-core conspiracy theorists. His assumption that Gull put the *Protocols* into effect is one example. But granting the assumption—not a wholly implausible one—Knight is correct to point out that it doesn't matter whether the *Protocols* are authentic or not. All that's important is what Gull read them to mean.

There is one final twist to Knight's hypothesis. While Knight believes that Anderson, as a good Freemasonic fanatic, was complicitous in covering up the true, composite identity of Jack the Ripper, he finds too many inconsistencies that preclude Anderson from taking part in the killings. The "third man" could only have been, Knight concludes, Walter Sickert.

Sickert's detailed knowledge of the Ripper killings could have derived only from on-site experience. Sickert's own motive can be nothing but survival and protection of the infant who was Eddy's illegitimate offspring and would years later mother Sickert's own son. The Masons must have coerced him with threats, Knight reasons.

Other than Knight's, the favored Ripper conspiracy theory has a syphilitic Prince Eddy himself as the Ripper, his already muddled thinking further warped by disease. A version synthesizing the two hypotheses puts Sickert at the scene of the crimes, but as a babysitter for Eddy, who is under some kind of Masonic mind control. Thus Sickert's guilt is doubled: He is complicitous not only in the killings but in the degradation of his former disciple.

Sickert's aching conscience led him not only to unburden himself to his son (with Anderson in his role) but to plant clues at the crime scenes—the Juwes message among them—to implicate Freemasonry in general and Gull in particular. All of these clues were eliminated or obscured by law-enforcement Masons purporting to investigate the murders. Frustrated, Sickert went on to paint clues into a number of his later works. He often said that certain paintings were inspired by the Ripper murders, or by his old friend Marie Kelly.

"He was a strange man," says Sickert's son Joseph at the conclusion of Knight's book. "He would start weeping for no reason sometimes, terribly moved by something long ago."

MAJOR SOURCES

Knight, Stephen. *Jack the Ripper: The Final Solution.* London: Granada Publishing, 1977.
Rumbelow, Donald. *The Complete Jack the Ripper.* Boston: New York Graphic Society, 1975.

24

Death Squad From the Desert

Nowadays, after a decades-long bombardment of Bundys and Dahmers and Sons of Sam, Night Stalkers, McDonald's massacres, and headless bodies found in topless bars—a world-without-end of pointless gore rushing forth from our TV screens—the impact of Charles Manson's crimes is hard to fathom. They sound almost routine by 1990s standards: five people killed one night, two the next. Stabbed and shot. Blood-writing smeared on walls. Maybe even a little blood drinking, just for good measure. Change the channel, honey, I think the Knicks are on.

On August 9, 1969, a group of Manson's cult followers crept into a house at 10050 Cielo Drive in the Benedict Canyon section of Beverly Hills. The home was rented by film director Roman Polanski and his gorgeous, pregnant bride, actress Sharon Tate. The intruders didn't leave until they'd slaughtered all five humans present (Polanski was out of the country at the time).

America wasn't ready for it. The Manson gang hacked up

supermarket magnate Leno LaBianca and his wife the next eve in similar fashion and from then on there has always been a touch of fear on the land. Even on the coziest, calmest American summer nights, there is indeed something very evil out there. And maybe, just maybe, it is coming for you.

Why did this happen?

Vincent Bugliosi, the prosecutor who put Manson and his (mostly female) killers away for life established a motive and wrote a book about it: *Helter Skelter*. This phrase, scrawled in victims' hemoglobin at the carnage scenes, was, in addition to being the title of a Beatles' song, Manson's term for race war. He hoped the murders would be blamed on black militants, thus sparking an apocalyptic conflict.

In Charlie's ultraracist view the physically superior but mentally inferior blacks would win the war, but then find themselves incapable of governing the wasteland. Thus Charlie and his "Family" cult would emerge from their desert hiding cave and assume control.

Charlie bought this cartoony-bigoted scenario, no doubt. But even the Wizard (as one-time Manson patron Dennis Wilson of the Beach Boys called Manson) acknowledged that "Helter Skelter" was not the true motive for the massacres. Bugliosi said he relied on Helter Skelter because the L.A. police failed to turn up anything else. It never made much sense anyway. If Manson wanted to start a race war, why give up after two nights of bloodshed?

As one female disciple noted, Manson had a selfish motive for everything. Indeed, the other murders he is known to have committed or ordered each had tangible motives involving either drug deals or silencing potential snitches.

Bugliosi sent Manson et al. to the slams with the Helter Skelter case, but he suspected there was more to the story. In the epilogue to his bestseller he notes that Manson appeared to have had some connection to the Process Church of the Final Judgment, the satanic cult whose leader, Robert Moore (aka DeGrimston) spouted rhetoric all-too-Mansonesque.

When Bugliosi asked Manson if he'd ever heard of Moore, Manson snapped. "You're looking at him. Moore and I are one and the same."

Perhaps concerned about its image, the Process Church dispatched two representatives from its Cambridge, Massachusetts, outpost to Bugliosi's office in Los Angeles. They had a nice, civil chat with the young prosecutor, but Bugliosi later found their names registered on the list of Manson's jailhouse visitors for that same day. Bugliosi never found out what kind of a chat they had with Manson, but whenever he tried to probe about the Process Church thereafter, Manson clammed up.

Bugliosi's inquiries were confined by the constrictions of a prosecutorial case, but underground journalist Ed Sanders and investigative reporter Maury Terry traced the "Family" tree with wider-ranging investigations. Sanders authored *The Family*, the most comprehensive treatise on Manson. Terry—a decade or so later—came out with *The Ultimate Evil*, in which he connected Manson (albeit tangentially) to the Son of Sam murders in New York.

Both reporters believe that a soured drug deal was the real motive for the Tate murders. Possibly the LaBianca killings as well. They agree that Manson was subcontracting his homicidal cult to some higher authority. The true target of the Tate murders was probably Vojtek Frykowski, a playboy and LSD dealer who had gotten in over his head. Frykowski, along with his girlfriend Abigail Folger (of the Folger coffee empire), and Hollywood hairstylist-to-the-stars Jay Sebring, were murdered along with Tate.

There are some indications that Rosemary LaBianca was involved in the LSD market too. Her husband, the supermarket mogul, also owed substantial gambling debts.

"Don't you think those people deserved to die?" Manson blurted to an interviewer who caught up with him years after the fact, as he mellowed into middle age. "They were involved in kiddie porn."

Outré porn reels are a potentially lucrative operation, and

kiddie or not, the Tate crowd could very likely have been up to something cinematic. The problem is, no such films have ever turned up.

Some sources in a position to know have gone on record stating that the house at 10050 Cielo Drive was something of a porno soundstage. Terry Melcher, who used to live in the house, was aspiring folkie Manson's major music biz contact. He was also the son of Doris Day, and he said in his mom's autobiography that he knew of at least one "orgy" that was filmed in his old haunt. Sharon Tate was among the ensemble cast. Reportedly other very recognizable Hollywood faces appeared in Cielo Drive epics, many of which had a bondage and pain theme.

Films of nonsimulated raunch and gore seem a popular entertainment (and revenue source, perhaps) for certain types of offbeat groups. One of Sanders's informants claims to have viewed a loop of some Family members dancing on a beach around a beheaded corpse. Films of scantily clad Manson girls ingesting blood and sacrificing animals have also been rumored.

Maury Terry believes that one of the Son of Sam murders was videotaped and that a cameraman was snuffed when the Sam cult came to recover the reel. Terry believes that another cinephile for that shooting of a shooting was the occult hit man dubbed Manson II, later identified as convicted murderer William Mentzer, who moved through the same late-sixties L.A. sex-drugs-porno scene as Manson and knew Abigail Folger.

Terry offers a secondhand quote from "someone in the intelligence community" who says of Mentzer, "We have it that he did a hit in Son of Sam."

The intelligence community?

But it seems the intelligence community may have taken an interest in Manson, as well as in Manson II. Two days after the Tate murders Charlie Manson was spotted driving a spiffy black Mercedes belonging to a big-shot LSD dealer whose boss—the LSD industry's Mr. Big—was, in Terry's description, "said to have been a former Israeli who had strong links to the intelligence community."

If one is truly conspiracy-minded, the name Ronald Stark comes to mind—the international LSD entrepreneur of the late 1960s. While not quite "a former Israeli," Stark was multi-lingually fluent and often passed for nationalities other than American. His ties to the CIA were apparently so evident that an Italian judge once dismissed a major case against him on grounds that Stark appeared to be working for that U.S. spook hive. And around the time Manson was prowling the West Coast, Stark was preeminent in the acid trade there.

The Los Angeles Police Department was far from the only agency investigating the Tate murders. Seems every law enforcement arm from the FBI on down took an interest. Israeli intelligence also, according to Terry.

Dazzled by the official interest, Sanders once wondered "if the Process was a front for some intelligence operation."

Such musings are, of course, pure speculation, and in the absence of definitive investigations, other intriguing speculations have also been offered regarding the Manson case. The former D.A. of California's Inyo County, Frank Fowles, not only probed Manson's links to the Process—Manson probably intersected with the cult in San Francisco, and according to some accounts, he did join—but also to the Bay Area's Zodiac killer. With an indeterminate number of victims, the Zodiac was never apprehended. He, or they, sent a number of taunting letters to the police chock full of occult cryptography and rambling. A few years later, Son of Sam would exhibit some of the same behavior.

Whoever ultimately ordered the Manson murders can take credit for one sorry accomplishment.

"Manson's Family seemed to wound the best qualities of a generation," wrote Ed Sanders. "Its sharing and self-reliance, its music and wild colors, its love of the outdoors and the natural beauty of America, its search for higher standards, its early sense of the need to protect the environment. Could it be that this one group would put a grotesque and hideous capstone upon a decade that had such a powerful and beautiful promise?"

Richard Nixon and J. Edgar Hoover in cahoots with the CIA could not have done a better job of that.

MAJOR SOURCES

Bugliosi, Vincent. *Helter Skelter*. New York: Bantam Books, 1973.
Newton, Michael. *Raising Hell: An Encyclopedia of Devil Worship and Satanic Crime*. New York: Avon Books, 1993.
Sanders, Ed. *The Family*. New York: Signet Books, 1989.
Schreck, Nicholas, ed. *The Manson File*. New York: Amok Press, 1987.
Terry, Maury. *The Ultimate Evil*. Garden City, NY: Dolphin Books, 1987.

25

"Hello From the Gutters"

T he string of .44 caliber shootings that panicked the Big Apple in 1976 and 1977 were plenty horrifying. But if the murders were not the work of a single, deranged gunman now idling in prison, if they were instead rituals of a nationwide drugs-and-death cult—that's scarier still. Turns out, reports journalist Maury Terry, that the Son of Sam killing spree marks the concentric point in a sphere of unsettling satanic conspiracies.

Because, of course, all serial killers without exception are either paranoid schizophrenics or sexually frustrated misfits incapable of involvement in any form of organized conspiracy whatsoever, when police zeroed in on a security guard and former serviceman named David Berkowitz (who had dutifully paid a ticket he'd been issued for illegally parking his car near one of the murder sites) the Son of Sam case was quite comfortably solved.

The alleged lone gunman claimed that he received orders to kill from a neighbor's dog, thus satisfying the "by gosh, there's just no explainin' it" prerequisite. As if it wasn't enough to be just plain bonkers, the overweight, baby-faced Berkowitz matched the other pop-prototype of a mass killer: loner, nerd, a bust with the babes (he was said to be a virgin). Supposedly he had botched two knife attacks on women the previous year. As so often happens, the official explanation proved inadequate when confronted by actual evidence.

Terry broke the conspiracy story in a 1981 article that ran in the Gannett newspaper *Today*. Berkowitz, the story said, may have participated in just two of the seven attacks. The remainder were planned and executed by other members of the cult. Terry fleshed out the theme in his 1987 tome, *The Ultimate Evil*.

The composite culprit, according to Terry (who's now built a career on his Samophilia), was a satanic cult called The Children that held campy if gruesome rituals (lots of drugs and dog-killings) in Yonkers' Untermeyer Park.

Berkowitz himself first revealed the cult connections in correspondence from prison and chats with cellmates. His reluctance to go into more than sketchy detail and refusal to use the cult angle as a defense argues against the possibility that Berkowitz concocted the tale self-servingly. He appeared comfortable enough to be characterized as a "homicidal exhbitionist" and cooperated on a book with the psychiatrist who diagnosed him as such.

But in late October 1978, David Berkowitz revealed knowledge about a murder that had happened three years before the Son of Sam spree and three thousand miles away.

North Dakota police received an anonymous package containing a book on witchcraft with the words "Arliss Perry, Hunted Stalked and Slain. Followed to Calif. Stanford University" in Berkowitz's handwriting. The book also contained references to the Process Church of the Final Judgment, one of those countercultural mutations that slithered from the dour side of sixties San Francisco. The Process Church's leader, ex-Scientologist Robert DeGrimston (né Moore) was an acknowledged influence on Charles Manson.

Around the same time, the convicted Son of Sam penned a couple of letters from prison going into greater detail about the 1974 murder of Perry, a newlywed devout Christian from North Dakota, whose body was found systematically and symbolically mutilated in a Stanford University campus chapel on October 12, 1974. That date, perhaps coincidentally, was the birthday of occult legend Aleister Crowley—*and* of John Carr, Berkowitz's buddy and a known satanist, who died in 1979 of a shotgun blast to the head on an air force base in North Dakota.

Carr's death was ruled a suicide, though someone had scratched the numbers 666 into the dried blood on his hand and smeared NY SS in his blood on the wall near where the body was discovered. NY SS appears an obvious reference to the Son of Sam slayings in New York and Carr was indeed a real son of Sam. His father was Sam Carr, owner of the dog from which Berkowitz claimed to have received his kill-commands.

Carr also matched eyewitness descriptions of the gunman in one of the Sam slayings, and in one of the Son of Sam letters, Berkowitz (or whoever wrote it) included a reference to "John Wheaties, rapist and suffocator of young girls." Carr had a sister named Wheat and for some reason, John Carr himself went by the nickname Wheaties.

With clues like that it's amazing that police ever had a suspect other than Carr.

There were other should-be suspects. Witnesses at the scene of the Perry murder described a sandy-haired young man skulking around the Stanford chapel shortly after Perry was seen entering it the night of her death. Their descriptions were close to those of the shooter in the second Sam slaying. Berkowitz confirmed that the two descriptions were indeed of the same individual, whom he identified only as Manson II.

According to Berkowitz's intimations, this dangerous fellow was an "occult superstar," an associate of the original Manson who now belonged to a team of satanic contract killers that carried out ritual murders coast to coast—knocking off renegade cultists, potential witnesses, outside meddlers, or just about anyone the cultists deemed worthy of execution. Perry's killing, under this hypothesis, stemmed from her missionary-like attempts to convert a coven of devil worshippers in her native North Dakota.

In 1988 Los Angeles police arrested William Mentzer, a cultist, drug dealer, and one-time bodyguard for paralyzed pornographer Larry Flint. Mentzer was charged with murdering Long Island sleaze impresario Roy Radin who, when he was killed in 1983, was engaged in trying to raise financing for the movie *The Cotton Club*. Radin was also tied up in various cocaine deals with a Miami drug runner named Karen Greenberger who also did business with Mentzer. Terry had long suspected that Radin—whose orgies at his Long Island mansion were known to include videotaped gang rapes, including one starring actress Melanie Hallor from the sitcom *Welcome Back, Kotter*—was the Mr. Big referred to by Berkowitz as the godfather of the Son of Sam cult. This Mr. Big, according to Terry's sources, commissioned the videotaping of one of the Sam murders for his collection of snuff flicks, and even more significantly, for sale throughout a national network of financially well-endowed weirdos and creeps.

In other words, Son of Sam was big business.

Tipped off that some sort of occult clue would be found near the scene of Radin's murder, Terry journeyed to California and examined the site. He discovered a Bible opened to a passage reading "Let us eat and drink, for tomorrow we shall die."

Mentzer, Radin's killer, turned out to be an associate of Charles Manson (in Manson's L.A. social scene; he was not part of the Family) and of Abigail Folger, the coffee heiress killed by Manson's followers at the Sharon Tate house. He was also reportedly in the Bay Area at the time of the Arlis Perry killing.

Berkowitz's inside knowledge of the Perry job came from Manson II himself, who regaled the Yonkers cultists with details of his grisly handiwork when he visited them in New York. The Los Angeles cops openly acknowledged Mentzer's membership in "some kind of hit squad."

Terry's prison source also said that Berkowitz conveyed
information that Manson himself was acting on orders when he
commanded his Family to slaughter the Tate party and the
LaBianca couple. Cultists make spiffy assassins.

If Mentzer is indeed Manson II, and Berkowitz wasn't
making the whole thing up, then his very existence links the Son
of Sam murders to the Manson massacres eight years earlier—
an occult conspiracy cutting through space and time. But how
far back?

The Son of Sam correspondence was inscribed with an occult
symbol drawn up by nineteenth-century black magic practi-
tioner Eliphas Levi. "I believe somebody put it in my mind to
write that," Berkowitz later explained. One of the shootings
happened outside a disco called Elephas. And in one of the Sam
letters the writer referred to himself as "the chubby behemoth."
An elephant?

"Could the Black Magic adept Eliphas Levi have programmed or shaped the Son of Sam happenings from the
nineteenth century," wonders hyper-imaginative conspirophile
Michael Hoffman II in a 1984 *Conspiracy Tracker* article.

Hoffman connects Son of Sam not only to Manson but,
straining credulity rather a bit, to the 1921 rape-slaying of
Virginia Rappe by "chubby behemoth" silent movie comic
Roscoe "Fatty" Arbuckle. Hoffman pegs that definitive Hollywood Babylon-ish incident as a black magic rite invoking the
"elephant force." Arbuckle (who was acquitted of the crime) is
said to have violated the unfortunately named Miss Rappe
(Virginia Rappe = Virgin Rape) with a wine bottle, a procedure
that, according to Hoffman, is a traditional magickal method
of simulating the "must" of the elephant, whatever that means.

In any event, the Arbuckle elephantine "ritual" took place at
the St. Francis Hotel in "California's mystical city named after
St. Francis." (Um, that would be San Francisco?) St. Francis has

special significance to occultists, particularly Mason, Hoffman reports.

About forty years later, San Francisco became home to the Process Church.

Hoffman's analysis deserves some sort of praise for its, shall we say, inventiveness. But his comment about the "programmed" Son of Sam may be worth a second glance. Bearing in mind Berkowitz's own comment that "someone put it in my mind" to scribble Eliphas Levi's symbol on his letters (and for that matter, his cover story about receiving orders to kill by remote control—albeit from a dog), Son of Sam may fall into the category of Manchurian Candidate assassins.

California conspiracy-radio-host Dave Emory in a multipart "documentary" copping the title *The Ultimate Evil*, embellished Terry's thesis to bring the "national security establishment" in on the plot.

Berkowitz experimented with LSD while stationed with the military in Korea. To suppose that he took part—wittingly or not—in an MK-ULTRA-style mind-control project is not terribly far-fetched. Nor does it transcend plausibility to postulate that satanic cults provide a perfect vector for nefarious national security types to breed their automaton assassins.

Does *everything* connect through the Son of Sam interface? Recall that in 1974 one of Manson's least repentant disciples, Lynette "Squeaky" Fromme tried to do away with President Gerald Ford. If she'd pulled it off, the presidency would have fallen to none other than Nelson Rockefeller, *appointed* vice-president by Ford—and whose name is synonymous with the Insider multinational corporate capitalist communist Illuminati occult conspiracy. And Ford himself is a Freemason who sat on the Warren Commission, which covered up the death of one president. Had Ford received his possibly poetic justice, Rockefeller would have ascended to ultimate power thanks to a member of the occultist Nazi-satan-worshipping Manson Fam-

ily, which sprung from the same Process Church that produced
the Son of Sam cult and whose offshoots act as killers-for-hire.

MAJOR SOURCES

Newton, Michael. *Raising Hell: An Encyclopedia of Devil Worship
   and Satanic Crime.* New York: Avon Books, 1993.
Terry, Maury. *The Ultimate Evil.* Garden City, NY: Dolphin Books,
   1987.

VI

Unified Field
Theories

26

The Enlightened Ones

When it comes to the Illuminati, the line between history and hysteria gets fuzzy.

To place them in their context employing some semblance of rationality, the Bavarian Illuminati, the most renowned of all groups to adopt that appellation, were one of many manifestations of the enlightened (illuminated?) spirit sweeping Europe in the eighteenth century, which saw no higher purpose than to eradicate the centuries-old monarchical/feudal domination that had trapped mankind in the dark ages. The Illuminati were as much products of their age as shapers of it.

On the other hand...

The society's founder, Adam Weishaupt, was a hotheaded, prodigious Ingolstadt University law professor—barely postadolescent at twenty-six—when he joined the Freemasons in 1774 and shortly set to work blueprinting a utopian schemata to move human civilization into a universal state of nature unshackled by authoritarian strictures. While not lacking in ambition, Weishaupt also possessed enough realism to understand that he required a dedicated bevy of accomplices to pull off this caper.

With a restless mind that rejected all normative systems of belief, young Adam grew into an occultist of sorts, with an enthusiasm for Greek mystery religions. While no one's 100 percent sure what went on inside these cults—they were, after all, mysterious—Weishaupt sussed out enough to pattern his own secret society on their structure. Recruiting five members from a prestigious Masonic lodge over which he'd gained a measure of control, on May 1, 1776 (a retroactively suspicious date, if ever there was one), Weishaupt inaugurated the Order of Perfectibilists, better known as the Bavarian Illuminati.

While Weishaupt himself may have talked a good game, he wasn't much of a "player" in the Masonic politico scene. Again, he shrewdly compensated for his own shortcomings. He executed a recruiting coup, signing up one Adolf Francis, known as Baron Knigge, who by 1780 was already one of the Continent's leading Masons. The baron had attempted for years to unite all the European lodges into one giant, spidery entity of subterfuge. With Knigge's talent for organization, Illuminati rolls quickly swelled to over three thousand—each name plucked from the cream of the Masonic crop—in what amounted to a bloodless coup of the European Freemasonic upper echelon.

On the Continent, Freemasonry was traditionally a refuge for radical intellectuals, politicians, and those who wanted to rub shoulders with them. The Illuminati selected the most dedicated and powerful of these and filtered them through initiation rites more grueling and esoteric than Freemasonry's own. The practice was designed largely to ensure allegiance to Weishaupt and the other chief executives of the order. The Illuminati, thusly, became a secret revolutionary cell whose influence far outstripped its numbers.

Alas, like so many secret organizations, it had a hard time keeping itself secret. After a few defectors spilled some of Weishaupt's classified info in the early to mid-1780s, the Illuminati was specifically decreed to be an outlaw organization and the Bavarian heat came down hard. Weishaupt and a few other leaders fled to neighboring provinces. Or somewhere.

Adam Weishaupt's trail appears to peter out at this point. New Age literary prankster-laureate Robert Anton Wilson has (spuriously) suggested that he escaped to America and knocked off and then impersonated our hemp-smokin', avidly Masonic founding president. Maybe Washington's idiosyncrasies were really Weishaupt's. That speculation is as good as any, because stories about the Illuminati refuse to go away. Almost instantly upon their forced dissolution, rumors began making the rounds that Weishaupt's subversive elitists were still up to their devious schemes. According to the classic exposé *Proofs of a Conspiracy*, published fourteen years after the Illuminati breathed their apparent last, the Illuminati metamorphosed into the German Union and had played a role in—if not caused—the French Revolution, an uprising whose motto, "Liberty, Equality, Fraternity" was explicitly Masonic.

In his wonderful, divagating history of the topic, *The Illuminoids*, Neil Wilgus reports that George Washington, whoever he was, read *Proofs* and felt that its charges deserved wider play. Though, of course, he added, American Masonic lodges engaged in none of the chicanery of their European counterparts. Thomas Jefferson, another Mason (as were most of the founding fathers) had a passing familiarity with Weishaupt's writings. He admired them, saying that he could understand the German radical's penchant for secrecy given the despotism that held dominion over Europe. But if Weishaupt had been in America, said the author of the Declaration of Independence, he "would not have thought of any secret machinery" to propagate his freethinking ideology.

Weishaupt's Illuminati have become the all-purpose conspiracy; the theory that explains everything and always applies. Various versions of the tale list Franklin Delano Roosevelt as an initiated Illuminatus. After all, it was under Roosevelt that the Masonic eye in the pyramid first appeared on U.S. currency.

One anecdote, which likely falls into the category of "urban legend," tells how Charles Manson was identified as a card-carrying member of the Illuminati—on the Oprah Winfrey Show.

One can't help but wonder, however, whether the entire Illuminati story is fabricated. Is it possible that an "Adam Weishaupt" ever existed? His very name smacks of hoaxery— Adam, the first man; Weishaupt, which translates "wise head." Nice moniker for the purported instigator of a world revolution.

While general consensus does seem to hold that such an individual did, at one point, stalk the Earth (though living perhaps not quite as spectacular a life as is often described), Weishaupt is a mythic character like any historical figure: JFK, John Dillinger, Hitler, Casanova, Babe Ruth. A living metaphor. For...what?

Wilgus took the most accurate approach, chronicling not the history of Illuminati but "illuminoids," a neologism defined as "like the Illuminati." Throughout history "enlightenment" or "illumination" has been one of humanity's greatest obsessions. Weishaupt's Bavarian Illuminati, though they receive the widest publicity, were a rather minor exponent of a tradition that probably dates back to the days of prehistory, when some cave shaman first freaked out his flock by sparking fire with flint and sticks. He or she quite literally saw the light. The quest for illumination can be simultaneously baleful and benign. The Force always has its Dark Side. To hear the right-wingers tell it, history has played host to a veritable army of Darth Vaders. Peering through the prism from a different angle, we can see the illuminoids as segments of humanity dissatisfied with our everyday lot on this mudball, reaching above, within, and elsewhere for a better way.

Early mystery sects of the type that inspired Weishaupt may have been among the first manifestations of organized illumination. Jewish cabalism, Christian gnosticism, and Islamic sufism followed, as did a liberal peppering of cults and secret societies from the fearsome Hashishim (assassins) and the ill-fated Knights Templar to smaller occult groups, some (as in Spain and France) actually calling themselves "Illuminati." Weishaupt's organization fits snugly onto this continuum. Since the Bavarian Illuminati's ostensible demise, the flame has burned brilliantly. Occult groups from Aleister Crowley's Ordo Templis Orientis to Anton LaVey's Church of Satan occupy one end of the spectrum, feeding the paranoia of that particular strain of Christian who exhausts a reservoir's worth of energy fretting about "satanism." Then who's to say they're so crazy? Who is satan but Lucifer, the fallen "Angel of Light"? The first Illuminatus.

On the more respectable side of things, we spot traces of Illumination in, first of all, the very existence of an "establishment," a ruling class that considers itself possessed of some special knowledge needed to lead, and even more so in establishment institutions: the Council on Foreign Relations, the Trilateral Commission (with its ominous triangular logo), the Bilderberg Group. All are private bodies composed of business, political, and academic "leading lights," so to speak, which, despite the contrary protestations of their members, do in fact wield considerable influence over how geopolitics shape up. The Council on Foreign Relations (CFR) was born as an American offshoot of Cecil Rhodes's British Round Table. Its roster has included most of the presidents and secretaries of state for the last six decades. Henry Kissinger was inducted as a young academic and the CFR published his breakthrough book, *Nuclear Weapons and Foreign Policy,* in which Kissinger originated the idea of "winnable" nuclear war.

When the CIA was founded in 1947, its "old boy network" also connected to the CFR. CIA officials still deliver off-the-record briefings to CFR meetings. The Trilateral Commission, founded by multinational banking demigod David Rockefeller, is an offshoot of the CFR, but with Japan included. Membership in the two groups overlaps considerably. Jimmy Carter was a Trilateral "commissioner," and when he became president, conspiracy theorists were greatly alarmed.

The Netherlands-based Bilderberg Group is more shadowy, but it's the same idea with many of the same members—only with a European accent.

The aim of these elite groups, according to anti-Illuminist lore, is to consolidate control through some form of "one-world government." That is, to set up a "new world order." Oddly, the "meditation room" in the United Nations building is decked out in eye-in-the-pyramid decor. A clue dropped to taunt those of us still in the dark? Not unlike George Bush's repeated public expressions of enthusiasm for creating a new world order. A photograph of Bush in his hospital bed, surrounded by little kids with a pyramid in his lap (can anyone say "fertility rite"?), is said to be the Skull and Bones president's favorite. If that's just a legend, the snapshot is certainly the conspiracy theorists' favorite. This is the same president whose initiation into his alma mater's premier secret society required that he lie naked in a coffin—masturbating.

The Illuminati are everywhere, in one guise or another. All it takes is the will to recognize them. In their Masonic persona, mad genius conspiracy researcher James Shelby Downard has identified their handiwork in the Kennedy assassination.

A writer named Jay Katz (né Jim Keith) in an intriguing monograph titled *Saucers of the Illuminati*, posits the enlightened ones as the all-too-human force behind the UFO phenomenon, while William Bramley in his book *Gods of Eden* makes an unsettlingly cogent case that the Illuminati overlords are in fact aliens—an argument put forth far more loosely by a wide variety of true believers from ultraconspiratorialist Bill Cooper to heavily armed cult priestess Elizabeth Clare Prophet, the millennialist leader of the Church Universal and Triumphant in Montana.

Adam Weishaupt and his cadre of bookworm revolutionaries come off as nickel-and-dimers compared to that lot.

MAJOR SOURCES

Robison, John. *Proofs of a Conspiracy.* Boston: Western Islands Press, 1967.
Wilgus, Neil. *The Illuminoids: Secret Societies and Political Paranoia.* Santa Fe, NM: Sun Books, 1978.

27

The Sorcerers

Some conspiracy theorists question not "the facts" so much as reason itself. James Shelby Downard is one of those mad geniuses with a talent for making the most improbable, impossible, ludicrous, and laughable speculations appear almost plausible. A self-described student of the "science of symbolism," Downard peels away the rational veneer of history and exposes an abyss of logic-defying synchronicities.

Downard dwells upon a confluence of the familiar and the esoteric that, to him, forms a portrait of political conspiracy the purpose of which is not power or money, but alchemy—the mystical science of transformation. By breaking apart and rejoining elements, it was long ago supposed, alchemy could effect most any miracle (for example, changing base metal into gold).

From ancient times through the Enlightenment, science and magic were one and the same. As far as Downard's concerned, the era when science was indistinguishable from sorcery never ended. The Age of Reason and its industrial, postmodern antecedents are facades obscuring the dream world of primeval urges that surfaces only in sleep.

Per Downard, the plotters are Freemasonic alchemists scheming for sovereignty over the realm of uncontrollable impulse. The relatively tame domains of politics, economics, and ideology are mere means to that end.

"Do not be lulled into believing," warns Downard, "that just because the deadening American city of dreadful night is so utterly devoid of mystery, so thoroughly flat-footed, sterile, and infantile, so burdened with the illusory gloss of baseball-hot dogs-apple-pie-and-Chevrolet, that it exists outside the psychosexual domain. The eternal pagan psychodrama is escalated under these modern conditions precisely because sorcery is not what 'twentieth-century man' can accept as real."

Drawing up a brief primer of Downardism seems an impossible task, though not quite as daunting as reading Downard's own essays, which have been set forth for public consumption largely through the good offices of publisher Adam Parfrey, whose small, outré firm, Feral House, has anthologized Downard's essays in a few collections of conspiratorial material. We can do no more than scratch the surface in this forum.

"The United States, which has long been called a melting pot, should more descriptively be called a witches' cauldron wherein the 'Hierarchy of the Grand Architect of the Universe' arranges for ritualistic crimes and psychopolitical psychodramas to be performed in accordance with a Master plan," Downard explains.

That Master plan necessitates execution of three alchemical rites: the creation and destruction of primordial matter; the killing of the king; and the "making manifest of all that is hidden."

Shakespeare's MacBeth is a "killing of the king" drama. MacBeth, who killed his king in accordance with a witches' (alchemists') plot and was himself later killed, is part of the same schemata.

The latter-day reenactment of the MacBeth ritual, says

Downard, was the assassination of JFK in Dealey Plaza, site of the first Masonic temple in Dallas and a spot loaded with "trinity" symbolism. *Three* is, for those not versed in such matters, the most magic of all magic numbers. Downard's observations include:

- Dallas is located just south of the 33 degree of latitude. The 33rd degree is Freemasonry's highest rank.

- Kennedy's motorcade was rolling toward the "Triple Underpass" when he was slain by, according to some analysts, three gunmen. Three tramps were arrested right after the murder. Hiram Abiff, architect of Solomon's Temple and mythic progenitor of Freemasonry was murdered according to Masonic legend by three "unworthy craftsmen."

- The MacBeth clan of Scotland had many variations of the family name. One was MacBaine, or Baines. Kennedy's successor was Lyndon Baines Johnson, a Freemason.

- *Dea* in Latin means goddess. *Ley* in Spanish can refer to law or rule. Dealey Plaza was "goddess-rule" plaza.

- Blamed for the assassination was a man named Oz, (Oswald) explained by Downard as "a Hebrew term denoting strength." Divine strength is integral to the king-killing rite.

- Oz was killed by Ruby, just as the ruby slippers freed Dorothy from the land of Oz in *The Wizard of Oz*, which writes Downard, "one may deride as a fairy tale but which nevertheless symbolizes the immense power of 'ruby light,' otherwise known as the laser."

- Dealey Plaza is near the Trinity River, which, before the introduction of flood control measures, submerged the place regularly. Dealey Plaza therefore symbolizes both the trident and its bearer, the water-god Neptune.

- "To this trident-Neptune site," writes Downard, "came the 'Queen of Love and Beauty' and her spouse, the scapegoat, in the Killing of the King rite, the 'Ceannaideach' (Gaelic word for Ugly Head or Wounded Head). In Scotland, the Kennedy coat of arms and iconography is full of folklore. Their plant badge is an oak and their crest has a dolphin on it. Now what could be more coincidental than for JFK to get shot in the head near the oak tree at Dealey Plaza. Do you call that a coincidence?" (For those in our audience still too puzzled by the whole *Wizard of Oz* thing to get that last bit: the "Queen" is Jackie and "Ceannaideach" is the Gaelic form of Kennedy.)

• An earlier "trinity site," in New Mexico, was the location of the first atomic bomb explosion. Chaos and synergy—breaking apart and joining together—are the first principles of alchemy. The atomic bomb broke apart the positive and negative (male and female) elements that compose primordial matter. Physicists refer to this fiendish trickery as "nuclear fission."

• The New Mexico "Trinity" sits on the 33rd degree latitude line.

• The Kennedy assassination's true significance was concealed by the Warren Commission headed by Freemason Earl Warren with Freemason Gerald Ford as its public spokesman. The commission drew its information from the FBI, headed by Freemason J. Edgar Hoover, and the CIA, which transmitted information through its former director, Freemason Allen Dulles, who sat on the commission.

• A decade later, Ford, when president himself, was the target of an attempted assassination in front of the St. Francis Hotel, located opposite Mason Street in the City of St. Francis, San Francisco. Members of the Freemasonic "Hell Fire Club," eighteenth-century London site of many a sex orgy involving such luminaries as Freemason Benjamin Franklin, called themselves "Friars of St. Francis."

• The St. Francis Hotel was also the site of sex orgies. On its premises occurred the rape-murder of Virginia Rappe by silent film comic Roscoe "Fatty" Arbuckle. Virginia Rappe's name is a variation on "virgin rape." The rape of a virgin is an important alchemical sex-magic rite.

• The serpent is a Masonic symbol of king-killing. The Symbionese Liberation Army, which kidnapped San Fran-

cisco newspaper heiress Patricia Hearst, pictured a serpent
on its emblem.
- The name Symbionese means "joined together."
- Patricia Hearst's grandfather, newspaper magnate William
  Randolph Hearst, built a vast estate called San Simeon (St.
  Simon) on La Cuest Encandata, The Enchanted Hill. On the
  estate is a "pool of Neptune" with a statue of Venus, the
  "queen of love and beauty." The Hearst family joined
  together the *San Francisco Chronicle* and *Examiner*.

As mentioned previously, we are able only to touch the most
superficial aspects of the alchemical conspiracy made manifest
in the message of James Shelby Downard. We have ignored his
hint that Marilyn Monroe's death was Freemasonically inspired, in part because "when she was mortal she was subjected
to sexual debauchery, as the innocent are in sorcery rites."

Nor have we covered Downard's argument that the advertis-
ing war "between Avis and Hertz car rental corporations
involves fertility symbolism."

Avis and Hertz? For God's sake, let us hope he's misguided.

MAJOR SOURCES

Downard, James Shelby. "The Call to Chaos." In *Apocalypse Culture*,
    expanded and revised, edited by Adam Parfrey. Los Angeles: Feral
    House, 1990.
————. "King Kill 33 degrees." In *Apocalypse Culture*, edited by
    Adam Parfrey. New York: Amok Press, 1987.
————. "Sorcery, Sex, Assassination." In *Secret and Suppressed*,
    edited by Jim Keith. Portland, OR: Feral House, 1993.
————. "Witches' Plot," photocopied manuscript in authors'
    possession.

28

Anglophobia

These days they seem a benign and rather comical lot, those British royals. Face it—when a guy is caught confiding to his mistress his fond wish to take the place of her tampon, as Prince Charles did to Camilla Parker-Bowles, it's hard to take him seriously as the next chief executive of a vast and malignant global conspiracy. But that is just the position to which Prince Charles ascends when he assumes the throne, according to the strain of conspiratorial theorizing that places "the British" at the center of its Copernican universe.

Lyndon LaRouche ranks as the most illustrious of this school of thinkers, such as they are. LaRouche has endured considerable, and perhaps not entirely unjustified, derision for his allegation, "The Queen of England pushes drugs."

But LaRouche is only the most seasoned self-publicizer among British conspiracy theorists. The crowd includes, for example, Lloyd Miller, the entrepreneur behind A-Albionic Research, which fashions itself as a news service à la the Kiplinger *Washington Letter*—only instead of recording the relatively quotidian gossip of Capitol Hill, Miller tracks the battle for world domination between the British Royal Family and the Vatican.

At least Miller places another party in the picture. For LaRouche, the Brits are all. In the definitive statement of LaRouchism, *Dope Inc.: Britain's Opium War Against the U.S.* (credited to "a U.S. Labor Party Investigating Team"), the LaRouche approach to the book's topic, and by extension to world history, is spelled out in bold type: "the entire world's drug traffic has been run by a single family since its inception."

And which family might that be?

But the LaRouchies in their somewhat overstated fashion have a point. Remember that we are dealing with a country that until relatively recently was the greatest colonizer of other countries the world had ever seen, with no particular reservations about taking over the world by any means necessary, covert or overt, forcing their cricket, crumpets, and marmalade down the throats of any sub-Saharan tribesman too slow to dodge a musket ball.

Indeed, state the *Dope Inc.* authors, "To call this a 'conspiracy' would be to abuse the meaning of the term...the British oligarchy is so much a part of the bedrock of events that it does not need to act in conspiratorial fashion: by its own description it merely is and always has been."

Their conspiratorial teleology, according to LaRouche and those like-minded, is a "New Dark Ages," (NDA for short) with a world population cropped to its bare minimum by AIDS, famine, and the occasional nuclear holocaust—until there is just enough soylent green remaining to feed the profligate indulgences of those ravenous, sex-crazed, slurping, sucking, yet fiendishly intelligent oligarchs.

But even the British aristocracy can't go it alone. They've formed a whole universe of secret societies, private policy groups, and connected intelligence agencies—involving not only Brits but Anglophiles from the United States and Europe—to implement the NDA agenda. These include not only the usual suspects—Bilderbergers, the Trilateral Commission, and the Royal Institute for International Affairs—but also some lesser-known entities. Chief among the latter is the Club of Rome (CoR) a Bilderbergerish body comprised of the political, financial, and intellectual aristocracy. The innocuously christened Club has spewed forth a generation of think-tanks, corporations, and other respectable entities working tirelessly to soften up the mass mind with their New Age claptrap, rock music, sex, and dope, at least according to the Anglophobic weltanschauung.

LaRouche, for example, pegs the Grateful Dead as a "British intelligence operation," spawned from the CIA's LSD trials at Stanford University and similar far-out Bay Area institutions of higher education. "That was an Allen Dulles-period operation which was run together with the Occult Bureau types in British intelligence, such as Aldous Huxley," LaRouche states dryly.

"This is part of this satanism business. Call it the counterculture. Call it the Dionysus model of the counterculture."

Okay, it's the Dionysus model of the counterculture.

"Rock is essentially a revival of the ancient Dionysiac, Bacchic ritual," LaRouche continues. "It does have a relationship to the alpha rhythms of the brain. If combined with a little alcohol and more, shall we say, mood-shaping substances, with youth, with funny sex, this does produce a personality change of a countercultural type."

Funny sex?

Dr. John Coleman, a self-described former British intelligence agent who has taken many of LaRouche's notions one better (if that's possible), though from a more "Christian" angle, goes into greater detail.

The Grateful Dead are small game. Coleman goes straight for the biggest prize around. The Beatles, he claims, are nothing more than a Club of Rome experiment cooked up by two famous and widely influential think-tanks: the CoR-managed British research organization known as the Tavistock Institute for Human Relations and its American sibling, the Stanford Research Institute (SRI).

"When Tavistock brought the Beatles to the United States nobody could have imagined the cultural disaster that would follow in their wake," writes Coleman. "The phenomenon of the Beatles was not a spontaneous rebellion by youth against the old social system. Instead it was a carefully crafted plot to introduce by a conspiratorial body which could not be identified, a highly destructive and divisive element into a large population group targeted for change against its will."

To provide tactical support for the Beatles, says Dr. John, Tavistock also "prepared" a new lexicon of "code words signifying the acceptance of drugs" which it deployed the Fab Four to disseminate. This new vocabulary included such words as *teenager, cool, pop music,* and *discovered.*

"Incidentally," Coleman notes, "the word *teenagers* was never used until just before the Beatles arrived on the scene, courtesy of the Tavistock Institute for Human Relations."

While Coleman proves himself no authority on etymology, he displays an affection for rock 'n' roll that makes Albert Goldman look like Lester Bangs. He hesitates to use such "beautiful words" as *music* and *lyrics* in reference to the Beatles because, "it reminds me of how wrongly the word *lover* is used when referring to the filthy interaction between two homosexuals writhing in pigswill."

The Brits have agents everywhere. What would the Beatles have ever amounted to without the assistance of "the scurrilous Ed Sullivan"? asks Coleman.

Now, lest one fall into the trap of supposing that this exercise in mass manipulation ended with the release of Paul McCartney's first solo album, Coleman assures us that through its intelligence agencies, "new sexually degenerate cults are even now being set up by the British Crown. As we already know, all cults operating in the world today are the product of British intelligence acting for the oligarchical rulers."

Coleman is not content to tab the British royals alone as those "rulers."

"That single entity," he writes, "the conspirators' hierarchy, is called THE COMMITTEE OF 300." (As much as Coleman hates rock music, he loves the Shift/Lock key.) "The Committee of 300 is the ultimate secret society made up of an untouchable ruling class," he writes in his book titled, predictably, *Conspirators' Hierarchy: The Story of the Committee of 300.*

"Note how the queen, Elizabeth II, performs the ceremonial opening of the British Parliament?" Coleman observes darkly. "There, in full view, is the head of the Committee of 300."

MAJOR SOURCES

Coleman, Dr. John. *Conspirators' Hierarchy: The Story of the Committee of 300.* Carson City, NE: America West Publishing, 1992.

U.S. Labor Party Investigating Team. *Dope, Inc.: Britain's Opium War Against the U.S.* New York: New Benjamin Franklin House, 1978.

Vankin, Jonathan. *Conspiracies, Coverups, and Crimes.* New York: Dell Publishing, 1992.

29

Those Christ Kids

The mysterious French organization known as the Priory of Zion may be a nine-hundred-year-old secret society possessing proof that Jesus Christ survived the crucifixion. What's more, it may also be the repository of Europe's secret history, and indeed the underground annals of all Christendom. Then again, maybe it's just an extremely elaborate hoax. Whichever, it launched a best-selling book, 1982's *Holy Blood, Holy Grail,* by BBC documentary filmmaker Henry Lincoln and historians Michael Baigent and Richard Leigh.

Lincoln and company set out to write about one of France's most enduring riddles, the legend of Rennes-le-Château, an antique village ensconced in the Pyrenees mountains. Legend has it that somewhere beneath its cobblestone streets, Rennes-le-Château harbors a fabulous treasure. Locals are partial to the theory that the stash belonged to the Cathars, Christian heretics stamped out by the Catholic church in the thirteenth century. New Age pilgrims and occultists trek there to partake of the town's supposed spiritual energy; treasure hunters prowl its windswept perimeters in search of more worldly goods;

others tie the source of the town's mystical fascination to UFOs. Whatever the theory, Rennes-le-Château owes its renaissance as a mystical landmark to a nineteenth-century cleric named Bérenger Saunière, and that is where Lincoln, Baigent, and Leigh began their quest.

The story opens in 1885, when the Catholic church assigned Saunière, thirty-three years old, handsome, well-educated—if provincial—to the parish at Rennes-le-Château. Saunière set about restoring the town's tiny church, which sat atop a sacred site dating back to the sixth-century Visigoths. Under the altar stone, inside a hollow Visigothic pillar, the young curé discovered a series of parchments. There were two genealogies dating from 1244 A.D. and 1644 A.D., as well as more recent documents created by a former parish priest during the 1780s. According to Lincoln and his coauthors, these more recent papers contained a series of ciphers and codes, some of them "fantastically complex, defying even a computer" to unlock their secrets.

Saunière took his discovery to the bishop in nearby Carcassonne, who dispatched the priest to Paris, where clerical scholars studied the parchments. One of the simpler ciphers, when translated, read: TO DAGOBERT II KING AND TO SION BELONGS THIS TREASURE AND HE IS THERE DEAD.

Whatever it all meant, apparently it became Saunière's entrée into a new world, with the accent on *worldly*. For during his short stay in Paris, Saunière began to mix with the city's cultural elite, many of whom dabbled in the occult arts. Contemporary gossip had it that the country priest had an affair with Emma Calvé, the famous opera diva who was also a high priestess of the Parisian esoteric underground. She would later visit him frequently in Rennes-le-Château.

When Saunière returned to his parish, he resumed restoration of the church and discovered an underground crypt, supposedly containing skeletons. At this point, his taste in interior design seems to have taken a turn for the, well, peculiar; among the eccentric fixtures he installed were a holy water basin sur-

mounted by a statue of a sneering red demon and an equally
garish wall relief depicting Jesus atop a hill at the base of which
is an object resembling a sack of money. The stations of the
cross had their oddities too: One, set at night, depicted Jesus
being carried into the tomb—or smuggled out of it? Saunière
also installed a series of cipher messages in the fixtures of the
church. He spent a fortune refurbishing the town and developed
extravagant tastes for rare china, antiques, and other pricey
artifacts. Yet how Saunière acquired this apparent windfall
remained a mystery—he stubbornly refused to explain the
secret of his success to the church authorities. When he died in
1917, he was supposedly penniless, yet his former housekeeper
later spoke of a "secret" that would make its owner not only
rich but also "powerful." Unfortunately, she never spilled the
beans.

Lincoln and his co-authors found no treasure, though they
speculated that Saunière might have exhumed *somebody's* loot:
Maybe it was the legendary Cathar hoard, or the nest egg of the
Visigoths, or perhaps the treasure of the Merovingian kings
who ruled the region between the fifth and eighth centuries—
the Dagobert II mentioned in the coded parchment was one of
them. Maybe it was a combination of all three treasures. Or, if
not treasure in the conventional sense, then perhaps Saunière
had discovered some form of forbidden knowledge and had
used it to blackmail someone, say, for instance, the church.

At any rate, during their investigation into the legend of
Saunière, what Lincoln and company *did* discover was less
cashable, yet just as mysterious: an unseen hand "discreetly,
tantalizingly" directing a low-key publicity effort on behalf of
the legend.

At the center of the underground PR campaign they found an
enigmatic and very real figure named Pierre Plantard de Saint-
Clair, apparently the source behind much of the recent literature devoted to the hilltown and its enigmatic priest. Shep-
herded to Paris's Bibliothèque Nationale, our trio of historical
investigators discovered there a provocative genealogy purport-

ing to link Pierre Plantard to King Dagobert II and the Merovingian dynasty. Hardly your run-of-the-mill blue blood, that Monsieur Plantard, for the Merovingians were considered in their day to be quasi-mystical warrior-kings vested with supernatural powers. Ah, but that was only one item on Plantard's impressive family résumé. More on that in a moment.

Throughout these *dossiers secrets* at Paris's national library were tantalizing historical references to a mysterious and ancient secret society called Prieuré de Sion, or Priory of Zion. The word *Zion*, of course, appeared in various ciphers connected with Rennes-le-Château. It also seemed to refer to Mount Zion in Jerusalem, site of the ancient Temple of Solomon.

According to the secret dossiers, the spectral Priory was linked to the famous Knights Templar, an order of warrior monks who defended the European occupation of the Holy Land during the twelfth century. The Templars took their name from the source of their authority and the site of their quarters, built on the ruins of the Temple of Solomon. Of course, this wasn't the first conspiracy theory to cast the Templars as cabalistic bugaboos, yet their supposed connection to the (possibly fictional) Priory of Zion was a new one. Taking a cue from the dossiers, Lincoln and company speculated that the clandestine Priory had hidden behind the Knights Templar, which served as the Priory's armed entourage and public face.

And if these secret dossiers were to be believed, the Priory of Zion was a covert force to be reckoned with. References to well-known historical events suggested that the Priory had been a secret power in Europe ever since the Crusades, a gray eminence manipulating kings and popes in the furtherance of some obscure mission.

According to the musty pamphlets and microfiche in France's national library, through the ages the Priory's leaders had included such luminaries as Leonardo da Vinci, Sir Isaac Newton, Charles Radclyffe, Victor Hugo, and the most recent entry on the list, Jean Cocteau, the twentieth-century artist and author. In all, the list named twenty-six such "grand masters" spanning some seven hundred years!

Could the group have survived into the late twentieth century? Lincoln and company checked with the French authorities and discovered that there was indeed a contemporary organization calling itself Priory of Zion. And who do you think was registered as the group's secretary-general but Pierre Plantard.

When Lincoln finally tracked him down, Plantard turned out to be a wily old aristocrat who had played a small part in the French Resistance. But his deliberate obfuscation seemed intended as much to conceal something as to lure the authors further into the mystery.

Just what was Plantard trying to hide—or *reveal* in his consciously eliptical way? What was the possibly sinister purpose behind the Priory of Zion?

The authors of *Holy Blood, Holy Grail* proposed a theory, as tangled and complicated as the *dossier secrets*, yet entertainingly mounted and surprisingly well argued. Was there a connection, they wondered, between the heretical Cathars of thirteenth-century France, Saunière's Rennes-le-Château, the Templars, and the omnipresent Priory of Zion?

But of course, they ventured. Lincoln and company hypothesized that the fabled Cathar treasure at Renne-le-Château was one in the same with the Merovingian cache *and* the Templars' treasure of King Solomon. At some point, according to Lincoln et al., the treasure had passed from the Merovingians to the Priory of Zion, whose Templar operatives later hustled the precious hoard from the Holy Land to the French Cathars, who, on the eve of their destruction by the church, squirreled the lucre away in the Pyrenees.

But what if the "treasure" was something other than gold? After all, legend had it that the Cathar heretics possessed a valuable, even sacred relic, "which according to a number of legends, was the Holy Grail," itself. During World War II, the Nazis supposedly excavated various sites in the vicinity of

Rennes-le-Château in their futile search for the Grail (which was dramatized in the movie *Indiana Jones and the Last Crusade*).

Was the lost Cathar/Templar/Merovingian/Saunière treasure, then, the fabled Holy Grail, itself? By suggesting that it was, our trailblazing authors were not suggesting that the ominous Priory revolved around a mere religious relic—and a rusty old goblet at that. Lincoln and company had something more ambitious in mind. Boldly reinterpreting centuries of folklore, they proposed that the Grail of medieval romance might have been a coded reference to something much more controversial: the literal bloodline of Christ.

Here's where Lincoln and company shifted into conspiratorial overdrive. Borrowing the thesis of Hugh J. Schonfield's book, *The Passover Plot*, and grafting it onto the enigmatic Plantard clues, Lincoln and his coauthors fashioned a, well, daring theory. Stripped of syllogistic elegance, it goes something like this: Christ survived the crucifixion by "faking" his death or otherwise being "fruitful" before Good Friday, either way leaving behind the wife and kids. The "Christs" subsequently legged it to the south of France where they intermarried with the royal Franks to found what eventually became the mystical Merovingian Dynasty. Ergo, the *real* mission of the Templars and Priory of Zion: to safeguard not just the treasure of the Crusades, but to preserve the Grail, which appeared in medieval texts as "Sangraal" or "Sangreal," and which Lincoln et al. translated to mean *sang réal*, or "royal blood." In other words: the dynastic legacy of Christ, literally.

This, then, might be the stunning secret—and the secret society that evolved through the ages to protect it—that Abbé Saunière stumbled upon in Rennes-le-Château: TO DAGOBERT II KING AND TO SION BELONGS THIS TREASURE AND *HE IS THERE DEAD*. Who He? J.C.

Suddenly, the meandering history of Europe develops a dramatic, cohesive plot line: The persecution of the Cathars by the church, the collusion of Rome in the assassination of King

Dagobert, the successful conspiracy of the Pope Clement V and Phillipe IV of France to suppress the powerful Templars—all were efforts to "eradicate it, Jesus' bloodline." For "it" constituted nothing less than a rival church with a more direct link to J.C.'s legacy than the Vatican could ever claim.

Whew. Fast forward to the twentieth century, and Plantard's Merovingian pedigree has obvious implications.

Of course, Plantard's response to all this virtuoso theorizing was that enigmatic Mona Lisa smile of his. He wasn't about to walk on water, at least not at the behest of three future bestselling authors.

Curiously, in their followup book, *The Messianic Legacy,* Lincoln, Baigent, and Leigh sounded at times almost as if they were proselytizing. Advocating the concept of the lost "priest-king," they argued that a dose of spiritual leadership might not necessarily be a bad thing for rudderless Europe, especially since the historically bickering nations were attempting to unify as an Economic Community anyway. A "theocratic United States of Europe" might be just what the doctor ordered, Lincoln and his associates suggested.

Yet their sequel ended on a decidedly down note, for their subsequent research raised doubts about the true nature of the Priory.

In piercing the confounding veil surrounding Plantard and his mysterious organization, Lincoln and company opened a sordid vault of modern conspiracies. Key Priory documents purporting to trace the royal lineage back to J.C., Himself, were said to have been smuggled out of France by British intelligence agents, possibly at the behest of American spooks. Why were these venal forces sullying the uplifting vision of the Lost King? There were other troubling elements lurking in the background, including Italy's crypto-fascist P2 Masonic lodge, which during the 1980s seemed to have reserved seating at every major conspiracy event.

Could Lincoln, Baigent, and Leigh have stumbled upon an

elaborate, tangled ruse set up for some abstruse objective of spycraft, or perhaps in the service of right-wing European politics? Was Plantard just a clever self-promoter with too much ancien régime leisure time on his hands? Or, if it wasn't a hoax from the get-go, did the Priory of Zion's ancient charter devolve at some point into a club for tweedy intelligence operatives? Was the Grail just a dirty cup filled with slippery spy dust?

During the 1980s, the books struck a ringing chord just about everywhere. The American clergy went ballistic at the suggestion that centuries of Christian dogma amounted to centuries of *false* dogma. Despite the fact that *Holy Blood, Holy Grail* restored the underappreciated French to the center of the cosmos (after all, the Messiah doesn't have an English or American accent, does He?), modern Gallic folk tend to be unimpressed with the trio's revisionist scholarship. And some even resent having their cherished national mysteries paraded on the international marketplace, by profiteering foreigners, no less. Of course, American and British book buyers have been much more generous.

By the 1990s, though, even Lincoln had soured on speculating about the Priory of Zion and its maddeningly hermetic chief executive, Pierre Plantard. "In my old age, I've decided to stick to that which can be verified," Lincoln groused when asked for an update on the secret society.

Though disillusioned, he hadn't finished with the mysterious hill town that launched his modern quest for the Holy Grail—not to mention his book-writing career. In his solo 1991 coffee-table book, *The Holy Place*, Lincoln announced that whatever else it may or may not be, the town called Rennes-le-Château is most certainly the "Eighth Wonder of the Ancient World," an "immense geometric temple, stretching for miles across the landscape." But sounding like the reformed heretic stung once too often by the critical flail, Lincoln offered a rather modest closing caveat: "This book does not claim to have solved the riddle."

MAJOR SOURCES

Baigent, Michael; Richard Leigh, and Henry Lincoln. *Holy Blood,
   Holy Grail.* New York: Dell Publishing, 1983.
Baigent, Michael; Richard Leigh, and Henry Lincoln. *The Messianic
   Legacy.* New York: Dell Publishing, 1986.
Lincoln, Henry. *The Holy Place: Discovering the Eighth Wonder of
   the World.* New York: Arcade Publishing, 1991.

30

The Gemstone File

The Skeleton Key to the Gemstone File, a twenty-three-page digest of an original sheaf of letters supposedly a thousand pages thick, was authored in 1975 by Stephanie Caruana, then a freelance journalist affiliated with that staid forum for elegant reportage, *Playgirl* magazine. The original Gemstone letters were penned by a mysterious and now long-deceased fellow named Bruce Roberts who was—well, no one's completely sure *who* he was.

Caruana's *Key* has been photocopied thousands of times. The exact number, like much of the information in the *Gemstone File* itself, is beyond verification. The contents are classic conspiracy theory: fact mixed with conjecture, blended with error, and expressed with certitude. Yet the document is so gripping and at the same time so obscure, always looking like a twentieth-generation Xerox, it begs credulity, even investigation.

Fade in.

1932.

Aristotle Onassis, the central figure in this epic—best known as the shipping magnate who married President Kennedy's widow, but described in the *Key's* opening lines as "a Greek drug pusher...who made his first million selling 'Turkish tobacco' (opium) in Argentina"—strikes a deal with bootleggers Meyer Lansky, Eugene Meyer, and Joseph Kennedy to ship illegal hooch into Boston. "Also involved," states *Gemstone*, "was a heroin deal with Franklin and Elliot Roosevelt." (Hmm.)

The chronology crackles through forty-three years of American cloak-and-dagger, fading out in April, 1975, at which time, to quote Caruana's typically delicate phraseology, "Ford, Kissinger, and Rockefeller squat like toads on the corpse of America."

Presumably, that date roughly coincides with the period when Roberts, bedridden by an undoubtedly suspicious ailment, ceased scribbling his original letters and unceremoniously passed away.

Along the way, the *Gemstone File* drops some tantalizing, sometimes puzzling tidbits and makes some outlandish, albeit intriguing assertions. The *File's* plotline concerns the malignant codependency between the U.S. government and the Mafia—a plausible enough hypothesis. But wait. This Mafia has more in common with James Bond's arch-nemesis SPECTRE than with the Sicilian secret society of *Godfather* lore.

And the "crowned head of the Mafia" is Ari O, himself. In fact, conspiracy researcher John Judge has speculated that Ian Fleming based his ubervillain Ernst Stavro Blofeld on Onassis, which would gibe with the *Gemstone File*, for if Bruce Roberts has the story straight Onassis was an evil mastermind and overlord who puppeteered presidents, gangsters, and popes.

Following the critical 1932 deal with Kennedy et al., there came two more watershed triumphs in Onassis's career-according-to-*Gemstone*. In 1957, he ordered Howard Hughes kidnapped and, later, doped to death, which accounts for the eccentric billionaire's storied reclusiveness. This caper gave Onassis control of Hughes's expansive fiscal shogunate, on top of his own already impressive domain.

Then, in 1963, Onassis seized ultimate power. John F. Kennedy, formerly under Onassis's control due to Daddy Joe's debt to the "Big O," unwisely wagged his presidential scepter by backing off on the Bay of Pigs raid, a Mafia (i.e., Onassis) operation to reclaim the Cuban cash cow. JFK "welshed" on the deal so Onassis ordered the president "hit" in Mafia style. Onassis, says *Gemstone*, lived up to "an old Mafia rule: if someone welshes on a deal, kill him, take his gun and his girl: in this case, Jackie and the Pentagon."

Some of the *Gemstone File*'s other provocative "revelations":

• Onassis immediately asserted control over Lyndon Johnson, relaying a message to him on Air Force One en route from Dallas: "There was *no conspiracy*. Oswald was a *lone nut assassin*. Get it Lyndon? Otherwise, Air Force One might have an unfortunate accident on flight back to Washington."

• J. Edgar Hoover possessed the *Gemstone File* and threatened to use it to expose what really happened in Dallas, but he was poisoned first. Someone slipped "sodium morphate" (whatever that is) in his apple pie; a gesture, it may be worth noting, rich in symbolism.

• Katherine Graham, the publisher of the *Washington Post* and daughter of Onassis comrade Eugene Meyer, was Bob Woodward and Carl Bernstein's Deep Throat.

• San Francisco's infamous series of Zebra killings— seemingly random shootings of whites purportedly perpetrated by black militant extremists—were really pulled off by Onassis/Mafia to deep-six a potentially dangerous witness, then distract attention from the murder's true motive, at the same time giving authorities an excuse to crank up the heat on "black terrorists."

• Richard Nixon, a Hughes pawn who became an Onassis vassal after Ari did the number on Howard, was forced to resign when Roberts started squawking. Mafia bosses worried Nixon'd blab about Big O. The eighteen minutes of "accidentally" erased Watergate tapes include Nixon ranting about "that asshole Roberts."

- Nixon made a deal with Gerald Ford, allowing Nixon to "murder anyone he needed to" to cover up Watergate/*Gemstone* (pretty much the same, in this universe).
- The pope was in on this whole thing too.

So who was Bruce Roberts and why was he saying all those terrible things about the good Mr. Onassis? Seems he was a genius of sorts who concocted a process for fabricating artificial gemstones. He tried to sell the invention to Howard Hughes's company only to see the multinational conglomerate rip him off. Righteously steamed, Roberts started digging—discovering that "Hughes" was not Hughes at all but in reality the sinister Onassis. That, anyway, is how Caruana tells the tale.

The two people who claim to have come into closest contact with the penumbral Roberts are Caruana and the ubiquitous Mae Brussell. Brussell said in a 1978 radio show that Roberts sought her out and passed her the file after reading her article "Why Was Martha Mitchell Kidnapped?" in the *Realist*. Caruana met Roberts through Brussell.

Brussell, of course, has been deceased for several years, but Caruana is still kicking. Interviewed by Jim Keith, editor of the definitive work on this topic (cited below), Caruana described Roberts as a real-life James Bond, whereas Brussell had dubbed him "Casper Milquetoast."

His letters, it seems, are widely discussed, but no one save Brussell and Caruana ever got a glance at them. For that matter, at this point, Bruce Roberts's former existence as an actual human being is mostly a matter of Brussell's and Caruana's sayso.

None of which is meant to imply that *Gemstone* is a ruse, or that Roberts is Stephanie Caruana's imaginary friend. If Caruana is a prankster, she is a peculiarly recalcitrant and testy one who engineered her fraud in such a way as to preclude any significant public impact or personal profit. And Brussell, while perhaps known to indulge in the occasional leap of logic, was anything but a hoax artist. Finally, if Roberts, or whoever presented himself as Roberts, was a disinformation artist, he must have specialized in low-impact disinformation.

If not a hoax, it's still tempting to dismiss the *Gemstone File* as the rantings of an admirably dedicated crank. But perhaps it would be kinder, and more accurate, to call the *Gemstone File* history by poetic license, the legacy of a man who was, if only in a peripheral way, history's victim.

MAJOR SOURCES

Caruana, Stephanie. *The Skeleton Key to the Gemstone File*: several photostatic versions in authors' files.
Keith, Jim, ed. *The Gemstone File*. Atlanta: IllumiNet Press, 1992.

VII

Conspiracy, Inc.

31

The White House Putsch

Few Americans know it, but during the Great Depression, a cabal of millionaire bankers and industrialists hatched a conspiracy to hijack the U.S. government and install a fascist dictatorship. It was, in the words of contemporary journalist John L. Spivak, "one of the most fantastic plots in American history."

Spivak's assessment in his 1967 book, *A Man in His Time*, certainly continues to hold true sixty years after the fact: "What was behind the plot was shrouded in a silence which has not been broken to this day. Even a generation later, those who are still alive and know all the facts have kept their silence so well that the conspiracy is not even a footnote in American histories."

Although a congressional committee confirmed the allegations, the findings were hushed up amid murmurs of a coverup. No wonder. The plotters were brand-name American financiers in the Morgan and Du Pont commercial empires, right-wingers bitterly opposed to Franklin Delano Roosevelt's New Deal and the president's sympathies toward organized labor.

Perhaps Americans would know all too much about the plot, and even celebrate it on "President Duce Day," if it weren't for a

patriotic military man, Major General Smedley Darlington
Butler. In the summer of 1933, the putsch plotters approached
Butler, the retired commandant of the U.S. Marines and a
popular war hero affectionately known as "the fighting
Quaker." They offered him the job of transforming the American Legion veterans group into a 500,000-man marauding
army, which was to spearhead an American coup d'état.

Unfortunately for facism, Butler's appeal to the plotters also
turned out to be the conspiracy's downfall. The conspirators
apparently chose the former general because of his enormous
popularity with rank-and-file soldiers; but it was Butler's
antielitist leanings and reputation for honesty that had made
him a populist favorite. In short, the conspirators couldn't have
selected a candidate more unlikely to agree to lead a fascist
takeover. Shrewdly, Butler decided to play along, feigning
interest in the plans in order to draw the plotters into the
daylight and expose the scheme to Congress.

As he told the House of Representatives' McCormack-Dickstein Committee, which was investigating Nazi and communist
activities in America, Butler was first approached by one
Gerald G. MacGuire, a bond salesman and former commander
of the Connecticut American Legion. As journalist Spivak
described him, "MacGuire was a short stocky man tending
toward three chins, with a bullet-shaped head which had a
silver plate in it due to a wound received in battle."

According to the former general, MacGuire described to
Butler "what was tantamount to a plot to seize the government,
by force if necessary." MacGuire, said Butler, explained that he
had traveled to Europe to study the role played by veterans'
groups in propping up Mussolini's fascist Italy, Hitler's Nazi
Germany, and the French government. MacGuire lauded
France's Croix de Feu as "an organization of super-soldiers"
with profound political influence. Then the man with the silver
plate in his cranium announced that "our idea here in America"
is to "get up an organization of this kind" because "the political
setup has got to be changed a bit."

According to Butler, MacGuire elaborated on the plot: "Now, did it ever occur to you that the president is overworked? We might have an assistant president; somebody to take the blame." MacGuire called the new super Cabinet official a "secretary of general affairs." And, he said, "You know the American people will swallow that. We have got the newspapers. We will start a campaign that the president's health is failing. Everybody can tell that by looking at him, and the dumb American people will fall for it in a second...."

Although MacGuire denied Butler's account under oath, corroborating testimony came from Paul Comly French, a *Philadelphia Record* reporter. Butler had asked French to look into MacGuire's plot and shed some light on "what the hell it's all about."

After checking with Butler, the voluble MacGuire agreed to see French. French testified that MacGuire told him, "We need a fascist government in this country...to save the nation from the communists who want to tear it down and wreck all that we have built in America. The only men who have the patriotism to do it are the soldiers, and Smedley Butler is the ideal leader. He could organize a million men overnight."

French continued: MacGuire "warmed up considerably after we got under way and he said, 'We might go along with Roosevelt and then do with him what Mussolini did with the King of Italy.'" If Roosevelt played ball, French summarized, "swell; and if he did not, they would push him out."

According to French, MacGuire dropped names to give the impression that American Legion brass were involved in the plot.

To impress Butler, MacGuire had flaunted a bank book itemizing deposits of more than $100,000 available to pay for "expenses." Later, he flashed a wad of eighteen $1,000 bills and boasted of "friends" who were capable of coughing up plenty more dough where that came from.

One of those friends was Robert Sterling Clark, a prominent Wall Street banker and stockbroker. When Butler demanded that MacGuire produce his superiors, the tubby intermediary made the introductions. According to Butler's testimony, Clark spoke of spending half his $60 million fortune in order to save the other half. What's more, Clark purportedly waxed ominous about the misguided FDR: "You know the president is weak. He will come right along with us. He was born in this class, and he will come back. He will run true to form. In the end he will come around. But we have got to be prepared to sustain him when he does."

Amazingly, the McCormack-Dickstein Committee (a forerunner of the infamous House Un-American Activities Committee) never bothered to haul Clark in for questioning. And the committee's members—who exhibited considerably more zeal ferreting out two-bit commies than they did big-shot American fascists—failed to grill a half-dozen other suspects named by Butler and French. In fact, the committee suppressed many of the names, even though French's newspaper articles caused a stir by naming the well-heeled conspirators (at the height of the Depression).

In addition to MacGuire and Clark, the leading plotters included:

- Grayson Murphy, a director of Goodyear, Bethlehem Steel, and a panoply of Morgan banks. Murphy was the original bankroller of the American Legion, which he and other wealthy military officers formed after World War I to "offset radicalism." He was also MacGuire's boss at the New York brokerage firm.
- William Doyle, former state commander of the Legion and purportedly the architect of the coup idea.
- John W. Davis, former Democratic candidate for president of the United States and a senior attorney for J.P. Morgan and Company.
- Al Smith, former governor of New York, a Roosevelt foe, and codirector of the newly founded American Liberty League, an organization described by MacGuire as the matrix on which the plot would be executed.

Other prominent businessmen lurked in the background,

including Smith's codirector at the American Liberty League, John J. Raskob, who was a former chairman of the Democratic Party, a high-ranking Du Pont officer, and a bitter enemy of FDR, whom he classified among dangerous "radicals." And in even deeper shadows was right-wing industrialist Irénée Du Pont, who established the American Liberty League. Grayson Murphy—MacGuire's boss—was treasurer of the same group. Clearly, this was no penny-ante whiner's club. Most astonishing was the presence among the plotters of heavy-hitting politicos from FDR's own party.

Mysteriously, though, the congressional probe expired with a whimper. The McCormack-Dickstein Committee released heavily edited excerpts from Butler's testimony but claimed it had uncovered "no evidence" other than "hearsay" linking prominent Americans to a fascist plot.

Had the committee backed down rather than take on a klatch of power-drunk millionaires? Did high-ranking Democrats—possibly one in the White House, as some reports had it—put the kibosh on the investigation for similar reasons, or to stave off political embarrassment, or to protect Democratic muckamucks who were in on the scheme?

All of the above would seem likely, for in fact the McCormack-Dickstein Committee's public report was utterly contradicted by its internal summation to the House. That document might have been lost to history had Spivak not somehow managed to liberate a copy. Contrary to the public whitewash, privately the committee acknowledged Butler's accuracy and MacGuire's lying. The report concluded:

> In the last few weeks of the committee's life it received evidence showing that certain persons had made an attempt to establish a fascist organization in this country....
> There is no question that these attempts were discussed, were planned, and might have been placed in execution when and if the financial backers deemed it expedient....
> MacGuire denied [Butler's] allegations under oath, but

your committee was able to verify all the pertinent statements made to General Butler, with the exception of the
direct statement suggesting the creation of the organization. This, however, was corroborated in the correspondence of MacGuire with his principal, Robert Sterling
Clark, of New York City, while MacGuire was abroad
studying the various form of veterans' organizations of
Fascist character.

Alas, as is so often the case, when truth finally emerged it was
greeted as yesterday's news—or worse, as last year's outmoded
fashion, which clashed with the committee's public dismissal of
the charges. Spivak's reporting appeared in a small left-wing
publication where it went largely unnoticed. After all, *Time*
magazine—hardly what you would call antagonistic toward
right-wing industrialists—had already dismissed the allegations as a joke.

"The fighting Quaker" went on national radio to denounce
the committee's deletions of key points in his testimony, but
history's loaded die had already been cast.

Ultimately, the plot's failure owes as much a debt to Butler as
it does to the hubris of the super-wealthy. Lacking a Mussolini-
calibre proxy, but swimming in ample cash to buy one,
America's elite fascists dispatched the man with a plate in his
head to build a better Duce. Of course, the revolution went
south when, in an act of inspired stupidity, they decided to buy
a dictator who happened to be a notorious democrat with a
small *d*.

MAJOR SOURCES

Archer, Jules. *The Plot to Seize the White House*. New York:
    Hawthorn Books, 1973.
Seldes, George. *Even the Gods Can't Change History*. Secaucus, NJ:
    Lyle Stuart, Inc., 1976.
Spivak, John L. *A Man in His Time*. New York: Horizon Press, 1967.

32

The Candy-Coated Conspiracy

As any local reporter who's ever covered a small-time city council meeting knows, the specter of fluoridation still haunts the public agenda. There's always some crotchety old buzzard who shows up, sheaf of documents clenched in fist, ranting about the impurity of precious bodily fluids. You'd think *Dr. Strangelove* had put the issue to rest once and for all.

In essence, the issue is "purity of essence," as the mad general Jack D. Ripper phrased it in Stanley Kubrick's 1964 flick (subtitled *How I Learned to Stop Worrying and Love the Bomb*). Beginning in the late 1930s, ostensibly as a public health measure, various academics, physicians, and bureaucrats began advocating the artificial enrichment of public water supplies with fluoride, a mineral known to prevent tooth decay.

To say this apparently public-spirited project was greeted less than warmly is an understatement. For the next forty years a significant lobby emerged dedicated to the proposition that fluoridation of public water supplies was not only unnecessary and potentially harmful, it was an insidious plot hatched by the worldwide communist conspiracy. Or something. At best, the plot's aim was to poison the U.S. public. At worst—to dissipate what President Kennedy might have later termed American "vigah."

The psychosexual subtext of this fear simmered barely beneath the surface. Somehow, this effort to improve the nation's dental health (widespread fluoridation has the potential to render cavities as passé as whooping cough) was being interpreted as an attempt to turn the home of the brave into a nation of gay blades.

Kubrick flayed fluoride paranoia with his General Ripper, for whom the pinko plot against "our precious bodily fluids" was but an excuse for his own impotence and implied homosexuality. But despite its pointed satire *Strangelove* left the anti-fluoridators undeterred.

As always, however, even with an issue this ridiculous, there is another side. The merits of government-mandated chemical modifications to the public drinking supply are certainly debatable. But is it really all part of a perfidious plot?

"In the words of the Communist Party itself," writes Phoebe Courtney in her 1971 tract *How Dangerous Is Fluoridation?* "anyone who promotes and supports fluoridation can be considered a 'radical'!"

Actually, what the *Daily World* article quoted by Courtney really said was that "such a well-documented and simple improvement in public health should be avidly supported by all who consider themselves radicals." Not that anyone who supports fluoridation is a radical. But logic was never the fluoride-baiters' strong point.

"An Ominous Precedent: Can Water Supplies be Used for Sinister Purposes?" Courtney asks in the title of just one of fifteen chapters in her 158-page paperback. Before you know it, nefarious liberals and cold-hearted physicians will be employing the water supply for "compulsory birth control" and the dissemination of "anti-hostility drugs."

"Perhaps 1984 is closer than we realize," warns the author. Perhaps indeed.

Among her other imprecations:

- "Fluoride pollution causes massive fish-kill."
- "The public seldom hears of it, but fluorides damage water-pipes as well as people....Automobile radiators were eaten out by fluoride corrosion."
- "It is common knowledge among all chemists and people interested in this particular subject that fluoride is one of the most electronegative active elements known to man."
- "Claim of 65 percent reduction in cavities not true!"
- "In his article in the March 1968 issue of *American Opinion* [a John Birch Society magazine], David O. Woodbury referred to sodium fluoride as 'violent enough in high concentrations to be the standard rat and roach killer and a first-rate pesticide.'"
- "Mrs. M.H., aged fifty-seven, a nurse, and Mrs. E.K., aged thirty-eight, had been in the habit of drinking one to two glasses of water before breakfast. For some unknown reason, they suddenly experienced abdominal cramps and vomiting immediately after their customary morning drink."

To combat the menace of fluoridation, Courtney suggests buying "extra copies of this book for your personal distribution. You may wish to send or give copies to: Officials of your city; Leaders of Parent-Teacher Associations, womens' clubs, fraternal and civic organizations; voters groups and patriotic groups; water works officials; the editor of your local newspaper as well as radio and TV commentators; your personal physician and dentist."

Incidentally, we also suggest that readers purchase extra copies of this book for distribution to physicians, water works officials, and patriotic groups.

As with so many of these theories, even the wackiest ones, there are two sides to the story. Courtney tends to play down the commie-conspiracy angle in favor of an even more nefarious culprit.

"For the sugar and candy interests, fluoridation was a heaven-sent proposal," Courtney writes. "Mothers who become convinced that fluorides strengthen their children's teeth and make them resistant to decay, are not afraid to allow them to eat all the candy and sweets they want. And this is exactly what the candy manufacturers planned when they endorsed fluoridation."

MAJOR SOURCE

Courtney, Phoebe. *How Dangerous Is Fluoridation?* New Orleans: Free Men Speak, Inc., 1971.

33

Reefer Madness

W hat if there was a plant that could feed and clothe the world, end global deforestation, replace smutty fossil fuels in the gas tank of your car, and offer salubrious therapy for dozens of ailments? What if George Washington and Thomas Jefferson had grown it, were required by law to grow it, so useful was this miracle shrub? Well, then, it stands to reason that a combine of jealous industrialists, shrieking demagogues, and yellow journalists would scurry to stomp the "demon weed" out forever and purge its distinguished legacy from the history books.

The name of this botanical martyr? The Founding Fathers, who drafted the Declaration of Independence on paper made from the plant, knew it as hemp. You may know it by another of its many appellations: Indian hemp, true hemp, bhang, dagga, ganja, muggles, muta, grefa, tea, boo, goo, gauge, herb, weed, "the kind," cannabis, reefer, buds, grass, pot—to wit, *marijuana*.

Beginning to get the picture? In his eminently civilized book, *The Emperor Wears No Clothes*, Jack Herer has exposed the "malicious conspiracy to suppress not a 'killer weed,' but the world's premier renewable natural resource, for the benefit of a handful of wealthy and powerful individuals and corporations." Herer is the founder of a group called HEMP (Help End Marijuana Prohibition). He sees the sixty-year war on pot as more than a pox on tokers: It's a latter-day Inquisition, a pernicious reprise of the Dark Ages, and, not least, "a conspiracy against mankind."

As do so many, this conspiracy began in smoke-filled board rooms—and you can bet the smoke wasn't a mellow sinsemilla haze. The year was 1937, and with the advent of new mechanical fiber stripping technology, hemp was poised to make a grand comeback as the nation's favorite, most versatile textile. But as Herer relates it, an unholy trinity of hemp enemies orchestrated the notorious prohibition of this "member of the most advanced plant family on Earth."

First, a brief history lesson, necessary because the story of hemp has indeed been obscured by a half century of suppression: Before the invention of the cotton gin in the early 1800s, hemp products made from the fiber of the plant's reedy stalk were everywhere in America—and the world. The word *canvas* comes to us from the Dutch pronunciation of the Greek *kannabis*. From the fifth century B.C. through the late nineteenth century, ships' sails and rigging were made from hemp. For thousands of years, cannabis fibers had been the chief source of the world's clothing, tents, carpets, rope, bedding, and flags—including Old Glory. As Herer helpfully reminds us, Washington and his troops would have frozen to death at Valley Forge were it not for their hemp threads. The Conestoga wagons that trekked across the American prairies were covered with cannabis canvas, and the settlers' Bibles were likely to have been printed on reefer paper. For thousands of years, hemp-seed oil did yeoman's duty as lamp fuel and even food. And during the nineteenth century, patent medicines utilizing the plant's more familiar chemical attributes were imbibed by God-fearing Americans of all stripes.

By the late 1930s, *Popular Mechanics* and other magazines were hailing technology that promised to make hemp, the strongest of the natural fibers, a "new billion-dollar crop." But there were those who connived to bury hemp's illustrious history under a mountain of slander, vilifying "marihuana" as the killer weed smoked by murderous Mexicans and insolent Negroes.

The first powerful player in the anti-hemp triad identified by Herer was William Randolph Hearst. The millionaire magnate deployed his sprawling Hearst newspaper chain in a hysterical crusade against marijuana.

The second, and most strident, figure in the plot to assassinate hemp was a corrupt hypermoralist named Harry J. Anslinger. Described in Albert Goldman's book, *Grass Roots*, as "a bull-necked, bald-headed, slab-shouldered cop" with "the demagogue's flair for sloganlike phrases," Anslinger was the spear carrier in the war on pot. His crude propaganda, laughable today, popularized spurious myths about pot in (Hearst) articles with headlines like MARIHUANA—ASSASSIN OF YOUTH and MARIHUANA MAKES FIENDS OF BOYS IN 30 DAYS: HASHEESH GOADS USERS TO BLOOD-LUST. Ax murderers, rampaging gunmen, and suicidal motorists were "depraved creatures" motivated by "reefer madness." In one publicized speech, Anslinger warned, "If the hideous monster Frankenstein came face to face with the monster marihuana, he would drop dead of fright." (Like many a morality cop, Anslinger was also a first-class hypocrite. He later admitted to illegally supplying morphine to the Red-baiting and drug-addicted Senator Joseph McCarthy. During World War II Anslinger helped the OSS, forerunner to the CIA, in unsuccessful experiments with a hashish derivative they hoped to use as a truth serum on spies.)

Forming the third flank in Herer's conspiracy theory was the powerful Du Pont corporation. All three had reasons for extinguishing the hapless weed.

Although most historians have explained the Anslinger-Hearst assault on pot as a product of the prohibition era, paranoia over creeping immorality, and old-fashioned Jim Crow racism, Herer has thrown an economic theory into the mix.

It seems that the Hearst Paper Manufacturing Division, with its sprawling timber acreage, was threatened by a new milling process devised by the U.S. Department of Agriculture to convert the woody stalks of hemp into reams of high-grade paper, cardboard, and fiberboard. Incidentally, the process produced fewer toxic chemicals than wood-pulp manufacturing and, according to the government, would save four acres of fragile forest for every acre of hemp cultivated. Concludes Herer: As far as Hearst and the wood-pulp-based paper industry were concerned, "Cannabis hemp would have to go."

As for Du Pont's motives, Herer postulates that hemp's natural fibers imperiled that company's mad dream of clothing the world in polyester.

In the campaign to assassinate hemp, Anslinger and the Hearst papers weren't above race-baiting. The bull-necked narc often described marijuana users as "ginger-colored niggers" with big lips, whose "satanic" music and demon weed drove white women "to seek sexual relations with Negroes." He warned Congress that most of the reefer fiends were "Negroes and Mexicans," or, worst of all, "entertainers." Hearst articles depicted languid, pot-smoking Mexicans who could turn into homicidal lunatics at the snap of a fried synapse. According to Herer, Hearst hammered (and misspelled) the Mexican slang term *marijuana* into the public consciousness in a campaign designed to confuse folks who might otherwise discover that the demon weed and the historic fiber were one in the same.

Soon enough the fix was in. Anslinger's Treasury Department bosses held closed-door meetings that yielded sneaky legislation to slap an exorbitant $100 tax on unregistered dealers selling hemp. (Anslinger, notes Herer, owed his job to his "uncle-in-law," Andrew Mellon, owner of the nation's sixth largest bank, who also happened to be...*a Du Pont banker.*) Thanks to the influence of House Ways and Means Committee chairman Robert L. Doughton, a dyed-in-the-wool (make that *poly-blend*)

Du Pont ally, the anti-marijuana law (posing as a tax law) breezed through Congress over the weak objections of hemp producers and the American Medical Association. Thus was born the Marihuana Tax Act of 1937, which effectively outlawed the drug—and the rest of the plant—in America.

And sure enough, shortly after the 1937 marijuana ban, Du Pont unveiled its "plastic fibers," which came to dominate markets previously served by hempen goods. The following year, Du Pont patented Nylon and a new super-polluting wood-pulp process.

As if to rub Rayon in hemp users' faces, in 1939 Lammot Du Pont boasted in *Popular Mechanics* of "conserving natural resources by developing synthetic products to supplement or *wholly replace natural products*" (emphasis added).

Maybe all of this is not exactly irrefutable proof, but as the *Emperor Wears No Clothes* points out, thanks to the governmental ban on cannabis, Du Pont continues to be the nation's "largest producer of man-made fibers, while no citizen has legally harvested a single acre of textile-grade hemp in over fifty years." Perhaps it's the price of progress: The snuffing of a versatile, clean, renewable resource paved the way for the Du Pont dynasty, dioxin, timber clearcutting and, of course, the leisure suit.

MAJOR SOURCES

Goldman, Albert. *Grass Roots: Marijuana in America Today*. New York: Warner Books, 1979.
Herer, Jack. *The Emperor Wears No Clothes: Hemp and the Marijuana Conspiracy*. Van Nuys, CA: Hemp Publishing, 1992.

34

New World Order

During the heady days of the Persian Gulf War, President George Bush dusted off an ancient phrase that immediately set teeth on edge—that is, the grinding teeth of conspiracy trackers.

"I hope history will record that the Gulf Crisis was the crucible of the new world order," Bush intoned in the wake of his greatest triumph, the American-led victory against Iraq. *New World Order*. The phrase had tripped from the president's lips at least half a dozen other times before and after American smart bombs had transformed the former "wimp" into a short-term war hero.

Of course, the *real* meaning of the term—bandied about for decades by a phalanx of elite bankers and industrialists—couldn't have been clearer to ultra-right-wingers of the John Birch Society ilk. Simply put, *New World Order* was code for "one-world government," a megalomaniacal communist plot to enslave the planet. In the words of the late Gary Allen, the prolific Birch Society author, "Communism is an arm of a bigger conspiracy to control the world by power-mad billionaires." Bush, the ultimate establishment insider, was clearly an agent of these crypto-capitalist/communist forces—as had been every sell-out president since FDR.

Lest we dismiss such concerns as the ranting of survivalist kooks, it's important to note that the New World Order is an equal opportunity conspiracy theory. Left-wingers were just as exercised by Bush's words, although progressives tended to see the preppy president more as a champion of capitalism run amok than as a creeping commie.

In fact, right-wing or left, suspicions about the New World Order are actually quite rational. The champions of the "NWO" are indeed a cadre of powerful industrialists, bankers, academics, and politicians who for three quarters of a century have been a gray eminence behind the governance of Britain and America. More to the point, perhaps, they *are* the governors of the Western world. Call them what you will, they are the "Establishment." Through vastly influential organizations like the Council on Foreign Relations and the Trilateral Commission, these elites formulate tomorrow's public policy today and staff the ship of state with their own.

If this network is something less than the Red devil depicted in many a right-wing conspiracy theory, it is nonetheless a kind of big business cabal that helps the elite of the private sector, if not "rule the world," then at least run it like a business.

The self-appointed historian of this power brokerage was Georgetown University professor Carroll Quigley, a distinguished scholar whom right-wingers regard as a smoking gun personified. In his massive history of the modern era, *Tragedy and Hope*, the late Professor Quigley wrote that there "does exist, and has existed for a generation, an international Anglophile network which operates, to some extent, in the way that the radical Right believes the Communists act."

Quigley admitted that he "had been close" to this "semisecret organization" of international manipulators—indeed, admired its goals—and had been allowed to examine its "papers and secret records."

According to Quigley, the network's benevolent aim is "nothing less than to create a world system of financial control in private hands able to dominate the political system of each country and the economy of the world as a whole"—thereby assuring peace and prosperity and, of course, profit.

This network grew out of secret political societies hatched by diamond baron/stealth fanatic Cecil Rhodes (Rhodesia, Rhodes scholarships) and a clutch of bleeding-heart imperialists resolved to prevent the sun from setting on the British Empire. By 1908, Rhodes was dead, but his dream and vast wealth lived on to sire the furtive Round Table Groups.

During the early part of this century, the aristocratic Round Tablers—who set up franchises in South Africa, Australia, the United States, and Canada—yearned to "civilize" native subjects of the British dominion. If properly instilled with liberal Oxford values and presumably an appreciation of cricket, even the most "backward" races could learn to be contented, perhaps "autonomous," citizens of empire. A connected dream was to yoke all of the English-speaking nations (America included) into a confederation of Atlantic states, with the capital in Washington, D.C.! (To Birchers' ears, this is an early echo of the dread "one-world government.") If their grander schemes flopped rather obliquely, the Round Tablers achieved a failure of spectacular proportions when they led the drive to appease Hitler.

In America, the Rhodes groups and J. P. Morgan banking interests incorporated the Council on Foreign Relations (CFR) in 1921 as a Round Table "front." According to Quigley, CFR and other Round Table cutouts became "a power structure between London and New York which penetrated deeply into university life, the press, and the practice of foreign policy" in both countries. This is the famous "Eastern Establishment" that continues to hold sway over the U.S. government, academia, Wall Street, and major American media outlets, including the *New York Times* and *Washington Post*.

The American arm of the network flourished under the

patronage of billionaire benefactors, including the Morgan and Carnegie interests—and of course the ubiquitous Rockefeller family.

Ah, the Rockefellers! Dons of the financial underworld! Godfathers of the commie/capitalist internationale! That, anyway, is what many a right-wing conspiracist believes. In Bircher fulminations, the four R's—Rhodes, Rothschilds, Rockefellers, and Reds—are demons that turbocharge the dry facts of Professor Quigley.

The radical-right theories were never synthesized more impressively than in Gary Allen's 1971 call to arms, *None Dare Call It Conspiracy*. Merging nativist strains of anticommunism, antielitism, and "gold standard" conservatism, Allen argued that the Rockefeller-CFR-Establishment cabal—dubbed the "Insiders"—had toiled for decades to "abolish the United States" and establish an "all powerful world socialist superstate."

Allen wasn't suggesting that supercapitalists like the Rockefellers were sincere Marxists, but rather that they used socialism "as the bait...the excuse to establish the dictatorship." According to Allen, the Rockefellers, the British Rothschild clan, and their various corporate agents had not only financed Lenin and the Bolshevik revolution, but David Rockefeller may have been the "paymaster" who later fired his employee, Soviet premier Krushchev! How did "the Rockefeller Foreign Office" keep unruly Moscow in line? Allen muses that the Insiders might have used "SMERSH, the international Communist murder organization described in testimony before congressional committees and by Ian Fleming in his James Bond books."

Allen's vision was nothing if not dramatic. In a successful effort early in the century to hijack the American economy and political arena, he reports, the Insiders established a central bank (the Federal Reserve System), lorded over by international bankers; they followed up by saddling citizens with the income tax, thereby fulfilling two key planks of Marx's *Communist*

Manifesto. The Insiders then "scientifically engineered" the stock market crash of 1929. They managed to top that feat by starting World Wars I and II (the latter through their appeasement of Hitler) *and* the Vietnam debacle, profiteering in all cases by arming both sides. Oh yeah, they also invented the nefarious United (communist) Nations as the keystone of their relentless New World Order.

In a rare instance of giving the Rockefellers a bit of a break, Birchers revived the old right-wing theory that the real powers behind the Insider throne—both communist and "cartel capitalist"—were those standby conspiracy bugaboos, the Illuminati, a secret Freemasonic society that definitely existed, albeit in eighteenth-century Bavaria.

(In an effort to cast the Illuminati as a "Zionist" cabal, anti-Semites—and Allen wasn't one—often invoke the Jewish Rothschilds and the old lie that the Bolshevik revolution was all a Jewish plot. Allen dismissed that "thinking," and typically had a more interesting angle: The Insiders themselves covertly promoted such anti-Semitic falsehoods in an effort to tar all their critics as racists. Of course, Allen offered no evidence for this theory, but perhaps he was on to something. More than one modern blowhard of the "there-are-no-conspiracies" school has offhandedly broadbrushed conspiracy theorists by yoking them with Holocaust apologists.)

Although the conspiratorial tapestry woven by the Birchers was a bit, well, *busy*, even the staid Professor Quigley grudgingly acknowledged that it contained "a modicum of truth." For one thing, the so-called Insiders "had no aversion to cooperating with the Communists," per Quigley. After all, big business is big business, and what better way of acquiring access to untapped natural resources than being neighborly? Likewise, the CFR-dominated U.S. Department of State was indeed very influential in midwifing the UN. And the Round Tablers did push for the income tax and the Federal Reserve.

As for the Rockefellers, the family *has* played a major role in the network since its early days. David Rockefeller, chairman of the CFR board, founded the Trilateral Commission in the early 1970s (same Euro-American "internationalists" but with the additional membership of Japanese power players). Another Rockefeller-Insider group arose as the retiring Round Tables passed the torch to the CFR (either that, or went deep underground, a hunch of many conspiracy theorists): This was the Bilderberg Group, named for the location of its first annual meeting, the hotel Bilderberg in Oosterbeek, Netherlands.

A super-secret riff on the CFR, the Bilderberg roll call featured Rockefellers and hordes of American officials, including U.S. State Department/CFR stalwarts Henry Kissinger, George Ball, Dean Rusk, and Dean Acheson. Its European contingent was infested by royals, including the founding Bilderberg chairman, Prince Bernhard of the Netherlands.

As we've seen, the CFR-Trilat-Bilderberg membership rolls were brimming with American officials and politicians eager to suck up to the power establishment. Even Richard Nixon, whose animus for the Eastern elite was famous, joined the CFR and later hired Rockefeller protégé Henry Kissinger. (Birchers haven't forgotten that President Nixon invoked the spooky phrase "new world order" during his trip to *Red* China.) Other U.S. presidents who were Insiders included Gerald Ford (CFR, Bilderberg), Jimmy Carter (CFR, Trilat), George Bush (CFR *board director*, Trilat), and even Bill Clinton (CFR, Trilat, *and* Bilderberg).

During the Carter era 284 CFR/Trilats held administration positions. Key Insiders included Vice President Walter Mondale, national security advisor Zbigniew Brzezinski (director of the Trilateral Commission), Secretary of State Cyrus Vance and CIA Director Stansfield Turner. By the end of Reagan's two terms, the number had risen to 313. Reaganite Insiders included secretaries of state Al Haig (a favorite candidate for Watergate's Deep Throat) and George Shultz (the tenth consecutive CFR alumnus to hold that job) and CIA Director William Casey.

Under Bush, "the conspiracy president," the number sky-rocketed to 382, including national security advisor Brent Scowcroft and the attorney general, Richard Thornburgh.

As for the Clinton administration, little has changed as far as CFR faces go. Secretary of State Warren Christopher, all five of his undersecretaries, and many of *their* underlings are CFR-ites. So are Clinton's national security adviser and CIA director, and so is his Republicrat aide, David Gergen.

Gergen is only one point of light in a constellation of media stars absorbed into the CFR. A partial list includes the late Walter Lippman (a CFR director in the 1930s), CIA propagandist/*Life* magazine publisher C. D. Jackson (who helped set up the Bilderberg Group), *New York Times*man Leslie Gelb (current CFR president), Dan Rather, Tom Brokaw, and Jim Lehrer, the non-Canadian half of the *MacNeil/Lehrer NewsHour*.

Though the CFR/Trilat connection runs deep into the blue veins of the Establishment, predictably its members scoff at the suggestion that they hold excessive influence over American "democracy" and world affairs. David Rockefeller once sniffed at what he called these "foolish attacks on false issues." With perhaps excessive modesty, he assured the skeptics that his Trilateral Commission is just "a group of concerned citizens interested in fostering greater understanding and cooperation among international allies."

Well, apparently all groups of concerned citizens are not created equal. As journalist Bill Moyers put it in a 1980 TV documentary: "David Rockefeller is the most conspicuous representative today of the ruling class, a multinational fraternity of men who shape the global economy and manage the flow of its capital. Rockefeller was born to it, and he has made the most of it. But what some critics see as a vast international conspiracy, he considers a circumstance of life and just another day's work."

If the New World Order isn't a blueprint for the "world super-state" of Bircher nightmares, it may simply mean a world more "orderly" for transnational big business. The implications are just as ominous, for although Trilats don't aim to raze Capitol Hill to make way for a U.N. high rise, they have made it clear that democracy often hampers their terribly important work. Not only have the Round Table progeny pushed for "limited," strongman "democracy" in third world countries, they have openly complained about the surfeit of liberty for the little people in this country.

A 1975 Trilateral Commission report concluded that the United States was plagued by an "excess of democracy," when "what is needed is a greater degree of moderation in democracy," to improve "governability." Trilat co-founder Brzezinski recommended a study on "Control Over Man's Development and Behavior" to devise "new means of social control," especially "in advanced societies."

In the coming New World Order, the natives apparently have yet to be civilized.

MAJOR SOURCES

Allen, Gary. *None Dare Call It Conspiracy*. Rossmoor, CA: Concord Press, 1971.

McManus, John F. *The Insiders: Architects of the New World Order*. Appleton, Wisconsin: John Birch Society, 1992.

Quigley, Carroll. *Tragedy and Hope: A History of the World in Our Time*. New York: MacMillan Company, 1966.

Sklar, Holly, ed. *Trilateralism: The Trilateral Commission and Elite Planning*. Boston: South End Press, 1980.

Wilgus, Neal. *The Illuminoids: Secret Societies and Political Paranoia*. Santa Fe, NM: Sun Publishing Company, 1978.

VIII

Tragedy and Trauma

35

This Means War

On the evening of December 6, 1941, Franklin Delano Roosevelt, the president of the United States, received a
message intercepted by the U.S. Navy. Sent from Tokyo to the
Japanese embassy in Washington, the message was encrypted in
the top-level Japanese "purple code." But that was no problem.
The Americans had cracked the code long before that.

It was imperative that the president see the message right
away because it revealed that the Japanese, under the heavy
pressure of Western economic sanctions, were terminating
relations with the United States. Roosevelt read the thirteen-
part transmission, looked up and announced, "This means
war."

He then did a very strange thing for a president in his
situation.

Nothing.

The Japanese secret declaration of war never reached the
people who needed to hear it the most—Admiral Husband E.
Kimmel, commander in chief of the United States Pacific Fleet
at Pearl Harbor, Hawaii, and the unit's commanding general,

Walter Short. Pearl Harbor, it was common military knowledge, was where the Japanese would strike. If they struck.

At dawn the next morning a Japanese squadron bombed Pearl Harbor and the surprise attack was just that, a complete surprise. At least to Kimmel and Short and the 4,575 American servicemen who died.

It may not have been such a surprise to Generals George C. Marshall and Leonard T. Gerow and Admirals Harold R. Stark and Richmond Kelly Turner. They were the military's top brass in Washington and the only officers authorized to forward such sensitive intelligence to outlying commanders. But the decoded war declaration did not reach Kimmel and Short until the morning, with the attack well underway off in the Pacific.

Marshall and Stark, supreme commanders of the U.S. Army and Navy respectively, later testified that the message was not forwarded to Kimmel and Short because the Hawaiian commaders had received so many intercepted Japanese messages that another one would simply confuse them.

Internal army and navy inquiries in 1944 held Stark and Marshall derelict of duty for keeping the Hawaiian commanders in the dark. But the military buried those findings. As far as the public knew, the final truth was uncovered by the Roberts Commission, headed by Justice Owen Roberts of the Supreme Court, and convened eleven days after the attack. Like another investigative commission headed by a Supreme Court justice on a different topic more than twenty years later, the Roberts Commission appeared to have identified its culprits in advance and gerrymandered its inquiries to make the suspects appear guilty. The scapegoats were Kimmel and Short, who were both publicly crucified, forced to retire, and denied the open hearings they desired. One of the Roberts Commission panelists, Admiral William Standley, would call Roberts's performance "crooked as a snake."

There were eight investigations of Pearl Harbor altogether. The most spectacular was a joint House-Senate probe that reiterated the Roberts Commission findings. At those hearings,

Marshall and Stark testified, incredibly, that they could not remember where they were the night the war declaration came in. But a close friend of Frank Knox, the secretary of the Navy, later revealed that Knox, Stark, and Marshall spent most of that night in the White House with Roosevelt awaiting the bombing of Pearl Harbor and the chance for America to join World War II.

A widespread coverup ensued. A few days after Pearl Harbor, reports historian John Toland, Marshall told his top officers, "Gentlemen, this goes to the grave with us." General Short once considered Marshall his friend, only to learn that the chief of staff was the agent of his frame-up. Short once remarked that he pitied his former pal because Marshall was the only general who wouldn't be able to write an autobiography.

There were multiple warnings of the Pearl Harbor attack concealed from the commanders at Pearl Harbor. The Winds Code was perhaps the most shocking. That was an earlier transmission, in a fake weather report broadcast on a Japanese short-wave station, of the words *higashi no kaze ame.* Which means, "east wind, rain." The Americans already knew that this was the Japanese code for war with the United States. The response of top U.S. military officials? To deny that the "winds" message existed and to attempt to destroy all records of its reception. But it did exist. And it was received.

Completely apart from the cloak and dagger of cryptography, the Australian intelligence service, three days before the attack, spotted the Japanese fleet of aircraft carriers heading for Hawaii. A warning went to Washington where it was dismissed by Roosevelt as a politically motivated rumor circulated by Republicans.

A British double agent, Dusko Popov, who siphoned information from Germany, learned of the Japanese intentions and desperately tried to warn Washington, to no avail. And there were others.

Why would Roosevelt and the nation's top military commanders sacrifice the U.S. Pacific Fleet, not to mention thousands of servicemen—an act that could justifiably be deemed treason? They had concluded long before Pearl Harbor that war against the Axis powers was a necessity. The American public disagreed. A strike against American territory would surely bring the public around.

"This was the president's problem," wrote Rear Admiral Robert A. Theobald who commanded Pearl Harbor's destroyers, "and his solution was based upon the simple fact that, while it takes two to make a fight, either one may start it."

"A small group of men, revered and held to be most honorable by millions," wrote Toland, "had convinced themselves that it was necessary to act dishonorably for the good of their nation—and incited the war that Japan had tried to avoid."

MAJOR SOURCES

Theobald, Robert A. *The Final Secret of Pearl Harbor.* Old Greenwich, CT: Devin-Adair, 1954.
Toland, John. *Infamy: Pearl Harbor and Its Aftermath.* New York: Doubleday, 1982.

36

The Lost Boys

The flag adopted by America's POW/MIA movement tells a provocative story: A downcast soldier languishes behind barbed wire, while an armed sentry looms in a distant watchtower. This mournful image, superimposed against a field of black, flies at veterans centers and lodges nationwide like an article of faith—but perhaps also as a symbol of *lost faith*.

This is because the banner also conveys another message: American prisoners of war were abandoned in Vietnam, "betrayed" by their own government, which for dark reasons continues to suppress evidence that live POWs remain behind enemy lines. The only thing missing from the flag is a cackling U.S. bureaucrat.

In recent years a ground swell of opinion has borne the theory of the "lost boys" out of America's conservative heartland and into the mainstream. But skeptics disparage the "MIA myth" as a mass pathology, a Rambo fantasy, a symptom of the jingoistic "Vietnam syndrome." Is it?

In the debit column, no living POWs have emerged from the jungles of Vietnam, Laos, or Cambodia in recent years to tell

harrowing tales of abandonment. The "evidence" that vaults
periodically into newspaper headlines is usually countered by
government "experts": The photograph of three aging MIAs? A
not-so-clever forgery. The Soviet "smoking gun" document
referring to some seven hundred American prisoners never
released by Hanoi? Probably a tally of "allied" POWs from
Asia, not red-blooded American boys.

But the debunkers tend to ignore an inventory of bizarre,
hard-to-explain details, incidents, and reports that do, in fact,
make an interesting case for "conspiracy."

Kiss the Boys Goodbye, the 1990 book by former *60 Minutes*
producer Monika Jensen-Stevenson and her husband, espionage
author William Stevenson, makes one of the more persuasive
arguments for the "lost boys" theory. "Hundreds of refugees
reported seeing Americans in all parts of Communist Southeast
Asia in the early postwar years," long after the government
announced that all American POWs had been released, they
write. Reportedly, American soldiers and intelligence officers
on covert missions in Indochina continued to report sightings of
U.S. prisoners in Vietnam and Laos throughout the 1980s. The
former head of the Pentagon's Defense Intelligence Agency
(DIA), General Eugene Tighe, claimed publicly that the secre-
tive DIA had intelligence to prove "there *are* live Americans
over there."

A key report came from a U.S. Marine private named Bobby
Garwood, who had been captured by the Viet Cong at China
Beach in 1965. Fourteen years later—at a time when there were
supposedly no American POWs in Indochina—the Vietnamese
government set Garwood free. Though Garwood claimed that
other live POWs remained in Vietnam, the military rather
hastily branded him a traitor, effectively discrediting his story.
(Years later, the government would quietly acknowledge it had
made a mistake in labeling Garwood an enemy quisling, but by
then his claim about live Americans was hardly timely news.)

How many POWs were wasting away in the jungle? Jerry
Mooney, a National Security Agency analyst who had

monitored American prisoners throughout Indochina up until 1976 (three years after President Nixon assured Americans that all POWs had been accounted for), claimed that he had tracked more than three hundred.

Douglas Applegate, a congressman from Ohio, announced in 1984 that he had obtained "very disturbing" CIA documents listing hundreds of "reports of live American prisoners in Laos." The DIA interceded and had Applegate's words stricken from the *Congressional Record*, supposedly because he had referred to satellite photographs showing Caucasian inmates—a breach of technological secrecy.

When POW/MIA families began requesting declassified documents, the military moved, strangely, to reclassify them. The official word remained that "there is no evidence to indicate that any live American POWs from the Indochina conflict remain alive."

Privately, though, the Reagan administration apparently thought otherwise. Reagan's National Security Counsel point man on POW families, Richard Childress, warned Jensen-Stevenson that her pursuit of the story "could jeopardize the lives of the prisoners still there." Huh? There weren't any POWs, yet Jensen-Stevenson was nevertheless endangering their "lives"?

President Reagan, himself, contradicted the official line (hardly a surprise, that), acknowledging in a letter to the wife of an MIA that his administration had planned a military rescue mission in 1981.

In 1986, the *Wall Street Journal* added a few details: That rescue mission had evolved after Hanoi offered to sell fifty-seven *live* American hostages to the United States for a price of $4 million. Reportedly, the Reaganites rebuffed the offer, unwilling to pay a ransom for hostages—if true, an ironic reluctance given the later Iran-Contra arms-for-hostage deals. According to the *Wall Street Journal*, Richard Allen, Reagan's crafty national security advisor, proposed an alternative: a Rambo-like rescue mission into Laos with the goal of retrieving live American prisoners. For some unexplained reason, though, the raid had failed.

According to a group of veterans who confronted Allen after the news story appeared, the Reagan aide said: "I know they're there, and it is my firm belief that live POWs are still being held in Indochina." By the time the mission got underway, Allen explained to the angry vets, the prisoners had all been moved.

But an assemblage of commandos and intelligence vets told a slightly different story. Yes, there had been a government-approved reconnaissance and rescue operation in 1981, but it had been scuttled—or sabotaged—at the last minute. Enter Colonel James "Bo" Gritz, the real-life Green Beret Rambo who inspired Sylvester Stallone's commie-crushing action hero. (One difference between fiction and reality was that Stallone wasn't known for making anti-Semitic remarks.) A super-stealth group within the Pentagon known as the Intelligence Support Activity (ISA) had indeed sponsored a Gritz mission to Laos, which was to supplement a larger Delta Forces raid. Before the Delta commandos got off the ground, though, the Pentagon shut the operation down. Then it shut off Gritz's mission.

But the cigar-chomping Green Beret had a plan B, and he launched his operation Velvet Glove, anyway. But as Gritz and his Special Forces troopers later told it, they arrived in Laos to discover their cover had deliberately been blown by the Voice of America, the U.S. government's propaganda broadcast. By the time Gritz trudged back to civilization, the international press was calling him a rampaging renegade. That's how it appeared, but it just wasn't true. The ISA continued to insist that its support of Gritz had been sanctioned by the Pentagon's joint chiefs; whatever else it was, Velvet Glove was not a "rogue" mission.

Given such wildly mixed signals from public officials, the conspiracy theorists were hardly unjustified when they began getting "paranoid." Wasn't the government acting mighty hinky, privately claiming there were live POWs in Indochina but publicly doing all it could to discredit anyone who tried to prove it? It seemed that every respected military official, competent government employee, straight-laced soldier, or inquiring reporter who broke ranks with the official line on POWs instantly became persona non grata, or worse, was dismissed as a "true believer," a crank, a nut, paranoid, even unpatriotic.

General Tighe, the former DIA chief whose internal Pentagon commission concluded that American POWs were being held in secret camps throughout Indochina, was publicly excoriated by Pentagon brass and privately maligned as maybe having a screw loose.

Journalists who stubbornly stuck with the story were getting threatening phone calls and being harrassed rather unsubtlely. Jensen-Stevensen's briefcase and notes were snatched in an airport; a BBC reporter was targeted by DEA officers who told him that somebody wanted to send him a warning; a Montana journalist looking into the suspicious death of an intelligence veteran involved in a POW mission received a scary phone call from a man warning her, "It's not in your best interests to investigate. Take it how you like. Do you need me to come out there and persuade you?"

The reaction to anyone claiming there were live POWs was so vitriolic, so over the top, it naturally inflated small suspicions to Brobdingnagian proportions.

Which brings us to that most famous of POW hunters, Texas billionaire and superpatriot H. Ross Perot. Perot had been hunting for POWs since the late Nixon epoch. In 1973, he financed a mercenary raid into the jungles of Laos and Vietnam, which failed despite the support of straight-shooting cowboys John Wayne and Clint Eastwood. According to the *New Republic*, Perot tried—and failed—again in 1983, this time with Bo Gritz wearing the fatigues. (Other reports have it that the ISA was in on the Perot-Gritz mission, which wouldn't be all that surprising considering Perot's eager-beaver support of Ollie North schemes during the early eighties, but Perot has denied these charges.)

Apparently in appreciation of his open billfold, Ross was given a spot on Reagan's Foreign Intelligence Advisory Board. There he could look into the POW issue as a "special investigator," and he later claimed that the government had current evidence of live POWs.

At some point, for whatever reason, the Reaganites got less cooperative with pesky Perot. The NSC snubbed his offer of "a hundred million dollars to buy back prisoners from Hanoi," and the White House also rejected his proposal to broker a deal with Hanoi. Perot jetted to Hanoi anyway and haggled with Vietnamese apparatchiks. "They said something to me that went so much to the heart of the matter," Perot told Jensen-Stevenson. "It confirmed...*the men are there.*" But the official U.S. delegation that followed Perot's opening, including POW point man Richard Childress, steered the negotiations to the subject of remains—teeth, bones, uniforms—sidestepping the issue of live prisoners, according to other delegates. Perot's advance work, apparently, was for naught.

But the last straw for gung-ho Perot seems to have been Vice President George Bush. For some reason, Perot had the odd impression that good ol' George, the former CIA director, was "a Boy Scout" who would jump at the chance to help an ol' pal save the Pee-Oh-Dubble-yuh's. But, if Perot is to be believed, Bush turned out to be the immovable object to H. Ross's irresistible force.

Clearly, Perot's falling out with his idol Bush over the POW issue set the stage for the billionaire's 1992 crusade for the presidency, which was as much Perot's personal vendetta against Bush as a strike against the tassel-loafered conspirators.

It all fell apart thus: Perot had gone to the thrifty and trustworthy Bush to spill the beans about the real stumbling block in the POW quest. "Well, George," Perot had explained, "I go looking for prisoners, but I spend all my time discovering the government has been moving drugs around the world and is involved in illegal arms deals...I can't get at the prisoners because of the corrupton among our own covert people."

That was the breaking point, Perot claimed; thereafter, he was "instructed to cease and desist" in his official capacity as a presidential investigator. But according to the *New Republic*, what really steamed Perot was that Bush had ignored the billionaire when he fingered the man he believed to be gumming up the POW search, Richard Armitage, who at the time was an assistant secretary of defense in charge of POW issues. Taking a leaf from the liberal Christic Institute (see page 310), Perot reportedly thought that Armitage was near the center of an old-boy network of intelligence vets who had dealt drugs, run guns, and left POWs out in the cold, among other conspiracies. (A federal judge subsequently threw out the Christics' lawsuit, which named Armitage and others, as frivolous.)

Drugs and illegal arms deals tied to the POW coverup? Was Perot off his King-size rocker?

Well, maybe. But that was precisely the underground story being traded by an assortment of clandestine operatives and government veterans. The sordid tale supposedly began during the Nixon administration.

"We negotiated the prisoners away," submitted Roger Shields, the Pentagon man responsible for POW/MIA affairs between 1971 and 1976. Shields wouldn't elaborate, but he told Jensen-Stevenson to ask Henry Kissinger, Nixon's secretary of state, why there had been such haste at the time of the 1973 Vietnam peace accord to remove the names of missing American soldiers and pilots from the official POW/MIA roster. Kissinger has maintained that no live Americans were left behind.

But the figures never quite added up. The answer to the puzzle, Perot and others believed, lay not in Vietnam, but in neighboring Laos, where the CIA and the U.S. military had fought a secret war against the communists for close to three decades. Although the North Vietnamese released 591 Americans in early 1973, they continued to refer to prisoners in Laos not covered under the Kissinger negotiations. On the eve of the accords, Pentagon books listed 317 men missing in Laos, men never accounted for, dead or alive.

"We can't make use of what we know about those lost in Laos because the whole war there was secret," claimed one of the sources, Nick Rowe, an army colonel and veteran of special intelligence operations.

The CIA's secret wars in Laos and Cambodia are a matter of record. Rowe, Gritz, and other military insiders described the secret wars, which, they claimed, had rendered the missing expendable:

- The illegal covert wars in Indochina continued even after the official end of the Vietnam conflict—and well into the late 1980s. Many of the missing in Laos disappeared during clandestine missions deployed *after* the 1973 armistice with Vietnam. Ergo, these secret soldiers drafted from the rank and file of the regular military were subject to "plausible deniability."

- The CIA helped fund its covert wars in Southeast Asia via sales of arms and narcotics, the latter produced by Laotian warlords in the opium fields of the Golden Triangle region, America's largest supplier of contraband heroin. (The CIA's involvement in Southeast Asian drug running has been well-documented through the years.) According to Ed Wilson, the CIA operative convicted for selling explosives and arms to Libya, those snooping around the MIA issue were bound to discover all sorts of embarrassing projects: heroin running; offshore banks set up by the CIA to fund "privatized" covert ops, à la Ollie North's Iran-Contra network; the arming of anticommunist guerrillas; etc.

- The government's official POW/MIA efforts—with offices and operatives on the ground in Southeast Asia—may have been used as a cover for continuing the secret wars and running the drugs that funded proxy armies. This might explain why several military rescue efforts planned during the early 1980s were scuttled before they got off the ground.

Bolstering the charges of secret warfare was the government of Thailand, which claimed it was used as a staging area for CIA-military covert training of guerrillas.

In early 1993, Senator John Kerry's select committee on POW/MIA affairs wrapped up its year-long investigation into the fate of American POWs. Their inconclusive conclusion—that they found no evidence of living POWs, but also that they couldn't disprove the theory—was embraced by the debunkers as the final nail in the coffin of the conspiracy theorists.

However, the Senate committee did produce evidence that supported part of what the conspiratologists had been saying all along: that the Reaganites, in their zeal to "roll back" global communism, used the POW/MIA issue as a cover for funding a covert guerrilla war in Laos. What's more, Senate investigators suspected that a private support group of POW families—backed by, yes, Childress and other Reagan officials—had raised private cash for an illegal war in Laos under the guise of funding POW reconnaissance missions.

If Perot and company weren't 100 percent on the mark in their suspicions, at least they were on the right track. Which begs an alternative conspiracy theory, the one favored by lefties who aren't inclined to sentimentalize heartland ideals like nationalism, valor, and the fallen warrior. To wit: *There never were any surviving POWs.* The Reagan-Bush administrations foisted the myth of the "lost boys" on its own constituency, the patriotic right, as a cynical hoax intended to rally cash and cover for yet another secret jungle war.

If you buy this theory, the sources claiming knowledge of live POWs fall into two categories: outright frauds spreading disinformation and deluded but well-intentioned believers. Certainly, there were some troubling super-sources navigating the POW/MIA waters, including Scott Barnes, a self-professed CIA contract agent who claimed to have restaged the aborted Bo Gritz mission. According to Barnes, he and his partner found American POWs in Laos—and were ordered to "liquidate the merchandise," a command they refused. Barnes's partner had been killed as a result of such insubordination, but, as luck would have it, Barnes lived to tell the tale.

A semiomniscent source peddling a number of conspiratorial tales, Barnes has been denounced as a charlatan and self-promoting scam artist. But he has bent the ears of many a POW tracker, including the cabal-sniffing Perot. Which, interestingly, may have helped undo the down-home billionaire's bid for the presidency. For Barnes was the guy who persuaded Perot he was the target of a Republican dirty-tricks campaign, a news flash that sealed Perot's image as a paranoid neurotic convinced that GOP malefactors were out to airbrush lesbians into photographs of his daughter. After Perot's self-destructing performance on *60 Minutes*, voters seemed to decide that maybe he wasn't the guy you'd like to think of as having his finger on "the button." Perot's credibility implosion certainly turned out to be good news for Bush, which makes Barnes a very interesting character indeed. It gives one cause to wonder who benefited from Barnes's hard-to-believe tales of POW double crosses.

Which isn't to say that all evidence on the POW front has been an outright swindle, as the lefties and centrists who disparage the lost boys theory like to claim. When *Kiss the Boys Goodbye* coauthor William Stevenson called on Vietnamese officials to ask about prisoners, they seemed blunt enough. "We had thousands of Americans after the release of 1973," offered the former chief of the secret police. "Until 1985, I knew about groups of Americans in several locations."

Submitted Truong Chinh, at one time the gray eminence behind Ho Chi Minh: "It is possible we shall embarrass the American government some day by sending some back."

It's been said that the discovery of aging American soldiers in Vietnam would prove embarrassing to both countries as they move toward normalizing relations. As the former Vietnamese chief of secret police put it to Stevenson, "It would help nobody today, not us nor the Americans, to let go of captured soldiers now. They're better dead."

Even if the theory of the lost boys is true, more than twenty years have elapsed since the (official) U.S. pullout from the Vietnam War. Even if the government was lying ten years ago when it said there are no living Americans POWs in Southeast Asia, when it says the same thing today it just might be telling the truth.

MAJOR SOURCES

Blumenthal, Sidney. "Perotnoia: The Strange Journey of Ross Perot." *New Republic*, 15 June 1992.

Jensen-Stevenson, Monika, and William Stevenson. *Kiss the Boys Goodbye: How the United States Betrayed Its Own POWs in Vietnam*. New York: Dutton, 1990.

Parfrey, Adam. "Bo Gritz Interrogated." *Flatland*, no. 10, 1993.

"Evidence Hints at Reagan Bid to Aid Laos Rebels." *San Jose Mercury News*, 24 January 1993.

37

The Evil Empire Strikes Back

When the Cold War's Reagan phase was in its most fevered stage, a Soviet fighter pilot made a badly timed boo-boo. He uncorked a missile at a Korean Air 747 and sent the plane with its 269 passengers swirling into the icy blackness of the Japan Sea.

The airliner had strayed 365 miles off course and was flying over not only Soviet territory, but some of the USSR's most sensitive military installations. It was the early morning of September 1, 1983.

In the Soviet Union, Yuri Andropov, chief of the feared and loathed KGB, was now premier. Back home, Ronald Reagan's "evil empire" rhetoric still rang fresh in American ears and the MX missile awaited congressional approval. Funding for the new missile system appeared in trouble, but after the KAL shootdown it sailed through as smoothly as an airliner through the calm Asian morning.

Within hours of the tragedy, Reagan, Secretary of State

George Shultz, and U.N. Ambassador/anticommunist poster lady Jeanne Kirkpatrick made public presentations defining the U.S. version of the tragedy: In cold blood the Soviets had fired on a civilian craft with no attempt to warn the plane's crew. If right-thinking Americans, at that point, needed further confirmation of the Soviet commies' callous contempt for human life, there it was.

As always occurs when the government manufactures an instant orthodoxy, a dissenting view also took shape. According to this theory, KAL 007 was the Reagan cold war's *Lusitania:* a civilian vessel sent on a provocative military mission—deliberately placed in harm's way and its inevitable destruction justified by the government's own aggressive intentions.

In other words, a provocation.

There was precedent. Seymour Hersh, one of the most honest and penetrating investigative reporters on intelligence and military affairs, details a lengthy history of U.S. sorties into Soviet space for purposes of testing Soviet defenses. As both Hersh and conspiracy proponent R. W. Johnson (an Oxford University Fellow in Politics) report, for a Korean airliner to wander into Soviet space for mysterious reasons was far from unprecedented. One had been shot down five years earlier.

And there was a motive for KAL to participate. Korean Air, whose financial survival depended largely on special favors from the U.S. government regarding routes and landing rights, was always willing to play ball with Uncle Sam. According to torts lawyer Melvin Belli, who represented relatives of some of the passengers, 007's pilot said to his wife shortly before departing, "Never again. This is the last trip. It's too dangerous."

A strange remark for an experienced airline pilot to make about a routine jaunt from Alaska to Seoul (a Korean Air 747 still takes the same route every day, though the flight is no longer numbered 007).

There is no question that the U.S. government conspired, as it were, to publicize a story that made the Soviets look as fiendish as possible—facts be damned. Even if KAL 007 was deliberately off course, nothing justifies shooting down a civilian airliner (though the U.S. government had little problem five years later when an American warship shot down an Iranian airbus, but that's another conspiracy).

But if the United States put KAL 007 over the Soviet Union on purpose, then the Soviet action seems more like lethal incompetence than unmitigated evil. The United States itself must share blame for the violent death of its own citizens.

The only piece of information about the flight and fate of KAL 007 that seems certain is that a Soviet fighter did indeed shoot it down—despite some conspiracy theories that hold that the United States deliberately bombed the plane (Robert Cutler's self-published *Explo-007* argues that hypothesis). More than ten years after the attack, the most important question about flight 007 remains open: Why did the plane wander into the most dangerous area in the militarized atmosphere?

Was it an accident, as argued by Hersh and, several years later, in a *New Yorker* magazine article written by Murray Sayle? Or was the plane, as Johnson believes, on some sinister, secret, and ultimately catastrophic mission?

According to Johnson, KAL-007 was sent at the behest of the Reagan administration-run CIA to trigger Soviet defenses. This would allow the numerous U.S., NATO, and Japanese electronic surveillance posts monitoring the Far East, a patch of the globe dotted with the highest of high-tech electronic intelligence collection stations, to get a good look at the Big Red Machine in action.

Not all the vantage points were Earthbound. A surveillance satellite orbited over the Sea of Japan at the time of the shootdown and—weirdly—the space shuttle Challenger, which two years later met its own untimely end, also flew over the Japan Sea four times during KAL-007's trip.

For some reason, the Challenger's cargo, a 3.5-ton satellite, had been replaced at the last minute with a "dummy satellite" of the same considerable bulk. Johnson has no evidence about the "dummy," but he suggests that it was in fact some kind of military monitoring device.

The CIA behaved strangely after it heard about the downing. Already knowing that the plane was in Davy Jones's locker, the agency put out the story to relatives of the dead passengers that the flight had landed safely on the Soviet-held island of Sakhalin.

The most persuasive counterpoint to the provocation theory (it should be noted that Johnson was merely the most articulate and credible proponent of that theory; its popularity was wide, helped along by some rather shameless Soviet propaganda) came after the end of the Cold War with the former Soviet intelligence and military agencies suddenly displaying a refreshing candor.

In an attempt to lay the conspiracy theory to a final rest, Murray Sayle presented the "error" case in his December 13, 1993 *New Yorker* piece cover-tagged, "A Cold War Case Closed." Unlike Johnson and Hersh he wrote with the benefit of access to Soviet information.

According to Sayle's piece, the Soviets recovered the plane's "black box" flight recorder (which was actually, Sayle seems pleased to point out, bright orange). The Soviets had always denied finding the recorder, but in the light of Boris Yeltsin's new dawn, the recordings found their way into the public domain.

Of course, no one would claim that Yeltsin is above a little trickery, but Sayle did not investigate the authenticity of the tapes.

"The voices can only be the real thing," he announces, as if pounding a gavel. He pursues the possibility of forgery no further.

That caveat dismissed, Sayle reports that the tapes reveal a sleepy, inattentive flight crew mumbling about the dinner menu and the pros and cons of exchanging currency at the airport. Not the stuff of Frederick Forsyth novels.

But no mild-mannered *New Yorker* reporter is qualified to interpret the contents of a flight recorder, so Sayle's "case closed" relies primarily on the conclusions of a French investigating unit working for the International Civil Aviation Organization (ICAO).

The ICAO team decided that the whole tragic problem stemmed from the captain's failure to engage the plane's inertial navigation system (INS), drowsily permitting the 747's "suicidally unreliable" magnetic compass to guide the plane.

That error is not unknown even to experienced pilots. But it is quite uncommon, despite Sayle's misleadingly phrased assertion that of "more than a hundred airline navigation errors involving the INS between September of 1978 and May of 1983" almost twelve percent were due to letting the compass rather than the INS itself guide the aircraft.

In other words, in a five-year period during which there were hundreds of thousands of commercial airline flights, the error apparently committed by the KAL 007 crew occurred approximately twelve times.

In his book *Shootdown*, Johnson dealt with the "drowsiness" issue long before the black-box tapes became available. He contends that the crew would have had to miss more than one blinking light to allow the plane to wander more than three hundred miles off course.

The pilots must have been feeling admirably casual given their flight path through perhaps the world's most heavily surveilled region. To allow their mistake to go uncorrected, they had to disregard their craft's ground-mapping radar, which would have revealed that the plane was flying over solid land, not sea as laid out in the flight plan.

The airliner, according to Johnson, made a sharp turn as Soviet fighters approached, presumably caused by the coincidental impulse of this highly improvisational flight crew to reprogram its computer at that moment.

If they knew they were in danger the flight crew would have reported this fact to its ground controllers. It didn't. Not then, or even after it was hit and began swirling downward toward the water. Not only did the pilot never say "Whoops!" he didn't even say "Uh, oh."

Johnson also notes one last piece of bizarre evidence: a fuzzy tape analyzed as the voice of KAL's first officer talking to Tokyo in the last seconds of KAL 007's existence.

The contents of the tape are barely intelligible and still uncertain, but some analysts think they hear the officer asking not for an air traffic controller but for a "director," as in "mission director." Only a military or intelligence flight requires a "director." The voice on the tape also refers to "bogies," a military term for enemy aircraft.

But scariest of all are the last words on the tape, according to analysts, recorded thirty-eight seconds after missile impact and delivered by the first officer, or Johnson suggests, someone in a nearby plane observing the confrontation, with unnerving calm.

"Gonna be a bloodbath," the level voice says. "You bet."

MAJOR SOURCES

Hersh, Seymour. *The Target Is Destroyed.* New York: Random House, 1986.
Johnson, R. W. *Shootdown.* New York: Viking Penguin, 1987.

38

Pan Am Flight 103

Four days before Christmas 1988, a Pan Am 747 was ripped from the sky by a powerful wad of plastic explosives. Perhaps it was happenstance that five CIA agents were among the 259 human beings who died in the crash. Perhaps it meant nothing that another squad of CIA agents showed up in Lockerbie, Scotland, a few hours after the aircraft splattered the country village with gruesome debris.

That the CIA agents on the crash scene, some posing as Pan Am employees, walked away with a mysterious briefcase seems somewhat more significant. It belonged to one of their downed men. By confiscating the case, they interrupted the sacrosanct "chain of evidence," imperiling prospective prosecutions. The half-million dollars found by two Scottish farmboys seems noteworthy as well. Detectives surmised that the cash also belonged to the deceased CIA team.

The ill-fated spies had traveled from Beirut. Their mission, investigators believe, was to locate American hostages held there by Islamic fundamentalist kidnappers. Pan Am flight 103, had it followed the bombers' schedule, would have exploded over the Atlantic ocean, but the bomb went off too soon. Wreckage, bodies, and passengers' personal effects all landed on the ground and meticulous Scottish investigators recovered everything except the briefcase. Among the fallout were two cryptic documents, both property of the CIA.

One was an intricate drawing of the interior of a Beirut building. Two crosses marked the map. The CIA agents had located two hostages. They may have intended to negotiate for the hostages' release, using the $500,000 to purchase information. Or, it is possible, the team headed by Charles McKee, an army major, was doing advance work for a rescue raid.

The other document was a Christmas card with a message either in intelligence cant or some kind of code. Investigators deduced the meaning of the message. It was addressed to one of the CIA agents and said that whatever they were planning would happen on March 11, 1989.

The bomb cost not only 270 lives (including the eleven Lockerbie dwellers who perished on the ground), but may have cost at least some of the hostages their immediate freedom. It undoubtedly impeded U.S. intelligence efforts in the Middle East. Recall that earlier, Beirut CIA station chief William Buckley had been grabbed, sent to Iran, and tortured to death in interrogation. Iran was the first suspect in the bombing of 103.

The CIA presence was publicly reported, though not widely known. A March 1990 *New York Times Magazine* excerpt from the book *The Fall of Pan Am 103* failed to mention the CIA officers, though the book itself goes into detail about who they were and why they were there. The *Times* version blamed the disaster on "bungling" German police.

Most media reports on the Pan Am 103 bombing endorsed the stereotype of irrational terrorists motivated by revenge. That there may have been a strategic and, by the warped logic of clandestine warfare, "rational" reason to bomb the plane— beyond retaliation for the shootdown of an Iranian airbus or the bombing of Tripoli (depending on who's getting blamed that day, the Iranians or the Libyans)—is not generally discussed. Admitting a motive (other than inscrutable fanaticism) for such a monstrous crime implies that the target of the crime, the United States, was involved in skullduggery of its own.

Far more incendiary were the conclusions of a private investigator, self-described former Israeli intelligence agent Juval Aviv. His New York firm, Interfor, conducted an investigation for Pan Am's insurance company. The Interfor report contains the grimmest conspiracy allegations in the Lockerbie case.

For two years the Interfor report circulated hand to hand in fax/Xerox form on the conspiracy circuit. The report went largely ignored by major news organizations. Then *Time* magazine suddenly discovered it and set off a bitter and highly personal internecine journalistic confrontation—all ignited by the following tale of intrigue, as told by Interfor:

A separate CIA team, stationed in Frankfurt and referred to as CIA-1 by Interfor, was also trying to free the hostages, Aviv reported. Because CIA-1 was an unauthorized "off the shelf" covert operation controlled from Washington, not from CIA headquarters in Langley, Virginia, it was at cross-purposes with the McKee team. The unnamed operatives hooked up with Monzar Al-Kassar, a Syrian arms and drug merchant, brother-in-law to Syria's intelligence chief (Syrian intelligence is a major terrorism sponsor) and paramour of Syrian fascist despot Hafez Al-Assad's niece. Not surprisingly, Al-Kassar was also deeply into terrorism, the politically correct thing to do for Syrian arms runners.

Al-Kassar, according to Interfor, assisted the French government in freeing French hostages. If he'd do the same for them, CIA-1 offered Al-Kassar, they'd protect his drug-smuggling route, which they had had under surveillance for some time.

"Al-Kassar agreed to the deal," says Aviv's report, "but continued his terrorism activities and told his cohorts that their smuggling through Pan Am/Frankfurt at least was now protected and safe to the U.S."

At the same time, Al-Kassar, who'd once been hired by Iran-

Contra conspirators Richard Secord and Albert Hakim to ship weapons to the Nicaraguan Contras, helped the Frankfurt-based CIA group by shipping weapons to Iran. The Americans hoped, once again tragicomically, to trade arms for hostages. According to Interfor, the drug-and-gun runner kept arms flowing to the Contras as well. In an effort to keep his American patrons happy, he even financed some of the Contra shipments with his own drug profits. "CIA-1 gave Al-Kassar a free hand," wrote Aviv.

Because CIA-1 was an unofficial operation run out of Washington, dealing arms for hostages and striking bargains with drug smugglers, comparisons to the Iran-Contra "enterprise" managed by Oliver North are inevitable. CIA-1 operated in 1988, when North was long since fired and CIA Director William Casey, the father of Iran-Contra, was dead from a brain tumor. Neither, then, could have been CIA-1's "control."

So who was? Much of Iran-Contra was coordinated, it now appears, from Vice President George Bush's office. Could former CIA chief Bush or his underlings be the "control" for CIA-1? Interfor doesn't touch that subject.

While CIA-1 was messing around with terrorists and heroin merchants, the official CIA and the State Department, blissfully unaware of its off-the-shelf counterpart's activities, sent the McKee team to Beirut. According to Aviv, their mission was, in fact, reconnaissance for a rescue mission. They found and photographed buildings where the hostages were incarcerated.

"After some time, the special team (McKee) learned of Al-Kassar and started investigating him," Aviv reported. "They also realized some CIA unit was protecting his drug smuggling into the U.S. via Frankfurt airport.... They had reported back to Langley the facts and names, and reported their film of the hostage locations. CIA did nothing. No reply."

While under surveillance, Al-Kassar and his associates in Syrian intelligence were surveilling the McKee team right back. When McKee and his cohorts became "frustrated and angry and made plans to return to the U.S.," Al-Kassar was watching.

He knew that the agents booked themselves a connecting flight in London: Pan Am flight 103, originating in Frankfurt. A week before that plane went down, Al-Kassar told CIA-1 of his problem, ratting out the McKee team, travel schedule and all.

All during this period, for political reasons of their own, Al-Kassar's terrorist overlords were plotting to bomb an American plane. They'd originally selected American Airlines as the victim. The target soon changed.

Warnings flowed in from every direction. German intelligence, the Mossad, and CIA-1 got word of a bomb attack in the making. No one did anything about it. The McKee team was in the dark and way out in the cold. Al-Kassar's associates slipped a compact "Semtex" device onto Pan Am 103, under cover of Al-Kassar's CIA-secured drug route. A German agent assigned to watch the route noticed that the drug suitcase was of a different make than usual. This agent heard the warnings. He knew right away that he wasn't eyeing dope, but a bomb.

The agent alerted CIA-1 to the bomb. CIA-1 called its Washington control. Control's reply: "Don't worry about it, don't stop it, let it go."

After its stopover in London, where it picked up a group of Syracuse University students returning home from a semester abroad, various American tourists, and the five CIA agents who knew where the hostages were held, the 747, nicknamed Maid of the Seas, exploded in mid-air.

The Interfor report first surfaced courtesy of James Traficant, an eccentric Ohio congressman with a populist's nose for conspiracies. He reportedly got it from Victor Marchetti, former aide to longtime CIA director Richard Helms. Marchetti, though his whistleblowing book *The CIA and the Cult of Intelligence* is now a classic, works for the ultra-right-wing Liberty Lobby these days and therefore has credibility problems.

Maybe, then, the Interfor report received scant publicity due to the questionable leanings of its leakers. More likely, the scandalous nature of its allegations are to blame. Much of the report gibes with public reality: the ignored warnings, for instance, and the botched raid by German police on a bomb-making enclave in October 1988. If properly carried out, that raid might have preempted the bombing.

The CIA-complicity charges erupted in April 1992. *Time* ran a rather lurid cover story, "Why Did They Die?" which conflated the Interfor allegations with additional details apparently from a dubious source named Lester Coleman. The story had a number of faults. The most glaring was its misidentification of a Christian Broadcasting Network cameraman (with photo!) as the traitorous CIA agent who sold out the McKee team.

Predictably, the story drew a torrent of attacks, particularly from Christopher Byron who wrote two major debunking pieces for *New York* magazine and from CNN correspondent Steven Emerson (in the *Washington Journalism Review*), co-author of his own book on Pan Am 103.

In his book, *The Fall of Pan Am 103*, Emerson dismisses the Interfor report as a "spitball," a hodgepodge of fact and unfounded speculation worthless as intelligence. The report had been echoed briefly on network news long before the *Time* story. On the day before Halloween 1990, NBC News reported that terrorists had infiltrated a Drug Enforcement Administration undercover operation to plant the Pan Am 103 bomb. Substitute *CIA* for *DEA* and the story mirrored the Interfor account. (Interfor did note that CIA-1 was working with the DEA.) The story was picked up by major dailies, including the *New York Times*, then quickly "investigated" and denied by the DEA.

In his attack on the *Time* piece—which followed Byron's closely—Emerson charged that *Time* "ignored evidence that contradicted its story." Both Emerson and Byron found some sizable holes in the *Time* story—though both spent an inordinate amount of ink on ad hominem attacks against Aviv and Coleman. They also made much of the fact that *Time*'s story appeared one week before a lawsuit against Pan Am was scheduled to go to trial.

Part of the problem was that *Time*'s story—perhaps thanks to the overzealous "hoaxster" Coleman—fleshed out the Interfor report with some questionable assertions that its critics were quick to seize upon.

Conspicuous by its absence from both Byron's and Emerson's articles was any mention of Monzar Al-Kassar. The omission was especially glaring because a key point of both attacks was the supposed mystery of how the bombers knew which flight the McKee team would take. According to the Interfor report, the information came from Al-Kassar.

Right about the time when Bush was recruiting Syria into the "allied coalition" against Iraq, the CIA shifted blame for the bombing from Syria to Libya, obviating more than two years of work by a multitude of investigators, from the Scottish police to ABC News, all of whom pointed to Ahmed Jibril and his patrons, Syria and Iran. Absolving Syria, of course, negates the Interfor scenario.

Late in 1991, the U.S. government indicted two Libyan intelligence agents for the bombing, and briefly, newspapers brimmed with bluster about the dire consequences to Libya if the pair weren't handed over. The legal tussle had not been resolved as of early 1994.

On the fifth anniversary of the bombing, in December 1993, the BBC aired a documentary, *Silence over Lockerbie.* The BBC debunked the CIA's Libya-damning evidence and, while not ruling out Libyan involvment, the documentary shifted blame back to the original suspects, Syria and Iran.

There are other conspiratorial tales to explain the mass murder aboard Pan Am flight 103. One, which briefly surfaced in the Italian press, puts the infamous, neofascist, quasi-Masonic P2 Lodge at the center of the conspiracy. But none are as detailed and internally consistent as the Interfor report. That doesn't mean Aviv got it right. It means only that the real story lies buried somewhere in the graveyard of geopolitics.

MAJOR SOURCES

Emerson, Steven, and Brian Duffy. *The Fall of Pan Am 103*. New York: Putnam, 1990.

Johnston, David. *Lockerbie: The Tragedy of Flight 103*. New York: St. Martin's Press, 1989.

Pan American Insurance Investigator's Report (copy in authors' possession).

39

The Jonestown Massacre

On November 18, 1978, in a cleared-out patch of Guyanese jungle, the Reverend Jim Jones ordered the 913 members of his flock to kill themselves by drinking a cyanide potion, and they did.

The cultists were brainwashed by the megalomaniac Jones, who had named their jungle village after himself and held them as virtual slaves, if not living zombies. Jones himself was found dead. He'd shot himself in the head, or someone else had shot him. Square-jaw, jet black hair and sunglasses, looking like a secret service agent on antipsychotic drugs, Jones takes his place alongside Charles Manson in America's iconography of evil.

But was Jones really a lone madman as Americans are so often advised about their villains? Is it plausible that more than nine hundred people took their own lives willingly, simply because he told them to? Or is there another explanation?

Not long after the slaughter in Jonestown, whispers began, strange hints of human experiments in mind control, even genocide, and the lurking presence of the CIA. At the very least, these stories maintained, the U.S. government could have prevented the Jonestown massacre, but instead it did nothing.

At worst, Jonestown was a CIA-run concentration camp set up as a dry run for the secret government's attempt to reprogram the American psyche. There are suggestions of parallel "Jonestowns" and that the conspiracy did not end with the deaths in Guyana.

Jim Jones was born May 13, 1931, son of a Ku Klux Klansman in Lynn, Indiana. His mother, he claimed, was a Cherokee Indian. That has never been verified.

An unsupervised child, Jones became fascinated by church work at an early age. By 1963 he had his own congregation in Indianapolis: The People's Temple Full Gospel Church. It was an interracial congregation, something then unheard of in Indiana. Young Jim Jones crusaded tirelessly on behalf of blacks. He also suffered from mysterious fainting spells, heeded advice from extraterrestrials, practiced faith healing, and experienced visions of nuclear holocaust.

Certain that Armageddon was imminent, that Indianapolis itself was to be the target of attack, Jones sought guidance. He found it in the January 1962 issue of *Esquire* magazine. An article in the occasionally ironic men's mag named the nine safest places in the world to get away from the stresses and anxieties of nuclear confrontation. One of those retreats was Brazil. Intimations of Jones's link to the CIA begin all the way back there.

According to an article in the *San Jose Mercury News*, Jones's neighbors in Belo Horizonte, Brazil (where he lived before moving to Rio De Janeiro), remembered his claim to be a retired navy man who "received a monthly payment from the U.S. government." They also remembered that Jones—who later claimed that he was forced to sell his services as a gigolo to support his family—"lived like a rich man."

"Some people here believed he was an agent for the American CIA," one neighbor reported.

Neighbors' recollections notwithstanding, Jones's biographer Tim Reiterman says that the Jones family "lived simply" in

Brazil, subsisting on rice and beans. When he returned to the United States, shortly after President John F. Kennedy was assassinated, Jones told his followers that he had spent his time in Brazil helping orphans. Eventually, he moved his church to Ukiah, California, then to San Francisco, where it became a fundraising force courted by local politicians.

Before Jones arrived in Brazil, he'd stopped in Georgetown, Guyana. Though his stop there was a quick one, he managed to garner some ink in the local media by publicly charging churches with spreading communism. According to Reiterman, it appeared a calculated attempt to "put himself on the record as an anticommunist."

Fifteen years later, he would tantalize his Jonestown flock with promises to move the People's Temple from Guyana to the Soviet Union. In a 1979 book, one former Jones devotee, Phil Kerns (whose mother and sister died at Jonestown), raises the possibility of a Soviet conspiracy behind Jonestown.

"Jones was a Marxist," Kerns wrote, "who had numerous contacts with officials of both the Cuban and Soviet governments." Among other suspicious facts, Kerns notes that shortly before the massacre two People's Temple members spirited $500,000 out of the cult's colony to the Soviet embassy.

Jones's deputies did meet frequently with Soviet officials—so frequently, in fact, that they became a running joke in Guyana's diplomatic circles. Jones told his followers that the CIA had "infiltrated" Jonestown.

Later, as we'll see, others raised the possibility that Jonestown *was* the CIA.

The temple's dalliance with the Soviets, however, is a wholly plausible point of contact between the cult and the Agency. Reiterman, a skeptic of the conspiracy theory, points out that "the CIA's presence in socialist Guyana...could be assumed." They certainly would have taken an interest in the temple's Soviet contacts.

Why exactly was Jones interested in the Soviets? He must have known that his professed dream of moving the temple to the U.S.S.R. was only that, a dream. He dropped it quickly in favor of mass suicide (a follower asked Jones, shortly before the suicides, if it weren't possible to forget the whole thing and escape to Russia; Jones said it wasn't). If the CIA had infiltrated the temple, or if the temple was, even in part, a CIA operation, then members' sojourns to the Soviet embassy would have had a more pragmatic purpose.

The CIA was first with news out of Jonestown, reporting the mass suicides. The suicides followed an attack, ordered by Jones, on a party led by Congressman Leo Ryan, in Guyana to investigate alleged human rights abuses at Jonestown. The gunmen struck at Port Kaituma airfield, as the Ryan party was preparing to depart. Ryan was assassinated in the attack. Four others died as well. Several more were shot, including Reiterman, then a reporter for the *San Francisco Examiner*. Among the wounded was U.S. embassy official Richard Dwyer.

Wounded, but ambulatory.

Did Dwyer stroll back to Jonestown after the airstrip assault? Was he there during the massacre? Reportedly, at one point on a tape recorded as the killings began, Jones's own voice commands, "Get Dwyer out of here!" Reiterman assumes that this was a "mistake" on Jones's part, that Dwyer was not actually there. If he was, however, the implications are chilling.

Dwyer was an agent of the CIA.

For his part, Dwyer neither confirms nor denies that he was a CIA agent, but he was identified in the 1968 edition of *Who's Who in the CIA*. A month after the massacre the *San Mateo Times*, a Bay Area newspaper (hometown paper of Leo Ryan), reported that "State Department officials acknowledge that a CIA agent was dispatched to Jonestown within minutes of the airstrip assault." Dwyer denied to the *Times* that he was there at the time. According to one report, Dwyer's next stop after Guyana was Grenada.

Nor was Dwyer necessarily the only intelligence-connected character in Guyana. The U.S. ambassador himself, John Burke, later went to work for the "intelligence community staff" of the

CIA. Richard McCoy, another embassy official, has acknowledged his counterintelligence work for the U.S. Air Force. The
socialist government of Guyana had piqued the interest of U.S.
intelligence for years. If there were covert operations going on
there, no one should be surprised.

Leo Ryan's aide Joseph Holsinger feared that the CIA might
have been running a covert operation there so sinister it would
shock even hardened CIA-watchdogs. In 1980 Holsinger, who'd
already discovered Dwyer's presence at Jonestown, received a
paper from a professor at U.C. Berkeley. Called "The Penal
Colony," the paper detailed how the CIA's mind-control program, code-named MK-ULTRA, was not stopped in 1973, as
the CIA had told Congress. Instead, the paper reported, it had
merely been transferred out of public hospitals and prisons into
the more secure confines of religious cults.

Jonestown, Holsinger believed, was one of those cults.

There were large amounts of psychoactive, i.e., mind-control,
drugs found on the site of the suicides. Larry Layton, the Jones
lieutenant who became the only person charged in any of the
killings (he was in the airstrip hit team, and somehow survived
the Jonestown massacre), was described as sinking into a
"posthypnotic trance" as he sunk ever deeper under Jones's
spell. Layton's own father called him "a robot."

Layton's brother-in-law, the man who arranged the lease on
Jonestown with the Guyanese government for Jones, was repor-
tedly a mercenary for the CIA-backed UNITA rebels in Angola.
Layton's father, according to Holsinger, was the biochemist in
charge of chemical warfare for the U.S. Army at its Dugway
Proving Ground in Utah.

Jones himself, the supposed Soviet sympathizer, was once a
fundraiser for Richard Nixon, around the same time Jones
declared himself the reincarnation of both Jesus and Lenin.

Then there was the problem of the bodies. The Jonestown
body count jumped by about four hundred within two days
after the suicides, leading to speculation that escapees may have
been hunted down and killed. In any case, Guyanese coroner

Leslie Mootoo testified that as many as seven hundred of the dead appeared to have been forcibly killed, not "suicides" at all. "I believe that it is possible that Jonestown may have been a mind-control experiment," Holsinger said in a 1980 lecture, "that Leo Ryan's congressional visit pierced that veil and would have resulted in its exposure, and that our government, or its agent the CIA, deemed it necessary to wipe out over nine hundred American citizens to protect the secrecy of the operation."

The "operation," if there was one, may have continued after the suicides. There have been attempts to repopulate Jonestown with Dominican and Indochinese refugees, backed by the Billy Graham organization. There was a Jonestown doppelgänger in Guyana even while Jones was still in business. Self-styled "Rabbi" David Hill, with his eight thousand-member Nation of Israel cult, was powerful enough to earn the nickname "vice prime minister" in his travels through the country.

One final, weird note: A memo that allegedly passed between Jones and People's Temple lawyer Mark Lane (who escaped the massacre) showed the two pondering the relocation of Grace Walden to Jonestown. Walden was a key witness to the assassination of Martin Luther King, Jr. Lane represented King's accused assassin, James Earl Ray. When the memo turned up, Lane denied that he had discussed moving Walden. (He claims that the memo was part of an "army intelligence coverup" of the King assassination, ostensibly an attempt to discredit him and, through him, Walden.) Most of the People's Temple rank-and-file were black. Most of the leadership was white. Joyce Shaw, a former member, once mused that the mass suicide story was a coverup for "some kind of horrible government experiments, or some sort of sick, racist thing...a plan like the German's to exterminate blacks."

In 1980, the House Permanent Select Committee on Intelligence announced that there was "no evidence" of CIA involvement at Jonestown.

MAJOR SOURCES

Kerns, Phil. *People's Temple, People's Tomb*. Plainfield, NJ: Logos International, 1979.
Kilduff, Marshall, and Ron Javers. *The Suicide Cult*. New York: Bantam Books, 1978.
Krause, Charles. *Guyana Massacre: The Eyewitness Account*. New York: Berkley Books, 1978.
Moore, Rebecca. *A Sympathetic History of Jonestown*. Lewiston, NY: Edwin Mellon Press, 1985.
Reiterman, Tim. *Raven: The Untold Story of the Reverend Jim Jones and His People*. New York: E.P. Dutton, 1982.
This chapter owes a debt to research assembled by John Judge.

40

AIDS: The Pentagon's Plague?

Dr. Donald MacArthur, a high-level defense department biological research administrator, showed up at a June 9, 1969, meeting of a House subcommittee on military appropriations begging for cash to carry out an unsavory endeavor.

"Within five to ten years," he prognosticated, "it would probably be possible to make a new infective microorganism which would differ in certain important aspects from any known disease-causing organisms. Most important of these," he continued—and this is the ominous part, "is that it might be refractory to the immunological and therapeutic processes upon which we depend to maintain our relative freedom from infectious disease."

This new germ, the one Dr. MacArthur desired so sincerely to whip up in his lab, would destroy the immune system. The good doc proffered the most hackneyed of Cold War rationales for this odious ambition.

"Should an enemy develop it there is little doubt that this is

an important area of potential military technological inferiority
in which there is no adequate research program."

He got his coveted taxpayer funding. In 1977 and 1978, at the
tail end of Dr. MacArthur's time frame, the first cases of
Acquired Immune Deficiency Syndrome (AIDS) emerged in
Africa.

As smoking guns, or smoking petri dishes, go, the Mac-
Arthur transcript leaves something to be desired. But the
coincidence is undeniably provocative. Is AIDS the ultimate in
biological warfare? This is a case with so many conundrums
that the JFK assassination seems like a District Court drunk-
driving rap by comparison.

U.S. representative Theodore Weiss—a New York congressman with a large gay constituency—speculated in 1983 that "as
far fetched as it may seem, given the attitudes toward homosexuals and homosexuality by some segments of society, the
possible utilization of biological weapons must be seriously
considered."

The demographics of AIDS also encourage the biowarfare
notion. Though no one is immune, several groups have been
especially hard hit: gays, Africans, drug users. Could those
groups have been deliberately targeted in some Pentagon-
operated biotech chamber?

Support for this biowarfare thesis is scanty at best. But then
the same holds true for the "official" explanation of how AIDS
entered the human population—that green monkeys spread it,
somehow—which rests on a rather flimsy foundation itself.

The generally accepted cause of AIDS is a virus labeled HIV
(Human Immunodeficiency Virus) "discovered" in 1984 by Dr.
Robert Gallo and, more or less simultaneously, by a team of
French scientists (the French doctors charge, apparently with
some justification, that Gallo ripped off their research—but
that's a conspiracy for another book). From what corner of the
ecosystem the virus arose remains an open question.

Gallo et al. note the similarity between a simian-borne virus
(STLV-III) and HIV. They muse that at some point the Cer-

copithecus aethiops carrying this virus transmitted it to an African human being. Within a few years thousands of people dropped dead from having sex and from blood transfusions.

It is barely worth scrolling down the litany of assumptions required to support this untested bit of fabulism (not the least of which is the massive and presumably instantaneous mutation of the simian virus). 'Nuff said that the green monkey scenario is at best an educated guess.

There are some gaping improbabilities in the AIDS-biowarfare mise-en-scène as well. Perhaps AIDS is indeed a biological bomb aimed to eradicate the world's useless eaters. The military and its politico-industrial cronies have certainly pulled some nasty stunts in their time. But who in their right mind would unleash a highly insidious, unstoppably lethal pathogen into the same population that includes oneself and one's All-American family?

A brief history of the U.S. biological warfare program appears elsewhere in this volume (see page 40). It includes on-the-record instances of military assaults on U.S. cities, unleashing various germs and toxins, though none as deadly as HIV (by a long shot). Nonetheless, there are some noteworthy examples of verifiable ruthlessness. Take the fiendish Tuskegee Syphilis Study. The U.S. Public Health Service ran the study on four hundred syphilitic black men, denying them not only treatment for their ailment but any information that they had the disease at all. This proceeded for forty years.

Then there was the 1931 Puerto Rico cancer experiment; self explanatory. A number of Puerto Ricans were deliberately infected with cancer by the Rockefeller Institute and thirteen died. Chief pathologist Cornelius Rhoades's justification?

"The Porto (sic) Ricans are the dirtiest, laziest, most degenerate and thievish race of men ever inhabiting this sphere....I have done my best to further the process of extermination by killing off eight and transplanting cancer into several more....All physicians take delight in the abuse and torture of the unfortunate subjects."

None too politically correct, that Dr. Rhoades. No one
prosecuted him, though. They brushed him off as "mentally
ill." The U.S. government must have disagreed. It placed
Rhoades in charge of two large chemical warfare projects
during the 1940s, granted him a seat on the Atomic Energy
Commission, and pinned him with the Legion of Merit.

Though biowarfare research was legislatively banned in 1972,
the Pentagon's "Department of Loopholes" took immediate
action and research pressed on. One of the germs that intrigues
military researchers is the *canis* strain of *brucella*. Symptoms of
this disease include headaches and fevers, malaise, muscle
aches, pharyngitis, and lymphadenopathy—the same roster
seen in AIDS-Related Complex, the precursor to full-blown
AIDS.

The first published charge of an AIDS-biowarfare connection
came in the *Patriot*, a newspaper in New Delhi. The July 4,
1984, report cited articles from an official U.S. Army research
publication about "natural and artificial influences on the
human immune system."

The Indian paper reported that scientists from Fort Detrick—
home of the National Cancer Institute's Frederick Cancer
Research Facility but until 1969 known as the Army Biological
Warfare Laboratory—ventured into darkest Africa in search of
"a powerful virus that could not be found in Europe or Asia."
The data from this excursion "was then analyzed at Fort
Detrick and the result was the isolation of a virus that causes
AIDS."

The U.S. government immediately labeled the article Soviet
disinformation, a case not harmed by the subsequent relentless
coverage given the story in Soviet media. A *Pravda* editorial
cartoon showing a doctor standing on a pile of corpses, and
handing a general a vial marked *AIDS virus* did draw a whine
of protest from the U.S. embassy. But it wasn't until a major
British newspaper splashed the story all over its tabloid pages
that American authorities began to react, their objections
echoed slavishly by the ever-enterprising U.S. media.

Next came the 1986 pamphlet *AIDS: USA Home-Made Evil* by two French-born East German scientists, Jakob and Lilli Segal. The pamphlet, with no listed publisher, floated freely throughout the English-speaking regions of Africa. Not an orthodox means of scientific publication, but the Segals' arguments formed the basis for much of the subsequent discussion, such as it was, of the AIDS-biowarfare theory.

HIV, the enigmatic Segals enigmatically claimed, is a genetically engineered hybrid of the visan virus (cause of a sheep-borne brain disease) and a virus called HTLV-I (HIV was originally named HTLV-III), which causes white blood cell cancer.

The Segals, too, fingered Fort Detrick as the lab that invented the virus. There has never been any hard evidence that HIV was synthesized at Fort Detrick—or anywhere else—but it can't hurt to inquire why the National Institutes of Health asked the army researchers at Fort Detrick, not the "civilians" there, to help develop a cure for AIDS.

In February of 1987 army colonel David Huxsoll, taken by a scoffing fit while discussing the AIDS-biowarfare charges, blabbed an intriguing bit of information.

"Studies at army laboratories have shown that the AIDS virus would be an extremely poor biological warfare agent," quoth the colonel.

What studies? Pentagon PR tells us that the military wants to put an end to AIDS in our lifetimes, not an end to our lifetimes. Huxsoll later denied making the statement. The reporter who wrote it down stands by the story.

The first American AIDS outbreaks—then confined almost exclusively to the gay male population—coincided with the onset of Reaganism and its attendant bitter backlash against gays. The biowarfare theory assumes that gays were singled out for destruction, or, at the very least, for scapegoating. But how?

In 1978 more than a thousand nonmonogamous homosexual adult males received experimental vaccinations against hepatitis B, courtesy of the National Institutes of Health and the Centers for Disease Control. Within six years 64 percent of those men had AIDS.

Coincidence is of course possible, even likely in this case. Under the conventional view of AIDS-transmission, non-monogamous homosexual adult males are prone to the disease anyway.

There was another vaccination program, for smallpox this time, in Africa. The World Health Organization ran the show. The regions where W.H.O. administered its program later became the most AIDS-wrecked in Africa. Again, however, the notion that this could be a coincidence is quite plausible, though among adherents of the AIDS-conspiracy theory the smallpox program stirs considerable alarm. But it's hard to knock the W.H.O.'s largely successful attempt to eradicate smallpox—a far worse killer than AIDS.

There are variations on the AIDS-biowarfare theme: Some rest on the argument that HIV, on its own, does not cause AIDS. Dioxins (used by the military in Vietnam) and dengue virus (used by the CIA in Cuba) have found mention as possible culprits, as has a mutated form of syphilis. Any of these would be simpler than a synthesized virus to administer as a weapon.

There's only one certainty: The epidemiology of AIDS is one case where neither the official nor the conspiratorial explanations comes off as particularly satisfying.

MAJOR SOURCES

Krupey, G.J. "AIDS: Act of God or the Pentagon?" *Steamshovel Press* no. 4 (Spring 1992).

Lederer, Robert. "Chemical-Biological Warfare, Medical Experiments and Population Control." *Covert Action Information Bulletin*, no. 28 (Summer 1987).

Lehrman, Nathaniel S. "Is AIDS Non-Infectious? The Possibility and Its CBW Implications." *Covert Action Information Bulletin*, no. 28 (Summer 1987).

Rappoport, Jon. *AIDS Inc.: Scandal of the Century*. Foster City, Calif.: Human Energy Press, 1988.

IX

State Secrets

41

The Return of Hitler's Spy

World War II had been kaput scarcely a week when a U.S. Army DC-3 touched down outside of Washington, D.C., ferrying a top secret German cargo. Stepping off the plane, possibly disguised as an American general, was Nazi legend Reinhard Gehlen, Hitler's master spy.

His slight physique—five feet eight, 130 pounds—belied his strategic importance to the U.S. officials who welcomed him with open arms. As chief of the Third Reich's Foreign Armies East, Gehlen had been Hitler's most senior officer on the Russian front. He had run an elaborate network of Nazi spies against the Soviet Union—the new villains in the budding Cold War.

Though he was forty-three years old, and Germany lay in ruin, Gehlen's best years were still ahead of him. He was about to make an offer that America's military and governing elites couldn't refuse: He would put his clandestine nexus of Nazi SS officers, underground fascist sympathizers, fugitive war criminals, and encyclopedic Soviet files into the service of Uncle Sam.

A shrewd survivor, Gehlen had buried his organization's plenary files on the USSR in the Austrian Alps as soon as Nazi Germany's collapse became imminent. Gehlen knew that the battle against communism would replace the war against fascist Germany as the overriding military and political goal of the capitalist West. "My view," he wrote in his memoir, "was that there would be a place even for Germany in a Europe rearmed for defense against Communism. Therefore we must set our sights on the Western powers, and give ourselves two objectives: to help defend against Communist expansion and to recover and reunify Germany's lost territories." (Apparently, Gehlen's bargaining chip was so valuable, his hosts were willing to overlook the general's still-current ideas about *Deustchland über alles*.)

Shortly after Germany's surrender to the Allies, Gehlen had descended from his Alpine retreat, audaciously turning himself over to American authorities. "I am head of the Section Foreign Armies East in German Army headquarters," he announced in his prepared speech. "I have information to give of the highest importance to your government."

"So have they all," snapped an army captain, who sent the arrogant, hot-tempered general packing to the camp at Salzburg with the rest of the Nazi prisoners. But he wouldn't stew there for very long. Within a month, with the Soviet Union demanding custody of Gehlen and his files, Hitler's spy master began to receive a stream of important American visitors.

At Fort Hunt near Washington, where an NCO butler and several white-jacketed orderlies catered to his needs, Gehlen conferred with President Truman's national security advisor, a gaggle of army intelligence generals, and Allen Dulles, a giant in America's wartime intelligence outfit, the Office of Strategic Services (OSS). Later Dulles would take the helm of the CIA.

After a year in Washington, Gehlen returned to the Fatherland—not as a prisoner, but as an influential agent in America's anticommunist war of nerves with Russia. Gehlen took command of his old organization and became America's foremost intelligence source on the Soviet Union. His influence over American policy would be sweeping; and like the proverbial Faustian pact, there would be later reverberations: His exaggerated reports of Russian military strength would escalate the Cold War to dangerous peaks.

How the U.S. government came to collaborate with Gehlen and hundreds of other high-ranking Nazis is a rarely told chapter of American history. American officials, increasingly paranoid about the threat of Soviet influence in postwar Europe and around the world, found expedient soul mates in the Nazi scientists and SS officers they recruited. After all, Nazi Germany's fascists were vehemently opposed to communism, too. Invoking the exigencies of the Cold War, Dulles explained away any misgivings about hiring Gehlen: "He's on our side, and that's all that matters."

Even as the U.S. military was hunting down Nazi war criminals, other branches of the U.S. government were quietly enlisting many of the same fugitives. Project Paperclip was the U.S. War Department's code name for its secret importation of Nazi scientists, using sanitized, rewritten "records" to sneak the Germans through U.S. immigration. In Germany, many of those scientists had benefited from fatal experiments performed on prisoners at Dachau and from slave labor at other concentration camps. During the early 1980s the U.S. Department of Justice identified numerous Nazi veterans who were still living in America.

Truman's National Security Council issued classified directives sanctioning the use of former Nazi collaborators. The paper trail was subject to a massive coverup, and the complete history of America's dalliance with Nazis remains partially obscured. They may not have saved Hitler's brain, as the B-movie conspiracy theory had it, but the Führer's intelligence apparatus found a new host, transplanted onto America's spy and military agencies. It's ironic that when President Truman demobilized the OSS, he warned against setting up a permanent

"Gestapo-like" intelligence agency, even as his administration was dotting the *i*'s and crossing the *t*'s on its make-work program for former and possibly not-so-former Nazis and their quislings.

Among the notorious Nazi fugitives quietly pardoned and employed by the postwar American government for intelligence work was Klaus Barbie, the SS "Butcher of Lyon." Barbie worked with Gehlen after the war and even lived for a time in the United States.

Though Gehlen promised his handlers, "on principle," that he wouldn't recruit former SS and Gestapo men, he immediately broke his official word, hiring at least six SS and Sicherheitsdienst (SD) veterans. And America's intelligence elite looked the other way.

Two of Gehlen's notorious postwar hires were Dr. Franz Alfred Six and Emil Augsburg, SS intelligence veterans involved in the mass extermination of Jews. They were both fugitive war criminals.

Franz Six was described by Adolf Eichmann as "a real eager beaver" when it came to the genocide of Jews. "The physical elimination of Eastern Jewry would deprive Jewry of its biological reserves," Six had announced at a conference on the so-called Jewish Question. He put his plan into practice in Smolensk, where his unit murdered some two hundred people in cold blood, among them "thirty-eight intellectual Jews who had tried to create unrest and discontent in the newly established Ghetto of Smolensk," he reported to headquarters.

Emil Augsberg, a staffer under SS chief Himmler, also had led a murder squad in Russia. According to his Nazi Party records, he achieved "extraordinary results...in special tasks," an SS euphemism for mass murder of Jews. Gehlen would find good use for Augsburg's specialty: overseeing assassinations behind "enemy" lines.

For the Gehlen Organization, both Six and Augsberg reactivated their Nazi spy networks in the Soviet Union and hired unemployed German intelligence veterans, many of whom were fellow fugitives. Gehlen must have realized that unofficial Allied policy favored the employment of war criminals: Augsberg was simultaneously moonlighting for several other U.S. intelligence agencies and a French government clandestine group, all the while serving in a private network of ex-SS officers.

When the U.S. Army's Counter-Intelligence Corps (CIC) caught up to Six, he was convicted of war crimes and got a twenty-year sentence. (Augsberg was luckier: the CIC didn't arrest him—it *hired* him.) After only four years in prison, though, Six won clemency—and U.S. permission to rejoin the Gehlen Organization as a valuable asset to Western security.

Gehlen's group not only formed the core in America's absorption of Hitler's espionage elite, it also helped midwife the newborn CIA: During the early postwar years, all of the Agency's anti-Soviet assets in Eastern Europe were managed and mastered by Gehlen. Sometimes his reports were retyped verbatim on CIA stationary and passed along to Truman. Gehlen also held great sway over NATO's intelligence and strategy. According to one estimate, the master spy generated 70 percent of NATO's information on the Soviet Union, Eastern Europe, and Europe.

In effect, the West's bulwark against the USSR was utterly dependent on information flowing from an operation run by former Nazis—and said information was often spurious, at that.

In his sobering book on America's recruitment of Nazis, *Blowback*, Christopher Simpson notes that Gehlen's alarmist reports helped ratchet up tensions between the United States and the Soviet Union during the Cold War: "Gehlen provided U.S. Army intelligence and later the CIA with many of the dire reports that were used to justify increased U.S. military budgets and intensified U.S./USSR hostilities," Simpson writes.

Gehlen's exaggerated reports about an imminent Soviet attack—when in fact the Russians were still licking their postwar wounds—came close to touching off war several times. According to Gehlen biographer E.H. Cookridge and others, in 1948

Gehlen nearly convinced the United States that the Soviets were about to launch an assault on the West. He advised that the West would be wise to strike first. Later, during the 1950s, his erroneous claims that the Soviets had outpaced America in the military buildup fueled fears about the so-called missile gap, which helped stoke up anticommie feelings to feverish levels.

"The [CIA] loved Gehlen because he fed us what we wanted to hear," former CIA officer Victor Marchetti told Simpson. "We used his stuff constantly, and we fed it to everybody else: the Pentagon; the White House; the newspapers. They loved it, too. But it was hyped up Russian boogeyman junk, and it did a lot of damage to this country."

Ironically, the Org also damaged the CIA's anti-Soviet work. The Org's underground groups were so riddled with Soviet double agents, that Western intelligence was compromised for decades. John Loftus, formerly the chief prosecutor of the Justice Department's Nazi-hunting section, summed up the Soviet infiltration of anti-East Bloc groups this way: "It really shows how Soviet intelligence was able to keep communism afloat for the last seventy years."

Intentionally or not, Gehlen undermined the very "national security" that had justified his recruitment in the first place.

Which brings us to some interesting, yet unsubstantiated, speculation. Some researchers propose that Hitler's haughty spy master had a plan B, an ulterior motive beyond the personal survival instinct and rabid anticommunism. Conspiracy researcher Carl Oglesby contends that Gehlen's postwar organization operated as a cover for the Odessa, an international underground set up by deputy führer Martin Bormann to preserve the defeated Nazi Reich. Oglesby calls Gehlen's group "by far the most audacious, most critical, and most essential part of the entire Odessa undertaking." Military intelligence historian (and espionage veteran) Colonel William Corson seconds this notion.

The Gehlen Org, Oglesby argues, provided a haven for fleeing Odessa members by putting them on the American intelligence payroll—a brilliant gambit. More than a few of Gehlen's operatives were indeed Odessa members. Oglesby's evidence is curious, if not entirely convincing. A declassified CIA document from the 1970s reports that while he was in a U.S. Army VIP prison camp in Wiesbaden, "Gehlen sought and received approval" for his deal with the Americans from Hitler's appointed successor, Admiral Karl Doenitz. "The German chain of command was still in effect," Oglesby concludes, "and it approved of what Gehlen was doing with the Americans."

Whether or not the Gehlen Org was a diversion to preserve an underground Nazi empire is an open question. But Gehlen did manage to attain his goal of splitting away from U.S. intelligence to serve the fledgling West German government. Gehlen's Org continues to live on, as Germany's BND intelligence service.

The Org's legacy also survives in America. The forty-year defense buildup that helped transform America into the world's largest debtor nation, as well as the ongoing exploits of Gehlen's godchild, the CIA, in the expedient realms of political assassination, propaganda, and covert operations certainly owe a debt to Hitler's master spy, and the men who signed him up to "our side."

MAJOR SOURCES

Cookridge, E.H. *Gehlen, Spy of the Century.* New York: Random House, 1971.
Gehlen, Reinhard. *The Service.* New York: World, 1972.
Higham, Charles. *American Swastika.* New York: Doubleday, 1985.
Loftus, John. *The Belarus Secret.* New York: Paragon House, 1989.
Oglesby, Carl. "Reinhard Gehlen: The Secret Treaty of Fort Hunt." *Covert Action Information Bulletin,* no. 35 (Fall 1990).
Simpson, Christopher. *Blowback.* New York: Weidenfeld & Nicolson, 1988.
Whiting, Charles. *Gehlen: Germany's Master Spy.* New York: Ballantine Books, 1972.

42

The Secret Team

A true period piece and document of an era, the Daniel Sheehan Affidavit even inspired a graphic novel—appropriately, because the document is less a court filing than a work of art; a Francis Ford Coppola-esque epic of secrets and subterfuge and omnipresent danger.

The affidavit was filed in December 1986 by Daniel Sheehan, a longtime activist-lawyer—he had worked, for example, on the Karen Silkwood case and for the Native Americans besieged at Wounded Knee. By the mid-eighties he was chief council for the Washington, D.C.-based Christic Institute, "an interfaith, public interest law firm and public policy center."

Wielding the unwieldy Racketeer Influenced and Corrupt Organizations statute (RICO) usually employed by prosecutors to bag mob bosses, Sheehan tried to nail an entire "secret team" of spies, mercenaries, gun runners, and their White House basement buddies by implicating them in the bombing of a renegade Contra leader's press conference in La Penca, Costa Rica.

The Contra, Eden Pastora, had tired of CIA hands-on

management of the anti-Sandinista rebellion. He called the press conference to explain his reasons for breaking with other Contra groups who paid greater homage to the CIA than to the cause. As soon as Pastora started to blab—boom! The Christic clients were two journalists scarred in the blast. With the broadly drawn RICO statute, if Sheehan could tie the bombing to the activities of this secret team, he could bring down the entire shadow government.

The affidavit came out around the same time that the Iran-Contra scandal hit the news and as the scandal unfolded some of its key names turned out to be among those men listed as the Christic Institute's twenty-nine defendants. Names like Richard Secord, Oliver North, John Hull, and Theodore Shackley; Thomas Clines, Albert Hakim, John Singlaub, and Edwin Wilson—all of them CIA operatives, military officers, arms dealers, or some combination thereof—populate Sheehan's counter-reality.

The affidavit, arising from Sheehan's own investigation involving seventy sources, spins the tale of an arms-for-drugs-for-guns-for-money enterprise extending from the far reaches of Southeast Asia three decades ago to Central America in the 1980s. The narrative picks up against a *Godfather Part II* backdrop of rip-roaring Havana circa 1959, overtaken by socialist revolution. Conspiracies unfurl posthaste. Richard Nixon meets with security-specialist-cum-private-spy Robert Maheu to discuss means of undermining the new Cuban government.

Maheu contacts the underworld elite: John Roselli, Sam Giancana, Santos Trafficante. They assemble a team of assassins to "supplement" the supersecret National Security Council "Operation 40," aimed at toppling Castro.

Members of Operation 40 also smuggle drugs into the United States from Cuba. Use of the Mafia leads to some "problems of control," but the operation carries on.

A few years later Operation 40 leadership relocates to Laos, the new frontier. The CIA's "Blonde Ghost," Shackley, and his chief lieutenant Thomas Clines form a new assassination squad using Laotian Hmong tribesmen.

The hit squad's commander is General John Singlaub, later founder of the ultra-right-wing World Anti-Communist League. North and Secord both served under Singlaub.

The unit backs an opium lord named Van Pao in a territorial war against two competitors in the Laotian jungle.

The fortunate Mr. Pao, with a little help from his friends, emerges victorious after his drug trade rivals are "mysteriously assassinated." Soon Van Pao meets in a Saigon hotel with Santos Trafficante and another drug-importing contract is finalized, according to Sheehan's allegations.

These types of activities proceed apace throughout the Vietnam era, most of the time with some kind of official sanction from the CIA or the military. The Phoenix Program, under which forty thousand Vietnamese local and municipal leaders were assassinated, was one such fully approved program of questionable ethical status. But good things come to an end. When Phoenix reached the end of its mandate, Shackley, Clines, and Richard Armitage—whom the affidavit describes as the "bursar" for this unusual quasi-corporation—"began a highly secret non-CIA authorized program setting up their own private anticommunist assassination and unconventional warfare program."

The secret team was born.

That, anyway, is the story according to Dan Sheehan. Opium-sales money "secretly smuggled out of Vietnam in large suitcases by Richard Secord and Thomas Clines—and carried into Australia where it was deposited in a secret, personal bank account," provided the wherewithal for the "Team's endeavors."

The affidavit contains any number of serious allegations against these men—who needless to say have denied them ad infinitum. It accuses Secord of brokering arms to Middle Eastern countries through middleman Albert Hakim in a scam that let the secret team skim profits away from the government—and into more secret team shenanigans.

Illegal? Sure. But good business. When the Reagan administration hit upon the "neat idea" of pawning off overpriced artillery to the "Islamic fanatics" in Iran—who were then engaged in a volley of mass slaughter with Iraq—and sending the skim to the "freedom fighters" in Nicaragua, the secret team got the job.

Not content with war profiteering, the secret teamsters turned also to their old standby, dope dough. Planes that flew weapons to the Contras sailed back packed with Colombian cocaine.

Among the accoutrements of death purveyed by the secret team, according to the Christic Institute affidavit, were liberal dollops of a plastic explosive called C-4, sold to (among other charming characters) Libyan terrorists. C-4 was the plastique of choice in a plethora of terrorist acts including the bombing of Pan Am 103. Sheehan swears that his evidence implicates one such Libyan using secret-team-supplied C-4 in the La Penca bombing.

But even more intriguing than the conspiracy described in the Christic Institute lawsuit was official reaction to the suit itself. Sheehan's case has been criticized, even by his ideological allies, for containing inaccuracies and (yawn) for taking an overly "conspiratorial" view of recent history. But Sheehan never had a chance to answer his critics in the one forum where his theories could have been laboratory-tested, the courtroom.

Judge James King threw the Christic's case out of the federal court in February of 1989, and he went a step further. He leveled a $1 million judgment against the underfunded Christic Institute on the grounds that the lawsuit was "frivolous." Given the non-profit group's precarious budget, the judgement amounted to an assassination attempt against the Christic Institute—until an anonymous fatcat came up with the cash.

The Christics' appeal was also rebuffed. Though the institute scrapes by, it has been crippled with discreditation, enduring the same treatment dispensed to, it seems, almost anyone who mounts a substantive challenge to U.S. covert operations. The case offers an instructive lesson in why conspiracy theories usually remain merely that: theories.

"If we were back in Vietnam in a fire fight," General Singlaub once remarked of his supposedly frivolous legal adversaries, "then I'd ask for an air strike to blow the bastards away."

MAJOR SOURCE

Affidavit of Daniel P. Sheehan, 12 December 1986.

43

Meet the New Boss...

Bill Clinton's presidency, like that of the previous Democrat in the White House, Jimmy Carter, has provided a bounty for right-wing conspiracy theorists. You know, cranky, disgruntled, out-of-touch-with-reality types like, say, Senate minority leader and presidential candidate Bob Dole.

Shamelessly, considering the Republicans' Iran-Contra imbroglio, Dole spearheaded the call for a special prosecutor to investigate the so-called Whitewater scandal. Named for a real estate deal in which the Clinton couple invested and lost a fair amount of cash about a decade before Mr. Bill came to Washington, dark allegations eddied around the case for months—charges ranging from influence peddling to assassination—but somehow, no one seemed to pin anything on the president and his supposedly equally culpable spouse.

The January 24, 1994, *Newsweek* declared, with remarkable candor, that "in the Whitewater scandal, Clinton's real problem may be letting his frustration overcome his judgment." Which, according to most judicial precedents has yet to become a punishable offense.

A few months later, a March 27 *New York Times* piece pored over the Clintons' tax returns, scouring for scuz. Clinton's lawyer, and Clinton himself, had acknowledged an error in reporting his Whitewater losses. Again, no big scandal. The best the *Times* could come up with was that the error "raises new questions about how the Clintons responded in 1992 to potentially damaging news accounts suggesting that Whitewater might have been a sweetheart deal."

"Questions" about "potentially" damning news stories "suggesting" that something "might" have been fishy: not exactly what you'd call "nailing down the story," but that's about what the "scandal" came to—not a question of Clinton's misdeeds, but how the First Couple handled their bad press. Whitewater looked more like a conspiracy against the president than one he was involved in.

Nonetheless, in June 1994 the Senate voted to hold limited hearings into the Whitewater affair. Muscling out a Republican proposal for drag-on-forever hearings, Democrats held the day, allowing the inquiry to zero in on just a few issues—including the suicide of Clinton crony Vincent Foster, which some on the Right (onetime Moral Majoritarian Jerry Falwell is tops among them) claimed was actually a Clinton-sanctioned rubout.

Most of the fussing over Whitewater came from the opposition party, the Republicans, who after twelve years found themselves squeezed out of the White House as well as outnumbered in Congress. But it all seemed rather hypocritical given their years of self-righteous posturing over the far more substantial and serious Iran-Contra affair. Republican reluctance to reopen that still festering wound may explain why they didn't seize on another Clinton peccadillo that makes Whitewater seem like a cartoon by comparison—one that could tie Clinton to Iran-Contra.

While the dovish draft dodger Clinton doesn't mingle so comfortably with the Ollie North clique, there is one noteworthy case that hooks him into an arms-for-drugs operation.

Seems that one of the secret airstrips from which the CIA—or someone—dispatched planes to Central America that carried weapons to the Contras in Nicaragua and, apparently, cocaine back into the United States, was located in a small Arkansas burg called Mena.

It was from this airstrip, in October 1986, that a plane carrying Eugene Hasenfus departed. Shot down over Nicaragua, Hasenfus survived to expose the CIA's part in the Contra insurgency (which until then had been sold to the public by the Reagan administration as the underdog effort of a ragtag troop of freedom-loving patriots).

The Mena coke smuggling endeavor was real. Massachusetts Senator John Kerry's Senate subcommittee examined the evidence and deemed it "sufficient for an indictment on money-laundering charges." Clinton was governor of Arkansas while this covert operation was underway. Nothing suspicious about that. But allegedly he knew about Mena and took no action—in fact, he is said to have aided the coverup.

"I have never seen a whitewash job like what has been executed in this case," said Arkansas congressman Bill Alexander, who, in what could be construed as a publicity stunt, sent Iran-Contra prosecutor Lawrence Walsh two boxes of the state attorney general's investigatory files on Mena. "There has been a conspiracy of the greatest magnitude that has not been prosecuted."

Pressed by Alexander in 1991, as he was gearing up to run for president, Clinton made his first public announcement regarding Mena. He claimed to have authorized a $25,000 allocation for a grand jury investigation of Mena way back in 1988. But the prosecutors who would have received the money deny that any such allocation was offered, and even the governor's office was forced to fess up that no record of any such funding authorization exists. After Clinton's statement and its subsequent failure to be borne out by reality, Alexander requested that the federal Justice Department allocate the $25K. Accord-

ing to a report in the *Village Voice* the money was granted to
Arkansas authorities but never reached the police authorities in
charge of the investigation.

What would possess Clinton to go along with a coverup of
the Mena operation and then apparently fabricate a butt-
covering tale about it? That is a matter for the imagination,
since no further link between the then-governor and the drugs-
and-guns operation has ever been established or even suggested
by evidence. Hard to believe he was protecting George Bush,
who probably knew a thing or two about Mena.

The best guess comes from Mark Swaney, grad student and
leader of a grass-roots group that once filed a one thousand-
signature petition demanding that the state look into Mena.
Swaney's hypothesis, as recounted in the *Voice*, involves one
Larry Nichols, a Contra enthusiast whom Clinton, for equally
unknown reasons, appointed to head the Arkansas Development Finance Authority (ADFA). The ADFA under Nichols's
stewardship, according to information Swaney gleaned from a
couple of shadowy informants who may or may not have
intelligence connections, might have been attempting to win
black-budgeted government programs for Arkansas. This policy could have tangled state authorities up with the Mena covert
operators.

The ADFA might even have been used to launder drug money,
which would clearly pose a PR problem for Clinton and his
wife, whose law firm counseled ADFA.

Clinton eventually sacked Nichols for allegedly making unauthorized phone calls to his Contra pals in Central America
and sticking the state with the phone bill. Nichols in turn sued
Clinton for defamation of character, and from that lawsuit
emerged revelations of Clinton's extramarital dalliance with a
cheesy blonde who later praised the governor's cunnilingual
prowess to *Penthouse* magazine.

All quite interesting, indeed. But perhaps shedding light on
Clinton's bizarre behavior in the Mena scandal may have
performed a greater public service.

Mena has produced not a peep from the Republican side, but when it came to Whitewater, Republican leader Dole rather sanctimoniously called on the attorney general to investigate the president, "for the president's sake and for the sake of the integrity of the attorney general's office."

Similar pleas were notably absent from the Republican side in the days of George Bush's malfeasance-ridden regime (from the Democratic side, too). Coupled with the barrage of playing-to-the-peanut-gallery charges of sexual hijinks aimed at Clinton from various shadowy corners (calling to mind the stories that toppled Gary Hart, who had the best shot of beating Bush in 1988), Dole's unctuous pronouncement makes one wonder if Clinton's presidency may not be the victim of sabotage—betrayed by the very cabal he's worked all his life to join.

Clinton acknowledged his ascendance into this cadre in his nomination acceptance speech at the 1992 Democratic convention when he coupled Professor Carroll Quigley with President Kennedy as the two most notable influences on his political development, thus acknowledging his affinity with the global banking-and-business elite that aspires to rule the world—at least in the minds of John Birchers and those of amenable perspective—who look upon Quigley's magnum opus *Tragedy and Hope* as the confessional that consummates their conspiracy theory (see page 249).

Quigley was a scholar, man of letters, and Clinton's favorite prof during his Georgetown University days. There aren't many politicians who'd use the most important speech of their careers to laud an author whose masterwork promoted the interests of a clandestine organization working to "create a world system of financial control in private hands able to dominate the political system of each country and the economy of the world as a whole." But Clinton did.

The same putative Anglo-American Establishment (to cop the title of Quigley's other major work) spewed forth Bush, who surprised Birchers not at all when he suddenly became infatuated with the phrase, "new world order."

Right wingers have built a cottage industry in imprecations against the "new world order." The late Gary Allen, author of the Birch classic *None Dare Call It Conspiracy*, titled his final paperback tract *Say "No" to the New World Order*. That was in 1987 when the Bush presidency was but a gleam in George's shifty eye.

Paranoia on the right was not only prescient, but substantive. The Council on Foreign Relations and related blue-blood cabals have been pushing for a "new world order" in their journals and symposia for years. Quigley was the self-appointed and highly affectionate historian of this meta-aristocracy. And Clinton announced to the world that he loves the guy. New world order redux.

Clinton always had more in common with Bush than he let on. Granted, he ran against Bush as an outsider. But where Bush was once a card-carrying member of the Council on Foreign Relations and the Trilateral Commission, Clinton notched those two plus the dread Bilderberg Group on his curriculum vitae. The difference, such as it is, is that while Bush was born into the Eastern Establishment his preppy portfolio prefabbed, Clinton—hailing from a town called Hope with a drunken dad and a gaggle of illegitimate siblings—is strictly a made guy.

Even Clinton's Rhodes scholarship seems sinister, taken in context. Cecil "Rhodesia" Rhodes, the zillionaire imperialist who endowed the scholarship fund, founded the Round Table, a British precursor to the Council on Foreign Relations. The idea behind the scholarships was to solidify British imperial dominion by inculcating the best and brightest from the colonies with British values at Oxford, then shipping them home to perpetuate the Empire among their native people.

The scholarships were "one component of Rhodes's plan to create a one-world government," writes conspiracy researcher Jim Martin.

Whitewater may not stick, but Clinton's credentials as a one-worlder are beyond reproach.

MAJOR SOURCES

Bainerman, Joel. *The Crimes of a President.* New York: S.P.I. Books, 1992.
Martin, Jim. "Quigley, Clinton, Straight and Reich." *Steamshovel Press*, no. 8 (Summer 1993).
Snepp, Frank. "Clinton and the Smugglers' Airport." *Village Voice*, 4 April 1992.
Kenn Thomas provided research for this chapter.

X
Random Shootings

44

Who Slew the Walrus?

The scene outside New York's spooky old Dakota apartment building on the evening of December 8, 1980, was as surreal as it was horrifying. John Lennon, probably the world's most famous rock star, lay semiconscious, hemorrhaging from four flat-tipped bullets blasted into his back. His wife Yoko Ono held his head in her arms and screamed (just like on her early albums).

A few yards away a pudgy young man stood eerily still, peering down into a paperback book. Moments earlier he had dropped into a military firing stance—legs spread for maximum balance, two hands gripping his .38 revolver to steady his aim—and blown away the very best Beatle. Now he leafed lazily through the pages of the one novel even the most chronically stoned and voided-out ninth grader will actually read, J. D. Salinger's *Catcher in the Rye.*

The Dakota doorman shouted at the shooter, Mark David Chapman, "Do you know what you've done?"

"I just shot John Lennon," Chapman replied, accurately enough.

It was a tragedy of Kierkegaardian pointlessness. There was only one apparent way to squeeze any sense from it; write it off as random violence by a "wacko."

"He walked past me and then I heard in my head, 'Do it, do it, do it,' over and over again, saying, 'Do it, do it, do it,' like that," Chapman, preternaturally serene, recalled in a BBC documentary several years after going to prison. "I don't remember aiming. I must have done, but I don't remember drawing a bead or whatever you call it. And I just pulled the trigger steady five times."

Chapman described his feeling at the time of the shooting as "no emotion, no anger...dead silence in the brain."

His unnatural tone sounded all-too-familiar. British lawyer/journalist Fenton Bresler took it as a tip-off. Chapman was a brainwashed hit man carrying out someone else's contract.

"Mark David Chapman," writes Bresler, "is in many ways as much the victim of those who wanted to kill John Lennon as Lennon himself."

Prosecutors, at a loss for motive, opted for the cliché: Chapman did it for the attention—the troublesome American preoccupation with grabbing that elusive fifteen minutes propels many a daily-newspaper-journalist-cum-pop-sociologist into raptures of sanctimony. But Arthur O'Connor, the detective who spent more time with Chapman immediately following the murder than anyone else, saw it another way.

"It is definitely illogical to say that Mark committed the murder to make himself famous. He did not want to talk to the press from the very start....It's possible Mark could have been used by somebody. I saw him the night of the murder. I studied him intensely. He looked as if he could have been programmed."

O'Connor was speaking to Bresler, and publicly for the first time. Bresler's book *Who Killed John Lennon?* offers the most cogent argument that Lennon's murder was not the work of yet another "lone nut."

Conspiracy theories abounded after the Lennon assassination, many rather cruelly fingering Yoko as the mastermind. Another focused on Paul who, by this line of reasoning, blamed Yoko for engineering his arrest in Japan on reefer charges. The Lennon conspiracy turns up on radio talk shows with some frequency, where hosts fend off callers with the "Why bother to kill that guy?" defense.

Only Bresler's thesis, that Chapman was a mind-controlled assassin manipulated by some right-wing element possibly connected to the newly elected (and not even inaugurated) Reagan apparatus of reaction, transcends the confines of pure speculation, extending into the realm of actual investigation.

Even so, Bresler's book a little too often substitutes rhetorical questions ("What does that steady repetition of a voice saying 'Do it, do it, do it,' over and over again in Mark's head sound like to you?") for evidentiary argument. We can forgive him for that failing. Bresler tracked the case for eight years, conducted unprecedented interviews, and extracted a ream of previously unreleased government documents. But unlike researchers into the assassinations of the Kennedys and Martin Luther King, he did not have volumes of evidence gathered by any official investigation, even a flawed one, to fall back on. The New York police had their man, the case was closed the very night of the murder—and, anyway, what political reason could possibly exist for gunning down the composer of "I Am the Walrus"?

In building his case, Bresler establishes some key points that put the lie to any "Who would want to kill an aging rock star?" brush-off.

Richard Nixon, his administration and other right-wing politicians (including ultraconservative ancient Senator Strom Thurmond, who personally memoed Attorney General John Mitchell on the matter) were fixated on what they saw as the Lennon problem. To them, the politically outspoken singer-songwriter was an insidious subversive of the worst kind, the famous and beloved kind.

• J. Edgar Hoover shared their concerns. One page of Lennon's FBI file bears the handwritten, block-lettered, under-

lined words, ALL EXTREMISTS SHOULD BE CONSIDERED
DANGEROUS.

- The government went all-out to deny Lennon his longed-for
  permanent U.S. residency, and more than that, to deport
  him altogether (that was the subject of Thurmond's memo).
- Lennon's FBI file—at nearly three hundred pages as chubby
  as Hoover himself—reveals that he was under "constant
  surveillance." Nor did the G-men keep a particularly low
  profile around the ex-Beatle, apparently attempting to
  harass him into silence or at least drive him nuts, similar to
  the tactic they had used on Martin Luther King, Jr., a few
  short but eventful years earlier.
- In late 1972, when the "surveillance" was at its peak,
  Lennon told humorist Paul Krassner, "Listen, if anything
  happens to Yoko and me, it was not an accident."
- The FBI and the CIA tracked Lennon at least from his "Free
  John Sinclair" concert in 1969 until 1976—even though by
  then Lennon had won his immigration battle and dropped
  out of not only political activism but public life altogether
  into what turned out to be a five-year period of seclusion.
  His apartment was watched, he was followed, his phone
  was tapped.

Placing a person under "constant surveillance" and ordering
that person executed are admittedly two different things.
Nevertheless, Bresler's point is that the government did not
consider John Lennon a harmless rock 'n' roller whose awk-
ward entrance into the world of political activism often carried
a high cringe factor (as in his Montreal "bed-in").

He was viewed as a dangerous radical who needed to be
stopped.

And in a way that official paranoia might have been justified,
because as embarrassing as Lennon and Ono's political publicity stunts occasionally became, John Lennon was always
capable of seizing the spotlight and speaking directly to millions of young people who venerated him.

With unfettered access to the media, his power was immense,

at least potentially so, and recognized by more experienced radicals like Jerry Rubin and Abbie Hoffman, who linked themselves to Lennon, clinging so close that they made the rock star uncomfortable.

Lennon was killed just four years after the intense FBI/CIA surveillance ceased. In those intermittent years, Jimmy Carter was president—a Democrat who kept the two gestapo-ish agencies more or less in check.

But in December 1980, when John Lennon's first album in half a decade was high on the charts, Carter was a lame duck chief executive, having lost his reelection bid to Ronald Reagan. Reagan's campaign was managed by career secret agent William Casey, who under President Reagan became the CIA's most freewheeling chief since Allen Dulles. The new far-right administration would reassemble the intelligence services and grant them a cheerful carte blanche.

The forces that tried desperately to neutralize Lennon for at least seven years lost power in 1976. Lennon's government dossier ends in that year. In 1980, as those forces were preparing to retake control of the government, "dangerous extremist" John Lennon emerged from retirement. Within a few months he was murdered.

The paper trail that might support the conspiracy theory is a little thin, however. It doesn't extend much beyond the airline ticket found in Chapman's hotel room; a Hawaii-New York connection departing December 5. But Chapman had actually purchased a Hawaii-Chicago ticket to depart December 2, with no connecting flight. The ticket found after his arrest had apparently been altered. None of his friends knew that he traveled on to New York. They thought he went to Chicago for a three-day stay.

Bresler concludes that the Lennon assassination, which, as Chapman himself noted in a rare interview, "ended an era," bears similarities to another assassination that took place twelve years earlier: the murder of Robert F. Kennedy.

RFK's apparent lone killer, Sirhan Sirhan, and Chapman

(coincidentally?) shared a defense psychiatrist. But while Dr. Bernard Diamond couldn't skirt the obvious fact that Sirhan was under hypnosis (Diamond wrote it off as self-hypnosis), he labeled Chapman a "paranoid schizophrenic."

The court disagreed. Chapman even now has never had more than routine psychiatric care since entering his guilty plea. He was not sent to a mental hospital, but to Attica State Prison. He was judged legally "rational."

Bresler clears up a few widely disseminated misconceptions about Mark David Chapman:

- While any mention of his name is now accompanied by the phrase "deranged fan," Chapman was anything but. He was no more or less ardent a Beatles/Lennon fan than anyone of his generation. His real rock hero was Todd Rundgren, a cynical studio craftsman who could not be further from Lennon in artistic sensibility.

- Notwithstanding Chapman's announcement months after the murder that he "killed Lennon to gain prominence to promote the reading of *The Catcher in the Rye*," Chapman never exhibited strong feelings about the novel until shortly before the shooting. (*Catcher*, Bresler muses, may have been used as a device to trigger Chapman's "programming.")

- After the murder, major media ran bizarre stories of Chapman's supposed growing identification with John Lennon—at one point he even "rebaptized" himself as Lennon, according to *Newsweek*. These stories were all quite fascinating, but there was no evidence to back any of them up. (It is true that when Chapman quit his last job he signed out as "John Lennon," then crossed the name out, but Bresler interprets this, reasonably, as Chapman saying, "John Lennon, I am going to kill you," rather than "John Lennon, I am you.")

- Chapman was not a "loner." He was for most of his life a normally social individual and a camp counselor who had a special rapport with kids.

Bresler also notes that when Chapman signed up for a YMCA

overseas program, he selected an odd destination: Beirut—a perfect place, says Bresler, for Chapman, a once gentle soul, to be "blooded," that is, desensitized to violence.

A final note to the mystery of Mark David Chapman: As he was ready to go to trial and his diligent public defender was winding up six months spent assembling Chapman's defense, the accused killer suddenly decided to change his plea to guilty. His lawyer was perplexed and more than a little perturbed. But Chapman was determined. He said he was acting on instructions from a "small male voice" that spoke to him in his cell. Chapman interpreted it as the voice of God.

MAJOR SOURCE

Bresler, Fenton. *Who Killed John Lennon?* New York: St. Martin's Press, 1989.

45

Potshots From the "Bushy Knoll"?

Talk about a small world! At about 2:30 in the afternoon of March 30, 1981, it became positively microscopic.

Crouching on the sidewalk in front of the Washington Hilton, a young man who modeled himself on Robert DeNiro's not-so-right Travis Bickle character from the movie, *Taxi Driver*, drew a bead on the new president. Steadying his .22-caliber pistol in both hands, John Hinckley, Jr., began firing explosive "devastator" bullets at Ronald Reagan. In the ensuing pandemonium, the sixth slug found its mark.

Apparently, before Secret Service agents could muscle the elderly president into his bulletproof limo, a shot had ricocheted off the armored sedan's fender, plowing into Reagan's armpit and puncturing the Gipper's lung. Had Hinckley scored a more direct hit that day, Vice President George Bush almost certainly would have ascended to the presidency, sloughing off his second-banana status eight years ahead of schedule.

Small world, indeed. For that very same day, John Hinckley's older brother, Scott, had a dinner date with an old friend of the

332

family: Neil Bush, son of the vice president. What some saw as merely an odd coincidence prompted more conspiratorially attuned eyebrows to arch like divining rods. After all, what are the odds of the president's constitutional successor and the president's would-be assassin knowing each other? Probably zero.

But the Bushes and Hinckleys went way back, to Texas of the 1960s, where both George Bush and John Hinckley, Sr., had amassed personal fortunes in the booming oil industry. Both were blue bloods who circulated in the same privileged circles, which the transplanted aristocrats liked to call their "Texas Raj."

Of course, socializing with the prominent family of a would-be assassin is hardly a hanging offense. Still, in the foggy nebula of a forming conspiracy hypothesis, circumstantial details have a way of radiating suspicious import:

- In the NBC special reports aired immediately after the shooting, correspondent Judy Woodruff said that at least one shot was fired from the hotel, *above* Reagan's limousine. She later elaborated, saying a Secret Service agent had fired that shot from the hotel overhang. Could Reagan's wound have been inflicted by friendly fire? Or, more ominously, did Woodruff glimpse a bona fide "second gunman"—à la JFK in Dealey Plaza? Either way, Woodruff's account might explain how a slug managed to strike Reagan when his limo's bulletproof door stood between him and Hinckley. Sizing up the Hinckley-Bush nexus, conspiracy researcher John Judge has theoretically dubbed this "the shot from the Bushy knoll."
- According to conspiratologist Barbara Honegger, White House correspondent Sarah McClendon made the somewhat more subjective comment that Reagan's Secret Service retinue wasn't in its "usual tight formation" around Reagan in front of the Hilton. Were the Gipper's bodyguards out to throw the game?
- Then there was Hinckley, himself. The Jodie Foster-obsessed

space cadet had been prescribed psychoactive drugs by a hometown psychiatrist. According to press reports, at the time of the shooting he was dosed with Valium. Before targeting Reagan (supposedly to gain the "fame" that would redeem him in the eyes of Foster and the world), Hinckley had stalked Senator Ted Kennedy and President Jimmy Carter. He devoured books on Sirhan Sirhan, Robert Kennedy's assassin (suspected by many conspiracy researchers to have been hypnotically programmed), and Arthur Bremer, who shot George Wallace. Theorists ask the inevitable question: Was Hinckley a mind-controlled assassin, a Manchurian Candidate programmed to "terminate with extreme prejudice"? They point to the CIA's longtime obsession with mind control and the fact that during the 1980 presidential primaries, Bush—the former director of Central Intelligence—enjoyed the zealous support of Agency regulars, who preferred their former boss to Reagan.

- For an antisocial pariah, Hinckley sure got around. In October 1980, he had flown to Nebraska in an attempt to contact a member of the American Nazi Party. Columnist Jack Anderson later claimed that Hinckley had ties to an American faction of the pro-Khomeini "Islamic Guerrilla Army." According to conspiracy author Barbara Honegger, a member of that group told Anderson he had warned the Secret Service about Hinckley's designs on Reagan—two months before the shooting. If Anderson's source is to be believed, the Secret Service did nothing to stop the Jihad-happy gunman.

- The day after his Nazi-seeking mission, Hinckley flew to Nashville to stalk Jimmy Carter, but was arrested at the airport when authorities discovered three handguns in his suitcase. Oddly, after only five hours in custody, this unstable character—who had attempted to transport weapons across state lines and into a city soon to be visited by the president of the United States—was fined and released without further ado. Even more oddly, the authorities apparently didn't bother to examine his journal, which in Dear Diary fashion, detailed Hinckley's plans to kill Carter. Was this a case of bumbling negligence or something more ominous?

• Finally, a pall of suspicion quite naturally fell over George "Poppy" Bush, the preppy achiever and future president whose spooky pedigree was longer than a Texas limo. Bush's father, Prescott Bush, Sr., had served as an army intelligence operative during World War I. Perhaps determined to prove himself a chip off the old block, George, like pater Bush before him, joined Skull and Bones, the elite Yale "society" that weaned more than a few powerhouse pols, Wall Street lions, and CIA superstars. Of course, everyone knows that much later in his life, Bush leap-frogged the career spies and became director of the CIA, where he deftly curtailed congressional investigations into various Agency misdeeds that had begun to ooze into public view following the wildcat gusher that was Watergate.

Of course, there is circumstantial evidence—denied by Bush—that he did in fact pay his dues to the Agency long before becoming its head honcho spook. As a young oilman, Bush founded the Zapata Offshore Oil Company, which, according to one former CIA operative, was used by the Agency as a front for clandestine operations during the early 1960s. "I know [Bush] was involved [with the CIA] in the Caribbean," the ex-CIA man told the *Nation* in 1988. Interestingly, according to retired colonel Fletcher Prouty, who acted as liaison between the Pentagon and CIA during the 1961 Bay of Pigs invasion, that disastrous operation was code-named Zapata, while two Navy ships assigned to the attacking armada had been rechristened *Houston* and *Barbara*. Could these have been sentimental references to Bush's adopted home and the future First Lady?

More evidence that George Bush had been a spook with portfolio as far back as the early 1960s would surface during the 1988 presidential campaign. Joseph McBride, writing in the

Nation, caused a stir when he reported on an interesting FBI memorandum signed by director J. Edgar Hoover, addressed to the State Department, dated November 29, 1963, and bearing the subject heading, "Assassination of President John F. Kennedy November 22, 1963." In it, Hoover reports that the FBI had briefed "Mr. George Bush of the Central Intelligence Agency" about the reaction of anti-Castro Cubans in Miami to the assassination. Twenty-five years after Hoover sent his memo, Bush would deny that it referred to him. "Must be another George Bush," a campaign flack muttered.

The CIA agreed, and, breaking with its longstanding policy of "neither confirming nor denying" the identity of its personnel, claimed that the employee referred to in the memo was "apparently" one George William Bush, who had left the CIA in 1964. Journalist McBride managed to track down the less famous Bush, who acknowledged that he had in fact worked for the CIA for about six months in 1963–64. But he certainly wasn't the George Bush of the memo, he said, because as a short-term "lowly researcher and analyst" he had never been briefed by the FBI or any other government agency, for that matter. "Is that the other George Bush?" he asked.

Indeed, there's another espionage link between George *Herbert Walker* Bush and outré characters orbiting the assassination of JFK. When Lee Harvey Oswald moved to Texas, the socially maladroit young man made an unlikely friend in the suave Baron George De Mohrenschildt, a White Russian emigré connected to the oil industry and, some suspect, the CIA. In 1978, Gaeton Fonzi, an investigator for the House Select Committee on Assassinations, called on De Mohrenshildt to question him about his unlikely friendship with Oswald. The baron's daughter told Fonzi that De Mohrenshildt wasn't home, so the investigator left his business card and said he'd call again. Later that day, Fonzi learned that De Mohrenshildt had returned home, gone upstairs, and lethally blasted his head with a .20-guage shotgun. (That is, if he wasn't "suicided.") When the police found him, the Baron had Fonzi's card in his pocket. In

De Mohrenshildt's address book, Fonzi found this entry: "George H. W. (Poppy) 1412 Ohio also Zapata Petroleum Midland."

If George Bush—the Skull and Bonesman who moved with equal ease among Eastern elites, Western oil tycoons, and Republican Party bosses—had also been a lifelong member of that fusty men's club of veteran intelligence operatives, his later fraternizing with the likes of Manuel Noriega, the Iran-Contra boys, Bay of Pigs/Watergate godfather Dick Nixon, and "new Hitler" Saddam Hussein would certainly make a lot more sense.

Of course, Bush's potentially Janus-faced background doesn't prove anything about the Hinckley hit. But it does suggest an underrated capacity and talent for deception, which is what keeps conspiracy trackers focused on the Bushy knoll.

So where was George, the future conspiracy president, on the day of Hinckley's dirty deed? Out of town, on official vice presidential business. Hmm.

OK, you could probably demolish the whole Bush-Hinckley theory by posing a simple question: Assuming the vice president had "foreknowledge," why on earth would Poppy's son risk meeting with a Hinckley sibling on the *very day* of the coup? Then again, we *are* talking about Neil Bush, whose common-sense deficit would later embarrass Dad when the Savings and Loan scandal made him its official poster child.

MAJOR SOURCES

Clarke, James W. *On Being Mad or Merely Angry: John W. Hinckley, Jr., and Other Dangerous People*. Princeton, NJ: Princeton University Press, 1990.

Fonzi, Gaeton. *The Last Investigation*. New York: Thunder's Mouth Press, 1993.

Honegger, Barbara. *October Surprise*. New York: Tudor Publishing Company, 1989.

McBride, Joseph. "The Man Who Wasn't There, 'George Bush,' CIA Operative." *Nation*, 16 July 1988 and 13 August 1988.

Vankin, Jonathan. *Conspiracies, Cover-Ups, and Crimes*. New York: Dell Publishing, 1992.

46

The Bulgarian Concoction

On a spring day in 1981, the almighty Cold War blasted its way into St. Peter's Square, Vatican City. Mehmet Ali Agca, a twenty-three-year-old Turkish terrorist and international fugitive, trained his pistol above the heads of the faithful and began to pump 9-mm slugs at the Holy Father himself, Pope John Paul II. Hit twice in the chest, the pope slumped in his popemobile, hemorrhaging blood. Police quickly wrestled the gun from Agca and collared the would-be assassin.

As did so many international incidents during the Cold War, the attempted assassination of John Paul II spawned dueling conspiracy theories. Version one, promoted by a consortium of anticommunists, vintage Western spooks and "terrorologists," proclaimed the assault a Soviet plot. Version two, proffered by critics on the Left (left behind in the American media's rush to endorse version one) argued that if there was an East versus West conspiracy, it had been launched not by communists, but by a clutch of Western cold warriors *after* the assassination attempt: a disinformation plot to frame the Soviets.

Which version was closer to the truth?

Agca, as the international press initially reported, apparently had nothing to do with the Soviets. In fact, the terrorist's background and associations all pointed quite clearly to a network of neofascist Turks—the terrorists behind Agca's earlier assassination of a liberal Turkish journalist and perhaps also the convicted killer's mysterious escape from prison.

The prospects for the Red conspiracy theory didn't begin to perk up until more than a year after the assault in St. Peter's Square. It was then that Agca confessed, from his Italian prison cell. Three Bulgarians living in Rome had put him up to the nefarious deed, he claimed. The anticommunist faction rallied to the cause and dubbed the affair, the Bulgarian Connection, a catchy title worthy of a Robert Ludlum spy novel.

To wit: the evil Kremlin, through its proxies in communist Bulgaria, plotted to assassinate the pope in an effort either to a) destabilize Turkey and NATO, or b) demoralize uppity Poland, the Holy Father's communist-infested homeland. According to this theory, the Bulgarians had activated Agca and his fascist cadres to execute the plot, thereby maintaining Soviet "deniability."

Yet apart from Agca's tardy "confession," there was little credible evidence to support the Bulgarian hypothesis. In fact, a fair reading of the evidence favors conspiracy theory number two: The Red conspiracy was a red herring.

For starters, the two key "journalists" promoting the so-called Bulgarian Connection in the American media had backgrounds as right-wing disinformationists. "Terrorologist" Claire Sterling had worked for the CIA-sponsored newspaper, *Rome Daily American,* and even Agency veterans found her books "linking" the Soviet Union to "international terrorism" notoriously unreliable, naively laden with CIA-planted propaganda canards.

The other Bulgarian Connection tout was Paul Henze, a

"former" propagandist and CIA veteran who had run the Agency stations in Ethiopia and Turkey.

But even before Henze and Sterling stoked up their Red Scare Redux, the Bulgarian-KGB theory had suspicious origins: Just six days after Agca's assault on the pope, Italy's corrupt intelligence agency, SISMI, produced a document claiming that a Soviet official announced at a meeting of the Warsaw Pact powers that Agca had been trained in the Soviet Union. The document later proved to be a forgery, but it helped buoy the anti-Soviet conspiracy theory.

Other "evidence" was equally chimerical. Sterling relied on a melodramatic cast of unnamed "insiders," such as the mysterious Bulgarian "Colonel X" whose "knowing Eastern eye could spot telltale signs" of commie conspiracies. In other words, Colonel X had a hunch that the Russians did it. Henze's supposed proof included vague rumors circulating in Italy, suspicions that the Vatican blamed Moscow, and assurances that a future defector with knowledge of the plot "is almost certain to turn up one of these days." (Ah, if only undiscovered theoretical future evidence were admissible in a court of law.)

Henze and Sterling, of course, were hardly deterred by the actual, *existent* evidence, which suggested that Agca's assassination effort had been sponsored by the neofascist Gray Wolves, the youth arm of Turkey's extreme-right Turkes party. Agca's neo-Nazi confreres generously supplied him with cash *and* the gun used against the pope. Undaunted by this superior evidence, Henze and Sterling speculated (without a scintilla of proof) that high-ranking members of the Gray Wolves, a fascist organization whose motto is "death to communists," decided to chuck their fanatic ideology and collaborate with the Bulgarian commies.

Yet there was always Acga's confession to fall back on. Or was it, too, suspect? In fact, there was plenty of evidence, largely unreported in the American press, that Agca had been cajoled and bribed to implicate the Bulgarians.

According to various sources, officials from the notoriously shifty SISMI pressured Agca during jail-house visits. During the

1985–86 trial of the Bulgarians implicated by Agca, a state witness accused former SISMI officials of hatching a plot to coerce Agca into implicating the Bulgarians. One of the named SISMI spooks, Francesco Pazienza, denied any complicity, but confirmed that *other* SISMI officials had in fact put the squeeze on Agca.

Pressure to blame the Soviets reportedly came from other quarters as well, including the prison's Catholic chaplain. (At one point, Agca fired off a stinging letter to the Vatican complaining of death threats from a Vatican emissary.) Also applying powers of persuasion were a Mafia leader incarcerated in the same prison (he claimed that SISMI pressured him to menace Agca) and the Italian magistrate who prepared the case against the Bulgarians.

Despite Agca's cooperation (or perhaps because of it) the long-awaited trial of the Bulgarians was something of a letdown for partisans of the Red Conspiracy theory. Agca set the tone for the proceedings when he promptly declared himself to be Jesus Christ. He continued to contradict, retract, and change his previous testimony, as he had done all along.

One example from many: Before the trial, Agca claimed to have attended a meeting at the Rome apartment of one of his supposed Bulgarian masters, Sergei Antonov. Agca described the apartment in detail. But when later challenged, Agca reversed his story, claiming that he had never visited Antonov's apartment, after all. The strange thing was that he had described the Antonov suite to a T—with the exception of one salient architectural detail present in every other apartment in the complex, but not Antonov's. If Agca had never been to chez Antonov, as he now claimed, how did he manage to describe it earlier? The fact that he screwed up one key detail suggests that Agca was coached by someone who had cased a neighboring flat.

Ultimately, the court dismissed the case against the Bulgarians for utter lack of evidence. Assessing the judicial fiasco, a major Italian newspaper commented that "Only one thing is clear: Agca is a liar."

In fact, the concerted efforts of Red-baiting journalists and investigators to pin the blame on the Soviets suggest a propaganda operation aimed at fomenting anticommunist sentiment worldwide and certainly in Poland, where the upstart Solidarity movement had been suppressed by the communist government. Although Cold War conservatives in the CIA pushed the Russkie conspiracy theory, a contingent of Agency analysts who had examined all the data argued that there was little, if any, credible evidence for Soviet involvement. (Future CIA director Robert Gates found himself in hot water when it was revealed during his Senate confirmation hearings that he had misrepresented the analysts' report in an effort to demonize the Evil Empire.)

As for Agca's motive in whacking the pope, some have suggested that the ultra-nationalist Gray Wolves intended to spread terror and chaos in Turkey and abroad in order to build support for a fascist putsch. Interestingly, this was the modus operandi of Italy's own neo-Nazi underground, which practiced the so-called "strategy of tension," in which neofascists bombed train stations and committed other acts of terror which were then blamed on the Left to build support for the far-Right.

Indeed, there are accounts of meetings between members of the Gray Wolves and Italy's right-wing terrorist groups, including the P2 quasi-Masonic lodge and Ordine Nuova (new order). Further, in the mid-1980s, Italians learned that P2 members had burrowed into prestigious positions in the press, government, and especially SISMI, the Italian intelligence agency accused of pressuring Agca to finger the Soviets. The 1980 terrorist bombing of the railway station in Bologna, initially blamed on the left, later resulted in indictments of P2 luminaries like Francesco Pazienza (the ex-SISMI official accused of helping to coach Agca), and Italy's public enemy number one, neo-Nazi terrorist Stefano della Chiaie.

On the lam from Italian authorities, Pazienza was later apprehended in the United States. He told U.S. customs officials of a Miami meeting in April 1981, a month before the assault on the pope. According to Pazienza, the meeting was attended by Gray Wolves, including Oral Celik—who reportedly accompanied Agca to St. Peter's Square—and Stefano della Chiaie. Although Pazienza's claim hasn't been corroborated, the attempted assassination of the pope makes more sense in the context of the Italian ultra-Right's "strategy of tension": like the Bologna bombing, a neofascist provocation blamed on the Left.

Finally, there are indications that Western intelligence agencies had some foreknowledge of Agca's plot—but did nothing to stop it. According to several reports, the CIA had thoroughly infiltrated the Gray Wolves. West German and Swiss authorities monitored Agca's phone calls as he passed through their countries—and apparently didn't bother to arrest the fugitive. Most interestingly, in the months before the Agca's attack, Count Alexandre de Marenches, the rightist chief of the French clandestine services, reportedly spread word of an East Bloc plot to kill the pope. Did de Marenches already know about the Gray Wolves plot or that cold warriors would subsequently attempt to. frame it on the Soviets?

There isn't evidence to prove definitively that Western spooks looked the other way, or even supported the Gray Wolves plot, but it is clear that ideologues exploited the outcome. And continue to do so. What propaganda/CIA veteran Henze wrote about the Soviets might also be read another way: "Disinformation can have a long shelf life."

MAJOR SOURCES

Henze, Paul B. *The Plot to Kill the Pope.* New York: Charles Scribner's Sons, 1985.
Herman, Edward S., and Frank Brodhead. *The Rise and Fall of the Bulgarian Connection.* New York: Sheridan Square Publications, 1986.
Herman, Edward S., and Noam Chomsky. *Manufacturing Consent: The Political Economy of the Mass Media.* New York: Pantheon Books, 1988.

XI

Twilight of the Idols

47

The Lincoln Conspiracies

As conventional history tells it, the conspirators who plotted the assassination of President Abraham Lincoln met justice at gun-point and on the business end of a hangman's noose. John Wilkes Booth, the actor who fired a derringer ball into Lincoln's brain at point-blank range, was shot dead by federal troops near Bowling Green, Virginia, two weeks after his grand exit from the scene of the crime at Ford's Theater. Later, four of Booth's coconspirators went to the gallows.

Yet from the moment of the president's murder on that drizzly Good Friday, suspicions about the actual nature of the conspiracy began to fester. Did the government have fore-knowledge of Booth's plot? Was Booth a pawn of high-ranking officials? Inevitably, 125 years after the crime of the nineteenth century, fact and lore are more than a little tangled. Still, given the abundance of odd "coincidences" and curious admissions of the players, in many ways America's first presidential assassination remains a genuine mystery.

The Booth plot, which included the attempted butchering of Secretary of State William H. Seward (he lived) and the planned

347

assassination of Vice President Andrew Johnson (never executed, thanks to a coconspirator with cold feet), involved nine
ne'er-do-well Northerners (including Booth) who harbored
Southern sympathies. But the bitter Civil War had only tenta-
tively concluded, so it fell upon the Northern government to
blame the plot on the South, not sparing Confederate president
Jefferson Davis from indictment. Of course, the North didn't
let a minor obstacle like lack of evidence hinder its case; at the
trial of Booth's peon cohorts, the government suborned testimony to implicate "the dirty Rebs."

Trumped-up evidence not withstanding, Booth did in fact
have provocative links to Southern brass. A rabid advocate of
the Confederacy (yet unwilling to don a uniform and fight), the
egocentric actor used his celebrity as a cover for smuggling
medicine to the South. Consequently, some historians have
claimed that Booth was a Confederate secret agent.

During an October 1864 trip to Montreal, Canada, Booth
conferred with Jacob Thompson, chief of the Confederate secret
service. At about the same time, Booth had been recruiting for
his grand plot to kidnap Lincoln, hoping to trade his eminent
hostage for Confederate POWs. "Did Booth propose his kidnap
scheme to Jacob Thompson?" asked historian Theodore
Roscoe. "Probably. Did he suggest Lincoln's assassination...?"
Roscoe thought that possible as well.

Another item often cited as evidence of a Southern role in the
Booth plot is a note found in Booth's steamer trunk and signed
by a "Sam." The note referred to seeing how Richmond, the
capital of the Confederacy, would feel about some unspecified
affair.

During the nineteenth century, a steady stream of pamphlets
linked Booth to the Copperheads—Northern Democrats seen
as Southern-symps—and their secret society, the Knights of the
Golden Circle. The Jack Ruby of the Lincoln affair, Boston
Corbett, the soldier who shot Booth in a burning barn,
purportedly was a religious nut who had castrated himself to

achieve spiritual purity. Though later locked away in a mental institution, he managed to escape and vanish without a trace. The altar on which the long-haired Corbett supposedly offered his eternal chastity? The Russian Skoptsi sect, a pagan goddess cult whose priests wore women's clothing. A pagan cult? Ah, cue the Illuminati: For conspiratologists who like to posit that all-powerful eighteenth-century Bavarian secret society at the center of history's nastiest moments wonder if the Illumined Ones had a hand in the Lincoln murder. If so, can we be sure that Brother (or is it Sister?) Corbett really killed Booth?

The more enduring—and earthbound—theories assert that Booth was working for traitors among Lincoln's own cabinet, that he escaped with their assistance, and that the rakish actor lived to a ripe old age on a handsome government pension.

"There was one man who profited greatly by Lincoln's assassination," historian Otto Eisenschiml announced in 1937. "This man was his secretary of war, Edward M. Stanton." A member of the Radical Republican faction that bitterly opposed Lincoln's lenient reconstruction plan for the South, Stanton stood to consolidate his own power if the North imposed a hard-line military occupation instead.

As Eisenschiml and other revisionist historians saw it, Stanton's behavior immediately preceding the assassination, and also after, was highly suspicious.

- Stanton refused a request by Lincoln to allow the secretary of war's assistant, Major Thomas Eckert, to accompany the president to the fateful performance at Ford's Theater. The implication, according to Eisenschiml, is that Stanton knew something Lincoln didn't.
- Despite the profusion of death threats against Lincoln— and an earlier kidnap attempt by Booth in which the actor shot the famous stovepipe hat clean off Abe's head—only one bodyguard accompanied the president to Ford's Theater. And he was hardly a stellar specimen at that, abandon-

ing the president in his hour of need to indulge in a snort at the corner pub. Apparently the bodyguard was never reprimanded for his gross negligence.

- The night of the assassination, commercial telegraph lines in Washington—controlled by the government during wartime—apparently went dead, delaying the news of Booth's escape. Some see this mysterious event as evidence that government insiders abetted the assassin in his flight.

- There is also the curious matter of Booth's diary, which disappeared into a Stanton safe after the assassination. It wasn't until several years after the conspiracy trial that the journal was made public, a revelation that caused a political tempest. Curiously, there were at least eighteen pages missing. Lafayette C. Baker, the scheming chief of the National Detective Police (NDF), forerunner of the modern Secret Service, testified that when his men turned the diary over to Stanton, all the pages had been intact.

  Others have explained Booth's vanishing diary in terms of a less sinister conspiracy. Thomas Reed Turner suggests that the government suppressed the diary, which detailed the failed kidnap plots, to avoid raising embarrassing questions about its own inaction in the wake of Booth's less-than-subtle abduction attempts. According to Turner, "There was more than just a suspicion that the government was aware of Booth's plot.... The fact that the government was able so rapidly to get on the track of the main conspirators indicates that this was a group it had under surveillance." Still, if this is true, the question remains: Why *didn't* the government put Booth and company out of business before all hell broke loose?

- In a strange cipher message written by NDF chief Baker (himself the object of many a suspicion) three years after the assassination, the corrupt top cop issued what some believe to be a rhyming confession: "In New Rome there walked three men, a Judas, a Brutus, and a spy. Each planned that he should be the kink [sic] when Abraham should die ...As the fallen man lay dying, Judas came and paid respects to one he hated, and when at last he saw him die, he said 'Now the ages have him and the nation now have I.'"

"Judas" obviously refers to Stanton, who rushed to the scene of the crime and uttered his famous "Now he belongs to the ages" quote. Brutus may refer to Booth's father, the famous actor Junius Brutus Booth; to Booth himself; or to Lincoln's close friend, Ward H. Lamon, the U.S. marshal for Washington, who had often warned Lincoln about assassination plots, but was out of town on that fatal evening. *Et tu*, Lamon? Whatever its real meaning, Baker's doggerel declaration concludes thus: "But lest one is left to wonder what has happened to the spy, I can safely tell you this, it was I. Lafayette C. Baker 2–5–68." Even anticonspiracist historians like Thomas Reed Turner concede that the text and signature seem to be authentic.

Baker died several months after penning that cryptogram, "at the robust age of forty-four." His wife believed he had been poisoned by government operatives.

Dead men tell no tales, of course.

It fell upon Schick Sunn Classic Productions, producers of searching documentary films on Bigfoot and Noah's Ark, to rejuvenate such arcana. *The Lincoln Conspiracy*, a 1977 book and feature film, is less the catalog of verities it professes to be and more of an imaginative compendium of assassination possibilities. Drawing on controversial "never before published documents," authors David Balsiger and Charles E. Sellier proposed a superconspiracy in which four separate (and not necessarily congenial) groups sponsored Booth's kidnap and assassination plots: Stanton and his Radical Republican confreres, who planned to seize the government with the aid of Baker; Jacob Thompson, the Confederate spy master, and his Graycoat superiors in Richmond; Northern bankers and cotton speculators, who made a mint on wartime contraband and hated to see the good times end; and Maryland planters whose malevolence toward the Negro-coddling Lincoln knew no bounds.

But Balsiger and Sellier managed to top even that ambitious theory by rallying the enduring legend of Booth's survival and escape from the massive federal dragnet. *The Lincoln Conspiracy* claimed that the man killed in the Garrett barn was not Booth, but a second Rebel-agent-cum-fugitive who had nothing to do with Booth's plot. His name was Captain James William Boyd, a man who, unfortunately for him, "bore a striking resemblance to Booth."

Lucky for Booth this amazing body double (who stood a full six inches taller than Booth) bore a number of other convenient similarities, including the initials J.W.B., which even *more* conveniently were tattooed on his arm. According to Balsiger and Sellier, both J.W.B.'s were hobbled by seriously injured legs. (Booth snapped his when he leapt from the president's box to the stage at Ford's Theater; Boyd's old war wound had flared up.) And as luck would have it, both men were accompanied by fugitive sidekicks, who themselves shared an uncanny resemblance. Not only that, but in his flight the hapless Boyd managed to team up with a bona fide Booth coconspirator.

When NDF chief Baker informed Stanton that his men had killed Boyd, and not Booth, the coverup began. This theory, like other tales of Booth's survival, draws on genuinely peculiar details surrounding the identification and disposal of the body, which were conducted in ironclad secrecy. Few saw the body; an official photograph of the corpse was consigned to oblivion; and Booth's own doctor had trouble identifying his former patient, who had never sported reddish hair *before*. (The folks at Sunn Classic tell us that Boyd had...reddish hair!)

Balsiger and Sellier's claims about body doubles and synchronized limping are a bit hard to swallow, as are their "newly discovered" documents, which include transcripts (yet not the originals) purporting to be the missing pages of Booth's diary.

However improbable, though, the legend of Booth's survival is incontestably deathless. During the 1920s, the mummified remains of a derelict painter, John St. Helen, billed as the once-worldy Booth, enjoyed a mildly successful postmortem career as a carnival sideshow. Before that, the latter half of the nineteenth century had been rife with accounts of a gracefully aging Booth, lately back from Europe, India, or points more mysterious, dropping in on relatives, or spouting deathbed "confessions" in unglamorous places like Enid, Oklahoma.

To loosely paraphrase Booth's often-alleged overboss, the redoubtable Secretary of War Stanton: Now the Lincoln conspiracies belong to the ages.

MAJOR SOURCES

Balsiger, David and Charles E. Sellier, Jr. *The Lincoln Conspiracy.* Los Angeles: Schick Sunn Classic Books, 1977.

Howard, Michael. *Secret Societies: Their Influence and Power in World History.* Rochester, VT: Destiny Books, 1989.

Roscoe, Theodore. *The Web of Conspiracy: The Complete Story of the Men Who Murdered Abraham Lincoln.* Englewood Cliffs, NJ: Prentice-Hall, 1960.

Turner, Thomas Reed. *Beware the People Weeping: Public Opinion and the Assassination of Abraham Lincoln.* Baton Rouge, LA: Louisiana State University Press, 1982.

48

The Long Aim of the Law?

It was just after 6:00 on April 4, 1968, and Martin Luther King, Jr., was standing on the second-floor balcony of Memphis's Lorraine Motel when a sniper's bullet cut through the evening air. Playfully bantering with his driver one moment, King was on his back the next, a pool of blood expanding around his head. Minutes later, the civil rights leader was dead.

The ostensible assassin, captured months later, was James Earl Ray, a petty crook who hadn't shown a previous aptitude for any criminal enterprise more elaborate than gas station stickups and a prison escape. As the result of a deal between his attorney and the prosecution, Ray pleaded guilty and received a ninety-nine-year sentence. But he immediately recanted and, insisting his innocence, has attempted to secure a retrial ever since, without success.

Did Ray kill Martin Luther King? Two and a half decades after the fact, a small mountain of accumulating evidence tends to corroborate Ray's broadest claim that he *didn't* fire the fatal shot. What we now know of that indelible day in Memphis shifts suspicion rather dramatically.

In the days and hours leading up to King's murder, an extraordinary phalanx of government agents, informants, soldiers, and spies quietly filed into Memphis. Their business remains murky, purposefully so—government documents that might shed light on the case are still stubbornly classified. However, they clearly had little interest in *protecting* King. His increasingly vocal opposition to the Vietnam War and outreach to impoverished whites had begun to stoke fears of revolution in the streets. Army intelligence, which had spied on King for decades, considered him to be a subversive and possibly a communist. Now they clambered to develop plans that might undercut King's agenda, especially his upcoming March on Washington, billed in a panicky Pentagon intelligence report as "a devastating civil disturbance whose sole purpose is to shut down the United States government." King was the domestic equivalent of the enemy being fought overseas: "a Negro who repeatedly has preached the message of Hanoi and Peking."

Against this martial backdrop, King had returned to Memphis, vowing to restage a nonviolent march in defense of striking sanitation workers. The previous week, a King rally there had erupted into a riot that injured sixty and left one person dead. Egged on by FBI director J. Edgar Hoover's hysterical "blind" leaks to the press, the media was now billing King's return as a "dress rehearsal" for looting and rioting in Washington.

Enter the feds, surreptitiously, almost as if they had declared war on King:

• In advance of King's visit, the army's 20th Special Forces Group, based in Alabama, had dispatched Green Beret soldiers to various cities in the South, including Memphis. Their mission: Making street maps, identifying landing zones for antiriot troops, and scouting sniper sites—*sup-*

posedly to crush civil disorder. But the 20th was chock full of Special Operations Group vets, who in Vietnam had worked with the CIA in clandestine operations, including assassinations. According to a former army counterintelligence major quoted in the *Memphis Commercial Appeal*, "They couldn't let a lot of these crazy guys back into the States because they couldn't forget their training." So the army "dumped" them in Birmingham's 20th SFG. "The rural South was 'in-country,'" the major said, "and at times things got out of hand." The Ku Klux Klan became the 20th's domestic intelligence network, dubbed "Klan Special Forces."

- According to army records obtained in 1993 by the *Memphis Commercial Appeal*, on April 3 army agents from the 111th Military Intelligence Group arrived in Memphis, where they shadowed King's "movements and monitored radio traffic from a sedan crammed with electronic equipment."
- On the day of King's assassination, "eight Green Beret soldiers from an 'Operation Detachment Alpha 184 Team' were also in Memphis carrying out an unknown mission," per the *Commercial Appeal*.
- According to then-Memphis police detective Ed Redditt, "an hour and a half, no more than two hours" before King's assassination, he was summoned from his command post adjacent to the Lorraine Motel and whisked away to police headquarters. Redditt was one of only two officers assigned to protect King. In the police chief's office, "It was like a meeting of the Joint Chiefs of Staff," he later told author Mark Lane. "In this room, just before Dr. King was murdered, were the heads and the seconds in command of I guess every law enforcement operation in this area...The sheriff, the highway patrol, army intelligence, the national guard. You name it. It was in the room."

Redditt was introduced to a U.S. Secret Service agent who claimed to have flown out from Washington to warn him that a group in Mississippi had put a contract on his head. Redditt, an African American, was ordered to relinquish his post and go home. The supposed "death threat," Redditt learned years later, turned out to have been a false alarm.

- The first person to reach the mortally wounded King was Marrell McCullough, supposedly a black radical, but in reality an undercover cop keeping tabs on the minister's entourage for the Memphis police and the FBI. According to Mark Lane, shortly after the assassination McCullough was also working for the CIA.

- The local cops behaved plenty suspiciously, too. Memphis's director of police and fire services removed the two black firemen stationed at the firehouse adjacent to the Lorraine Motel. That firehouse, Station 2, became the stakeout where Detective Redditt would surveil and protect King—until Redditt, too, was yanked from the site.

According to FBI documents, the Bureau had recently heard of some fifty threats against King's life, the latest just three days before his death. Despite the warning signs, the local police withdrew their tactical units several blocks away from King's motel. They also failed to seal off streets or issue an all-points-bulletin after the shooting. Consequently, the killer—or killers—had an open escape route.

The assassination was immediately dubbed the work of that familiar American archetype, the nonpolitical loner. And two months after the murder, London authorities arrested James Earl Ray, the leading suspect. Ray, a forty-year-old white fugitive, had indeed fled Memphis moments after the fatal shot was fired. Without a doubt, he had some connection to the killing—a fact he has never contested.

The evidence aligned against Ray certainly looked convincing, perhaps too convincing. It included fingerprints on a .30–06 rifle with sniper's scope, which was found on the sidewalk outside a seedy rooming house opposite the Lorraine

Motel. Ray had in fact checked into a room there under an alias earlier that day. Bundled with the gun were an assortment of Ray's personal items, including his prison-issued radio taken during his escape from lock-up the previous year.

Witnesses at the boarding house reported seeing a dark-suited man, presumed to be the new "tenant," rushing through the second-floor hallway moments after the shot rang out. He was described as carrying a long package. A minute or so later, patrons in a record store beneath the boarding house saw a similarly clad man rush by the store window, dropping the package onto the pavement with a conspicuous thud. Moments later, they saw a man in a white Mustang bolt away from the curb in a screech of burning rubber.

It didn't look good for Ray, to put it mildly. Not only did the window in Ray's room face the Lorraine Motel balcony, but so did the window in the common bathroom on the same floor, where several witnesses claimed the gunshot originated. The furniture in Ray's room had been rearranged to facilitate access to the window, and among Ray's personal effects ditched on the sidewalk below was a pair of binoculars he had purchased that afternoon.

Ray's inarticulate claims didn't help his case. He insisted that he had been the dupe in a plot organized by a mysterious character named Raoul, whom he described variously as a "blond Latin," a "red-haired French Canadian," or an auburn-haired "Latin Spanish." According to Ray, Raoul had hired him in Montreal the previous year as a courier in a gun-smuggling venture.

As Ray told it, he had purchased the damning rifle and binoculars at Raoul's behest. The rifle was to be a demo model for prospective illegal buyers. Although his boss told Ray to stay near his car parked below the flophouse, Ray claimed that he had driven to a nearby gas station. When he returned to the boarding house, he later asserted, pandemonium was in full swing. Assuming that Raoul's gun deal had gone awry, Ray claimed that he hightailed it out of town, only learning later that King had been gunned down.

Though the official version of events seems to present an open-and-shut case against Ray—bolstered by his initial guilty plea—there are more than a few discrepencies:

• Numerous witnesses reported that there were two white Mustangs parked outside the fleabite boarding house in Memphis. Could a man of a similar physical build and attire have impersonated Ray, conspicuously dropping the rifle for the benefit of bystanders, and then peeling away in a car just like Ray's?

• For Ray to pack his easily traced personal effects with the supposed murder weapon is the height of criminal stupidity. For him to then dump the incriminating package in plain view of witnesses, a few steps away from his car, is just plain unbelievable. On the other hand, someone trying to frame Ray might do just that.

• Only one "witness," Charles Stephens, identified Ray as the man seen fleeing from the boarding house. At first Stephens denied that Ray was the man who rushed from the bathroom, but after languishing in jail for a spell as a "material witness," Stephens changed his story. Later, however, he recanted and complained that he was coerced into signing a false affidavit.

According to Grace Stephens, her husband wasn't even in the building when the shot rang out. It was *she* who saw a man fleeing down the hall, not her husband. "There's no doubt in my mind," Mrs. Stephens claimed from the beginning. "That wasn't James Earl Ray. It was an entirely different man."

To be sure, the Stephenses aren't the most reliable of witnesses; at the time both were drinking heavily. In a move that certainly seems suspicious, though, soon after her husband was jailed, Grace was illegally confined to a

mental institution. According to her lawyer, she was "shut-
tled off" to the nuthouse because her loud claims threatened
the Memphis prosecutor's case against Ray.

• Though the rifle and sundry items packed around it were
  covered with Ray's fingerprints, uncharacteristically it took
  the FBI weeks to match them to Ray the escaped convict.
  And none of Ray's prints were found in his room, nor on a
  box filled with bullets.

There are other mysterious occurrences that belie the lone-
nut scenario: On the lam in Toronto, while he was holed up in a
boarding house, Ray was visited by a person who has come to
be known as "the fat man." The fat man hand-delivered an
envelope to the frightened fugitive. Apparently Ray wasn't
concerned that this supposed stranger might be a policeman,
for according to the hostel keep, her reclusive guest uncharacteristically met the man at the front door. It would seem that the
mysterious stranger delivered a wad of cash, for the very next
day Ray bought a plane ticket to London.

Canadian authorities later located the fat man, who rattled
off an implausible story that nonetheless satisfied the police: He
had stumbled upon an envelope bearing Ray's address and
decided to return it to its owner. But when author Philip
Melanson tracked him down and confronted him years later,
the fat man said that he had refused to testify in 1968 in order to
avoid getting "a bullet in my head." Later, he added, without
elaborating, "Ray and those people are gangsters. They'll kill
anyone."

But the best and spookiest evidence of a conspiracy consists
of Ray's use of sophisticated aliases during the months leading
up to the assassination and directly thereafter.

All four of Ray's aliases have one very crucial connection:
they were names of real people living in close proximity to one
another in Toronto, Canada. But Ray visited Toronto only once
in his life: while on the lam, just *after* King was assassinated.
Yet he had been using several of the false identities months

before the assassination. How had Ray come by these names? Typically, Ray's explanations have been evasive.

Melanson tracked down the Canadians, and the scenario he details in his 1989 book, *The Murkin Conspiracy*, is downright chilling. Months before the assassination, Ray was using the alias, "Eric Starvo Galt." Melanson discovered that, during the same period, the Toronto man named Eric Galt was signing his middle name, St. Vincent, as "St. V.," scribbling lopsided circles for the periods, so that the full name looked to the uninitiated like "Eric Starvo Galt." In an impressive bit of detection, Melanson found that at some point, the real Eric St. Vincent Galt changed his signature, and began signing documents and personal checks as Eric S. Galt. At about the same time, the recidivist American crook James Earl Ray changed his alias to "Eric S. Galt." And this was months before Ray's first and only visit to Toronto!

There were other uncanny parallels between Ray and the Canadians whose names he apparently filched—especially Galt. Ray bore a striking resemblance to Galt. Both had scars above their eyes. In fact, the other Canadians also had facial scars. Four months before the assassination, Ray—the two-bit holdup man—underwent plastic surgery, which modified his "very distinctive pointy nose," according to Melanson, and made him look even more like the real Galt. Moreover, the Canadian Galt was a skilled marksman who often toted guns in his car to and from the shooting range and who had visited cities of the American South frequented by Ray.

Melanson's point is very persuasive: These parallels cannot possibly be coincidences. Was someone trying to draw attention to these four hapless Canadians? In fact, that's just what happened. During the search for King's assassin, they became unwitting victims of Ray's aliases. At the time of "the greatest manhunt in history" Galt saw his name blazoned in banner headlines. Had the FBI not identified Ray's prints on the rifle, the innocent Galt would almost surely have become the prime suspect.

What was the point of this sophisticated legerdemain with Ray's aliases? According to Melanson, Galt was the key. "Galt was more than simply a cover: He was a man who could be implicated in the crime, at least temporarily, while Ray made his escape." The other two Canadians lived conveniently near Galt, and police might erroneously conclude that the real Galt had stolen his three "aliases" from them. In short, the unsuspecting Galt was set up to be the "wrong man."

The parallels "were surely the result of conspiratorial planning rather than coincidence," concludes Melanson, adding that "This was beyond the capacities of a small-time loser like Ray."

Melanson argues that the conspirators probably selected Galt and cribbed his vital stats by gaining access to his top-secret security clearance file. For Galt was an employee at a Canadian defense firm working on a classified missile project for the U.S. military. His file was kept by the Royal Canadian Mounted Police (RCMP).

The CIA routinely trades information with the RCMP, raising the possibility that American intelligence had a hand in Ray's elaborate odyssey—and the murder of Martin Luther King, Jr.

While some assassination researchers believe that Ray was a completely innocent "patsy," others suggest that he played a part in the plot, albeit maybe not as the triggerman. Melanson, who belongs to the latter school, suggests that had Ray reached his ultimate destination, Angola, he would have been discreetly murdered.

Which brings us full circle to the quasi-chimerical "Raoul," Ray's purported master. Ray had supposedly met Raoul in Montreal. In 1968 a Canadian journalist tracked down a "Raoul-like" character in that city. Named Jules Ron "Ricco" Kimble, this American expatriate also was known as "Rolland" or "Rollie."

Although the House Select Committee on Assassinations report stated that Kimble denied any evidence of the murder, in

1989 he told reporters John Edginton and John Sergeant that he had in fact been involved in the conspiracy that killed King. According to Kimble, the plot involved agents of the CIA and FBI, the "mob," and Ray. (Kimble is serving a double life sentence in El Reno, Oklahoma, for two murders he says were political.)

Kimble now claims responsibilty for introducing Ray to a CIA operative in Montreal who arranged for Ray's aliases. But was Kimble, himself, the mysterious Raoul? Unfortunately, the story gets murkier, for reporters Edginton and Sergeant cite an anonymous "ex-CIA agent" as confirming that the Agency employed a Canada-based operative who specialized in creating false identities. That operative's name? Raoul Maora.

The evidence of government involvement in the King assassination is admittedly circumstantial. But taken together— the massive presence of U.S. intelligence and law enforcement operatives in Memphis, the discrepencies in the evidence against Ray, the Canadian aliases, and the fact that Ray seems to have had a sophisticated support network that kept him on a payroll—the scenario gets, well, curiouser and curiouser.

The FBI's alleged absence from the scene of the crime is particularly odd. The Bureau claimed that it hadn't had King under surveillance in Memphis. For years, however, he had been the target of Hoover's pathological crusade to destroy the "Black Messiah," as King was known in Bureauspeak. That the FBI would innocently call off its unrelenting dogs just as King's "threat" to law-and-order types was cresting stretches credulity to the snapping point.

Did the FBI's illegal campaign against King go beyond its well-documented character assassination? An FBI memo dated less than a year before King died in Memphis seems prescient: It stated that a CIA informant "feels that somewhere in the Negro movement, at the top, there must be a Negro leader who is 'clean' who could step into the vacuum and chaos if Martin Luther King were either exposed or assassinated."

No heir apparent ever emerged—although ultrasuspicious

conspiracy trackers note Jesse Jackson's public appearance soon after the shooting in a shirt stained with the fallen martyr's blood—but by hook, crook, or sheer dumb luck, Hoover and his bully boys got their wish.

MAJOR SOURCES

Edginton, John, and John Sergeant. "The Murder of Martin Luther King, Jr." *Covert Action Information Bulletin*, no. 34 (Summer 1990).
Lane, Mark, and Dick Gregory. *Murder in Memphis: The FBI and the Assassination of Martin Luther King.* New York: Thunder's Mouth Press, 1993.
Melanson, Philip H. *The Murkin Conspiracy: An Investigation Into the Assassination of Dr. Martin Luther King, Jr.* New York: Praeger Publishers, 1989.

49

RFK Must Die!

The killing of Robert F. Kennedy, the senator who would have surely been president had he not been gunned down, is at the same time an ostensibly simpler yet more mysterious crime than the assassination of his brother, the president.

The many possible keys to the JFK assassination lie in documents, events, and witness testimony, much of it accrued by two separate government commissions. The interlocking intelligence, military, and underworld operations that seem somehow to bear on the Dallas events speak more or less for themselves. Lee Harvey Oswald may have taken the final secret of JFK to his premature grave, but he left a paper trail behind him.

The secrets of Robert Kennedy's assassination lie locked in the most secure vault of all—a man's mind. Sirhan Bashira Sirhan, who still sits in jail today, his sentence commuted from death to life, has never been able to remember what happened the night of June 5, 1968, when he lunged out of a crowd and opened wild fire in Kennedy's general direction. Unlike the

politically preoccupied Oswald, Sirhan never had any strong
political convictions. And unlike Oswald, the globetrotting
marine whose biography is a cryptogram of curious connections, Sirhan's life leading up to the assassination is remarkable
only for its unremarkability. No satisfactory motive for his
action has ever been revealed because even he does not know
why he shot Kennedy—or even if he did.

First, the facts. Then, the questions:

On California's primary election night, Bobby Kennedy—
senator from New York, former U.S. attorney general, and, of
course, younger brother of the president slain four and a half
years earlier—celebrated his crucial victory in that large state
with a speech at his campaign headquarters in Los Angeles's
fashionable Ambassador Hotel. The win in California looked
certain to propel him past Hubert Humphrey—Lyndon
Johnson's waffling vice-president—and fuzzy-minded liberal
Eugene McCarthy into the Democratic presidential nomination
when the party convened that summer in Chicago.

After rousing his supporters with the exhortation, "On to
Chicago! Let's win there!" Kennedy made his way off the
podium through a pantry in the kitchen of the Ambassador.
The place was jammed with warm bodies. These were the days
before the Secret Service received a mandate to guard presidential candidates as well as the president, and for some reason the
Los Angeles Police Department (LAPD) was off the case (the
department would later claim that Kennedy had ordered them
away, a claim never substantiated and apparently designed, like
any number of notions promulgated by defenders of the official
version in the *first* Kennedy assassination, to somehow hold the
victim responsible for his own death).

As Kennedy pushed through the throng, a dark-skinned
young man—later identified as the partial amnesiac Sirhan—
leaped at the senator and shouted, "Kennedy, you son of a
bitch!" Flailing a .22 caliber pistol, he squeezed off a string of
shots. Kennedy crumpled, blood oozing from the back of his
head and spreading smoothly into a pool on the pantry floor.

A day later he was dead.

Five months later, Richard Nixon, who eight years beforehand had lost the narrowest election in U.S. history to Kennedy's older brother, defeated Kennedy's replacement on the Democratic ticket (Humphrey) by the second smallest margin.

The Los Angeles Police Department, at that time the most respected municipal law enforcement agency in the country thanks to its spiffy *Dragnet* image, took over the investigation, forming a task force dubbed Special Unit Senator. Determined not to repeat "the mistakes of Dallas," the LAPD formulated an impenetrable case against the lone assassin who was subsequently easily convicted.

But there were discrepancies and omissions from the official version. Some of the most important:

- The blood seeping from Kennedy's head came from a wound behind his right ear. Powder burns indicated that the shot came from no farther than two or three inches away. Sirhan was at all times in front of Kennedy. Even granting the ad hoc (and false) explanation that Kennedy suddenly turned his head away from the gunman, Sirhan never got closer than a few feet. Given that single piece of evidence there is no physical possibility that Sirhan could be the sole assassin. The coroner who ascertained the position of the fatal wound, Thomas Noguchi, was fired and had to sue to get his job back.
- Based on evidence of bullet holes and bullets found in the pantry, at least thirteen shots were fired. Sirhan's pistol held just eight shots and they were accounted for, having been recovered from Kennedy's body and the bodies of other wounded victims. The LAPD explained some of the extra bullet holes as "dents caused by food carts" and suppressed photographs of its own officers examining other holes. Ceiling panels and door jambs where extra bullet holes were sighted and photographed were destroyed.
- At least five witnesses—according to police reports—saw a

woman in a polka-dot dress fleeing the scene of the assassination. Some of the witnesses—notably a young Kennedy campaign worker named Sandra Serrano—heard the woman shouting, gleefully, "We shot him!" Serrano asked the mystery woman whom they shot. "Senator Kennedy," the woman replied, on her hurried way out. A couple identified only as "the Bernsteins," who were interviewed briefly by a patrolman, told the same story, but they were outside the hotel, about one hundred feet down a staircase from Serrano's position when they had a brief exchange with the woman who was still screaming "We shot him! We killed him!" The "Bernsteins" (who could not be located later) also asked the woman "Who was shot?" and received the same reply.

Sirhan has always maintained that prior to being hauled to the ground by, among others, pro football player Rosy Grier, who was Kennedy's bodyguard that evening, his final memory of the evening was of drinking coffee with a young woman. Serrano and another witness, Thomas DiPierro, reported seeing Sirhan in the company of the polka-dot woman before the shooting.

The LAPD responded to their statements by dispatching Enrique "Hank" Hernandez to administer polygraph examinations designed not to ascertain the truth of their stories but to browbeat them into recanting, which, under Hernandez's relentless and often abusive pressure, they both did.

The patrolman's report of "the Bernsteins'" account vanished from the LAPD files. The police investigators claimed the woman in the polka-dot dress was Valerie Schulte, an attractive coed from U.C. Santa Barbara who was also a Kennedy hanger-on. Schulte was there and wearing a polka-dot dress, but the dress and its attendant dots were the wrong color and she did not fit the description given by Serrano and DiPierro (both of whom noted that the polka-dot-dress woman had a "funny nose"). Nor, presumably, did Schulte, something of a Kennedy groupie, flee the scene shrieking "We shot him!" in a fit of joy.

These three points by themselves should have been enough to first of all, point the investigation in the direction of an assassination conspiracy; and just as important, to take it away from the LAPD, which clearly decided in advance that its own interests were best served by closing off any embarrassing avenues of inquiry that might reveal a plot to kill the probable next president of the United States hatched within their own inviolate jurisdiction. After all, shouldn't the hypercompetent godchildren of Joe Friday have ferreted out such a nefarious caper before it came to fruition?

Besides face-saving, there are other possible—though more highly speculative—reasons why the LAPD would stymie rather than expand on conspiracy leads. The chief investigator for Special Unit Senator, the man who made all the decisions, was Manny Pena, an LAPD officer brought out of "retirement" for the occasion. In fact, he had never really retired. He was working for the CIA.

The intelligence agency had a cooperative deal with the L.A. cops and Pena allegedly had engaged in numerous assignments for the CIA under cover of the Agency for International Development (AID). Supposedly known to insiders as the CIA's "Department of Dirty Tricks," AID-cover units were said to specialize in assassination techniques.

Through Pena—and possibly Hernandez, who also boasted of taking part in secret operations overseas—the CIA becomes a suspect in the whitewash of facts that point toward conspiracy. Why the coverup?

Sirhan himself is the strangest element of a strange case. Not that the lad himself was terribly odd. But his memory blackouts; his "automatic writing" including the repeated scrawl, "RFK must die!" scribbled randomly in notebooks that the LAPD for some reason saw fit to label "diaries"; the analysis of a former army intelligence officer who gave Sirhan a Psychological Stress Evaluation; and the testimony of a witness in a later civil trial who quoted acquaintances of Sirhan's as describing him in "a trance"—they all add up to one bizarre but unavoidable conclusion: when he shot Robert Kennedy, Sirhan Sirhan was hypnotized.

The defense psychiatrist, Dr. Bernard Diamond, explained away the diagnosis he could not deny by speculating that Sirhan must have hypnotized himself. After Sirhan was placed on death row, Dr. Eduard Simson-Kallas—then chief of the prison's psychological evaluation program—spent thirty-five hours examining Sirhan. In an interview with FBI-agent-turned-investigative-reporter William Turner, Simson-Kallas labeled Diamond's diagnosis "the psychiatric blunder of the century."

Quoted in Turner's book *The Assassination of Robert F. Kennedy*, Simson-Kallas asserts that self-hypnosis never runs so deep that it induces memory blocks, and while partial amnesia can result from schizophrenia, Sirhan showed no other indication of that mental malady.

Turner and his coauthor Jonn Christian argue that Sirhan was a Manchurian Candidate assassin, the "robot of another," firing at Kennedy not of his own twisted but otherwise free will, but as a result of a posthypnotic suggestion. They also believe, based on the basic physical evidence, that Sirhan did not actually shoot Kennedy (in fact, unspent .22 shells were found on Sirhan's person, leading Turner and Christian to believe that Sirhan fired no bullets at all—only blanks).

The fatal shot was likely fired, the authors (and any number of assassination researchers) hold, by a security guard named Thane Eugene Cesar who was stationed right behind Kennedy and admitted drawing his gun—and even privately admitted firing it. Cesar somehow lost his clip-on necktie during the confusion. In the famous photo of a dying RFK sprawled on the pantry floor, a stray clip-on tie lies just a foot or so from Kennedy's clutching right hand.

With the number of bullets flying around the pantry, however, Turner and Christian also believe that there must have been a third gun somewhere on the scene. Sirhan was nothing but a decoy; a mind-controlled patsy.

One deficiency in most Manchurian Candidate conspiracy theories is the absence of any identified programmer for these "hypnoprogrammed" assassins. Turner and Christian find a candidate, though their evidence is rather thin. They zero in on William Joseph Bryan, "the world's leading expert" on hypnosis—or so Bryan claimed. Bryan's moment of greatest acclaim came when he helped solve the Boston Strangler case by hypnotizing the suspect, Albert DiSalvo. Sirhan's notebooks contained—among other ostensibly senseless jottings—the name "DiSalvo" written over and over again. Confronted with this "diary entry" Sirhan was baffled and said the name was meaningless to him.

When a journalist (an attractive female journalist, which with a character like Bryan is not an insignificant detail) asked the effusively self-promoting hypnotist for his opinion on Sirhan, the world's leading expert on hypnosis became inexplicably enraged.

"I'm not going to comment on that case because I didn't hypnotize him," Bryan snapped, then terminated that interview.

Bryan's dead body turned up in a Las Vegas motel room in 1977. Two call girls who "serviced" him regularly for the final two years of his life told Turner and Christian that Bryan not only boasted to them about hypnotizing Sirhan, but also about working for the CIA on "top secret projects."

It may well have been bluster. But whoever hypnotized him, the fact that Sirhan was hypnotized is not really in doubt. Whether he was a subject of some CIA MK-ULTRA-related mind-control program or whether, as has been occasionally speculated, he was affiliated with some sort of occult group—another form of mind control—or both or neither, is one of those secrets locked and perhaps now lost in the cozy confines of Sirhan Sirhan's securely sealed mind.

MAJOR SOURCES

Charach, Ted. *The Second Gun.* Film documentary, 1973 (video copy in authors' possession).

Kaiser, Robert. *RFK Must Die!* New York: E.P. Dutton Co., 1970.

Turner, William, and Jonn Christian. *The Assassination of Robert F. Kennedy: The Conspiracy and Coverup.* New York: Thunder's Mouth Press, 1993.

50

JFK: Conspiracy of Confusion

Michael Scott's father, Winston, had been chief of the CIA's Mexico City station from 1956 until his retirement in 1969, so in 1985 when Scott dropped in at CIA headquarters in Langley, Virginia, he was greeted more cordially than one might expect from the not-entirely-inviting spy agency.

Scott's father, a career secret agent, died in 1971, apparently from complications of a household accident. At the time of his passing he had just put the finishing touches on a memoir of his cloak and dagger career. He planned a trip to Washington to voluntarily (even enthusiastically) have the text vetted by his former boss, director of Central Intelligence, Richard "Man Who Kept the Secrets" Helms. But due to his demise, the elder Scott's travel plans were canceled. Within hours after Mrs. Scott found her husband's body drooping over the breakfast table, the CIA's legendary and consummately creepy counterintelligence chief James Angleton showed up on the Scott family doorstep in Mexico City, searching for the manuscript.

In 1985, Michael Scott was making ends meet as a Hollywood producer. Out of curiosity, he asked to see the never-published book. He hoped it would help him better understand his father's mysterious life. An inquiry to the CIA prompted the invitation to Langley. As he told the story to reporter Dick Russell, Scott was introduced to a "high-ranking officer who had obviously read the manuscript," who told him that "they had been forced to delete portions of the manuscript for national security."

What portions? the surviving Scott inquired.

"Well, there was some mention of Lee Harvey Oswald in some area," the CIA officer said, "and we don't want to make that public."

The CIA treated the son of one of its veteran officers no differently than it treated Congress and the American public. It held back or destroyed who-knows-how-many documents that could have illuminated the background of the JFK assassination—many relating to its formerly supersecret alliance with the mob to clip Castro.

Helms lied to the Warren Commission when he testified that the CIA never "contemplated" using Oswald as a contact. In fact, in 1960, according to internal CIA memos, the Agency "showed intelligence interest" in the then-obscure Oswald. During his condolence call at the Scott residence, Angleton scooped up a tape recording, purportedly of Oswald. The CIA tape came from Oswald's now-famous visit to Mexico City in the summer of 1963, just a few months before the Kennedy assassination.

Oswald—or someone pretending to be Oswald or someone identified as Oswald—went to the Cuban and Soviet embassies in Mexico City petulantly and obstreperously demanding a visa to Castro's Cuba. He also reportedly met with Soviet intelligence agents and tried to obtain a visa back to the Soviet Union where he had once defected (and returned to the United States strangely unmolested). Why? There are a number of theories. Perhaps Oswald was a disaffected nut smitten by

JFK: Conspiracy of Confusion

delusions of Marxist grandeur (who later took out his private frustrations on JFK). Or perhaps he was working for an intelligence agency in an anti-Cuban operation. There were many underway at the time.

Or perhaps someone was trying to make Oswald look like a communist so that, the theory goes, the Soviets could take the blame for the subsequent assassination. After the assassination, there was an attempt by CIA operatives and powerful right-wingers (led by oilman H. L. Hunt) to finger Castro and/or Kruschev as the kingpin.

In any case, Oswald's voice was recorded in Mexico City and Winston Scott saved one of the recordings in his home. He kept it even after he retired. The CIA did not admit that such a recording existed until 1976. Then it lied that the recordings were all destroyed before the assassination. The FBI later said that the voice on the tapes was not Oswald's at all.

Someone impersonating Oswald prior to the assassination?

The Mexico City episode is crucial to any portrayal of Oswald as an emotionally volatile crank, but in a 1978 debate with attorney and pioneering conspiracy researcher Mark Lane, the CIA's former Western hemisphere chief David Atlee Philips announced that "there is no evidence to show that Lee Harvey Oswald visited the Soviet embassy." If he didn't, who did? Lane described Philips's startling statement as a "confession."

Philips was the CIA spokesman before Congress about the Oswald tapes. This is the same David Philips suspected by the House Select Committee on Assassinations of doubling as "Maurice Bishop," CIA controller of the Cuban "Alpha 66" anti-Castro brigade. The same David Philips in charge of exculpating the CIA in the Oswald-Mexico City incident may have engineered the "Mexico City scenario" in the first place, according to Lane, who has made a legal and literary career out of blaming the CIA for JFK's death.

Alpha 66's Cuban leader, Antonio Veciana, claimed that at one of his hundred or so meetings with "Bishop," Oswald was there, not saying anything, just acting odd. "I always thought

Bishop was working with Oswald during the assassination,"
Veciana told reporter Russell.

Veciana's cousin worked for Castro's intelligence service.
After the assassination, Bishop wanted Veciana to bribe his
cousin into saying that he met with Oswald, in order to
fabricate an Oswald-Castro connection.

Investigators never established for sure that Bishop and
Philips were one and the same, but descriptions of Bishop's
appearance and mannerisms mirrored Philips's. A police artist's
sketch of Bishop based on Veciana's description jogged the
memory of Senator Richard Schweiker, a member of the
assassination committee, as being the spittin' image of Philips.
When the select committee's ace investigator Gaeton Fonzi
finally brought Veciana and Philips together, the two started
acting weird around each other. After a short conversation in
Spanish, Philips bolted. Witnesses to the encounter swear that a
look of recognition swept Veciana's visage, but Veciana denied
that Philips was his case officer of more than a decade earlier.

"But," Veciana added cryptically, "he knows."

Veciana's reluctance to make the ID, Fonzi theorized,
stemmed from two unfortunate events that had befallen the
Cuban of late: one, he was convicted of running drugs and
suspected that Bishop set him up; two, he was shot in the head.

Later Fonzi put the question to Veciana in a more comfortably roundabout way. "Would you have told me if I had found
Maurice Bishop?" he asked. "Well, you know," said Veciana
with a smile, "I would like to talk with him first."

Russell interviewed a retired army colonel named, coincidentally, Bill Bishop, who claimed to be a CIA-employed hit man
(in his talk with Russell, Bill Bishop took credit for pulling the
trigger on Dominican Republic dictator Rafael Trujillo). Bill
Bishop said that he worked for the CIA's Mexico station with
Philips and that he and Philips ran Veciana together. He later
produced a tape recording of a phone call between Veciana and
himself in the mid 1980s. The two clearly know each other.

There was definitely something the CIA did not want publicized about Lee Harvey Oswald. The Veciana saga might contain at least a clue. However, because no conspiracy theory has been more widely written about than the JFK assassination, no conspiracy theory has come in for more strident attacks. The credibility of the attacks rests on the lack of credibility of one Lee Harvey Oswald, a personage painted as so twisted and pathetic that he is precluded from even unwitting participation in any act more complex than a temper tantrum.

That view finds its most recent outlet in Gerald Posner's pompous book, *Case Closed*. To make sure that readers get his point, Posner gives his Oswald chapters such subtle titles as "He Looks Like a Maniac," "Our Papa is Out of His Mind," and "His Mood Was Bad."

When his treatise came out in 1993, marketed to coincide with the thirtieth anniversary of President Kennedy's death, the enterprisingly smug Posner supplanted the Warren Commission as the final arbiter of JFK truth as far as the major media were concerned.

Jonathan Kwitny, himself a journalist of notable repute, explained the media's attraction to *Case Closed*.

"All the good young reporters and public officials who mistakenly swallowed the official FBI-CIA line on the assassination thirty years ago have been waiting all this time for someone to relieve them of the self-doubt they are too smart not to have suffered under," Kwitny wrote in the *Los Angeles Times*, giving Posner a rare negative review.

Posner's method of evading evidence that punctured his thesis was to obfuscate with unsupported assertions stated in a tone of unshakeable authority. The counterevidence was usually buried in a footnote. Nowhere was his technique more apparent than in his treatment of the incendiary Veciana-Bishop/Philips-Oswald story.

Posner states that "there are doubts" about whether Maurice Bishop ever existed. He does not state the source or substance of these "doubts," nor does he note that former CIA director John McCone did say that a "Maurice Bishop" worked for the agency. And in fact, a number of other CIA employees inter-viewed by Fonzi said the same, including one who spon-taneously named Philips as "Bishop."

"The CIA denied that any case officer had ever been assigned to Veciana," says Posner. So what? The House Select Commit-tee in its report "found it probable that some agency of the United States assigned a case officer to Veciana." Given the CIA's deep involvement in anti-Castro plots at the time, that agency was most likely the CIA.

It is true, as Posner (foot)notes, that the committee in its report said it "could not...credit Veciana's story." It also said, as Posner does not report, that "no evidence was found to discredit Veciana's story" and "there was some evidence to support it." In a footnote of its own, the committee acknowl-edged that it "suspected Veciana was lying, when he denied that [Philips] was Bishop." At the same time, said the report, Philips "aroused the committee's suspicions" by claiming that he didn't recognize Veciana, especially because Philips "had once been deeply involved in Agency anti-Castro operations."

The committee, mainly through its penchant for vacillation and its unwillingness to offend the CIA, created more confusion than it cleared up. Confusion has indeed been the one consistent quality of the now three-decade-plus JFK case. Posner's ag-gravating work simply stirred the fog.

So who killed JFK? The CIA? Anti-Castro fanatics? The Mafia? The military? A cabal of wealthy right-wing extremists? Or were they all somehow in league? There is evidence for any of the above. And all. Perhaps there were multiple plots against Kennedy that coalesced into one gigantic coverup with each party protecting its own interests but not necessarily cognizant of its counterparts' involvement.

Dick Russell writes that there were three plots against JFK in 1963. His primary source is a man named Richard Case Nagell who tells of working for an array of intelligence agencies, domestic and otherwise. The first plot was to bomb JFK's speech at the Orange Bowl in Miami. The alleged CIA hit man Bill Bishop corroborated that story.

Plot number two—also corroborated independently by Bill Bishop—was scheduled for Los Angeles. Nagell's involvement was to shadow a Los Angeles leftist named Vaughn Marlowe who was "considered for recruitment to hit JFK," Nagell told Russell. The recruiters were L.A. members of Alpha 66. Marlowe didn't know he had been, potentially, the original Oswald until years later when Russell informed him. But he did know that Nagell was shadowing him. During New Orleans district attorney Jim Garrison's highly publicized investigation of the JFK case, Marlowe wrote Garrison to tell him about Nagell.

Nagell was also aware of the third plot—so aware that Russell believes he was hired by the KGB to terminate the plot by terminating Oswald. Instead, Nagell deliberately got himself arrested by firing a gun inside a bank in El Paso on September 20, 1963.

According to the recollections of Nagell's arresting officer, Nagell said, upon being taken into custody, "I'm glad you caught me. I really don't want to be in Dallas."

"What do you mean by that?" the policeman asked.

"You'll see soon enough," Nagell replied. Two months and two days later, in Dallas, President Kennedy was shot and killed.

Russell, unlike Posner, makes no claims to unimpeachable veracity. Far from it. But starting with Nagell, Russell winds through a menagerie of grim characters who fit in all of the categories mentioned above. Among the scariest and most powerful was Retired General Charles Willoughby, formerly intelligence chief for General Douglas MacArthur, but whose political leanings made MacArthur look like, well, JFK. MacArthur once described his underling as a "little fascist." Self-described hit man Bill Bishop also worked as an "intelligence aide" to MacArthur, according to a document turned up by Russell. "If true," Russell emphasizes, "that would mean Bishop

380 TWILIGHT OF THE IDOLS

had served under MacArthur's intelligence chief, Charles Willoughby."

Willoughby formed an ultra-rightist network whose most visible spokesman was fire-and-brimstone preacher Billy James Hargis and which included Texas oil baron H. L. Hunt and CIA-agent-turned-journalist Edward Hunter (credited with inventing the word "brainwashing"). Willoughby stayed in close touch with Allen Dulles, director of the CIA later fired by Kennedy—and subsequently appointed to the Warren Commission to investigate the slaying of the president who had fired him.

In 1975, after Russell wrote an article about the assassination for the *Village Voice*, he received an anonymous letter identifying "a famous American general who was born in Heidelberg, Germany, in 1892" as "having masterminded the assassination." The odd letter named this "famous general," cryptically, as "Tscheppe-Weidenbach."

Years later, while Russell was reading the book *The Origins of the Korean War* by Bruce Cumings, he came across "an obscure mention that Adolf Tscheppe-Weidenbach of Heidelberg, Germany, had changed his name, upon arrival in the United States shortly before World War I, to Charles Willoughby."

Finally there is the story, recorded by Fonzi, of Dave Morales, a self-proclaimed CIA assassin who one night, with only close friends present, went into a boozy diatribe against Kennedy for sacrificing his CIA-trained comrades at the Bay of Pigs.

"Suddenly he stopped," Fonzi writes, "and remained silent for a moment. Then as if saying it only to himself he added: 'Well, we took care of that son of a bitch, didn't we?'"

MAJOR SOURCES

Fonzi, Gaeton. *The Last Investigation*. New York: Thunder's Mouth Press, 1993.
Hurt, Henry. *Reasonable Doubt*. New York: Henry Holt and Company, 1985.

Lane, Mark. *Plausible Denial*. New York: Thunder's Mouth Press, 1991.

Posner, Gerald. *Case Closed: Lee Harvey Oswald and the Assassination of JFK*. New York: Random House, 1993.

Russell, Dick. *The Man Who Knew Too Much*. New York: Carroll and Graf, 1992.

Summers, Anthony. *Conspiracy*. New York: Paragon House, 1989.

Any writing about the JFK assassination owes a debt to the work of hundreds of researchers. Some, but by no means all, of the most important are: Peter Dale Scott, Jim Garrison, Jim Marrs, Sylvia Meagher, and Carl Oglesby.

The idea of the paranoid style would have very little contemporary relevance or historical value if it were applied only to people with profoundly disturbed minds. It is the use of paranoid modes of expression by more or less normal people that makes the phenomenon significant.

—Richard Hofstadter

We ought not to be too paranoid about paranoia, ought not to be too afraid of ambiguity and irreducible doubt, too afraid of confronting worst-case scenarios and outer-limits possibilities on the grounds merely that they disarm, dehumanize, and defeat us.

—Carl Oglesby

Perhaps if we clearly defined this thing we call paranoia it would not cause us to behave so foolishly. Genuine paranoia actually contains at least three ingredients, fear, suspicion, and mystification. Technically, it is heightened awareness, but not yet perfect awareness.

—Kerry W. Thornley

Index

More Fun Facts and Interesting Trivia

Ask for any of the books listed below at your bookstore. Or to order direct from the publisher, call 1-800-447-BOOK (MasterCard or Visa), or send a check or money order for the books purchased (plus $4.00 shipping and handling for the first book ordered and 75¢ for each additional book) to Carol Publishing Group, 120 Enterprise Avenue, Dept. 1576, Secaucus, NJ 07094.

Aardvarks to Zebras: A Menagerie of Facts, Fiction and Fantasy About the Wonderful World of Animals by Melissa S. Tulin
Illustrated with photographs & drawings
$14.95 paper   0-8065-1548-1   (CAN $20.95)

The Almanac of Fascinating Beginnings: From the Academy Awards to the Xerox Machine by Norman King
$9.95 paper   0-8065-1549-X   (CAN $13.95)

The Book of Totally Useless Information by Donald A. Voorhees
$7.95 paper   0-8065-1405-1   (CAN $9.95)

The Business Disasters Book of Days: The World's Greatest Financial Mishaps, Follies and Remarkable Events by Jill Herbers
$ 9.95 paper   0-8065-1585-6   (CAN $13.95)

The "Cheers" Trivia Book by Mark Wenger
Illustrated with photographs throughout
$ 9.95 paper   0-8065-1482-5   (CAN $11.95)

The Complete Book of Sexual Trivia by Leslee Welch
$7.95 paper   0-8065-1347-0   (CAN $9.95)

Death by Rock & Roll: The Untimely Deaths of the Legends of Rock by Gary J. Katz
Illustrated with photographs throughout
$9.95 paper   0-8065-1581-3   (CAN $13.95)

The Encyclopedia of Popular Misconceptions: The Ultimate Debunker's Guide to Widely Accepted Fallacies by Ferris Johnsen
$9.95 paper   0-8065-1556-2   (CAN $13.95)

50 Greatest Conspiracies of All Time: History's Biggest Mysteries, Cover-ups and Cabals by Jonathan Vankin and John Whalen
$12.95 paper   0-8065-1576-7   (CAN $17.95)

Film Flubs: Memorable Movie Mistakes by Bill Givens   Illustrated with photographs throughout
$7.95 paper   0-8065-1161-3   (CAN $10.95)
<u>Also available:</u>
Son of Film Flubs: More Memorable Movie Mistakes by Bill Givens
Illustrated with photographs throughout
$7.95 paper   0-8065-1279-2   (CAN $10.95)

Film Flubs: The Sequel - Even More Memorable Movie Mistakes by Bill Givens
Illustrated with photographs throughout
$7.95 paper   0-8065-1360-8   (CAN $9.95)

George Washington Had No Middle Name: Strange Historical Facts by Patricia Lee Holt
$5.95 paper   0-8065-1074-9   (CAN $7.95)

How a Fly Walks Upside Down and Other Curious Facts by Martin A. Goldwyn
$7.95 paper   0-8065-1054-4   (CAN $10.95)

Light Your House With Potatoes: And 99 Other Off-the-wall Solutions to Life's Little Problems by Jay Kaye   Illustrations throughout
$7.95 paper   0-8065-1376-4   (CAN $9.95)

Old Wives' Tales: The Truth Behind Common Notions by Sue Castle   Illustrations throughout
$7.95 paper   0-8065-1378-0   (CAN $9.95)

1001 Toughest TV Trivia Questions of All Time: Brain Teasers for the Thinking Couch Potato by Vincent Terrace
$9.95 paper   0-8065-1499-X   (CAN $11.95)

Peculiar Patents: A Collection of Unusual and Interesting Inventions from the Files of the U.S. Patent Office by Dr. Rick Feinberg
Illustrated throughout
$9.95 paper   0-8065-1561-9   (CAN $13.95)

The "Seinfeld" Aptitude Test: Hundreds of Spectacular Questions on Minute Details from TV's Greatest Show About Absolutely Nothing by Beth B. Golub
$8.95 paper   0-8065-1583-X   (CAN $12.95)

Sophomore Slumps: Disastrous Second Movies, Albums, Songs and TV Shows by Chris Golden   Illustrated with photographs throughout
$9.95 paper   0-8065-1584-8   (CAN $13.95)

Why Do They Call It Topeka?: How Places Got Their Names by John W. Pursell
$9.95 paper   0-8065-1588-0   (CAN $13.95)

(Prices subject to change; books subject to availability)